LINGUISTIC MINORITY STUDENTS GO TO COLLEGE

"This book addresses the complexities of immigrant education through important, timely research studies. It is a text whose time has come."

Robin Murie, University of Minnesota. ESL Programs Duluth Campus

Currently, linguistic minority students—students who speak a language other than English at home—represent 21% of the entire K–12 student population and 11% of the college student population. Bringing together emerging scholarship on the growing number of college-bound linguistic minority students in the K–12 pipeline, this ground-breaking volume showcases new research on these students' preparation for, access to, and persistence in college.

Other than studies of their linguistic challenges and writing and academic literacy skills in college, little is known about the broader issues of linguistic minority students' access to and success in college. Examining a variety of factors and circumstances that influence the process and outcome, the scope of this book goes beyond students' language proficiency and its impact on college education, to look at issues such as race/ethnicity, gender, SES, and parental education and expectations. It also addresses structural factors in schooling including tracking, segregation of English learners from English-fluent peers, availability and support of institutional personnel, and collegiate student identity and campus climate.

Presenting state-of-the-art knowledge and mapping out a future research agenda in an extremely important and yet understudied area of inquiry, this book advances knowledge in ways that will have a real impact on policy regarding linguistic minority immigrant students' higher education opportunities.

Yasuko Kanno is Associate Professor of TESOL in the College of Education, Temple University.

Linda Harklau is Professor of the Teaching Additional Languages program and the Linguistics program at the University of Georgia.

LINGUISTIC MINORITY STUDENTS GO TO COLLEGE

Preparation, Access, and Persistence

Edited by

Yasuko Kanno
TEMPLE UNIVERSITY

Linda Harklau
UNIVERSITY OF GEORGIA

 Routledge
Taylor & Francis Group

NEW YORK AND LONDON

First published 2012
by Routledge
711 Third Avenue, New York, NY 10017

Simultaneously published in the UK
by Routledge
2 Park Square, Milton Park, Abingdon, Oxon OX14 4RN

Routledge is an imprint of the Taylor & Francis Group, an informa business

Library of Congress Cataloging in Publication Data
Linguistic minority students go to college : preparation, access, and persistence / [edited by] Yasuko Kanno, Linda Harklau.
    p. cm.
    Includes bibliographical references and index.
    1. Linguistic minorities—Education (Higher)—United States. I. Kanno, Yasuko, 1965–
II. Harklau, Linda.
    LC3727.L56 2012
    378.1'982900973—dc23
    2011037628

ISBN: 978-0-415-89061-8 (hbk)
ISBN: 978-0-415-89062-5 (pbk)
ISBN: 978-0-203-82938-7 (ebk)

Typeset in Bembo and Stone Sans
by EvS Communication Networx, Inc

Printed and bound in the United States of America on acid-free paper
by IBT Global

CONTENTS

PREFACE

Linguistic minority students, students who speak a language other than English at home, are the fastest growing subgroup of the entire K–12 public school population in the United States. Already over 20% of the school-age population are linguistic minorities; about half of them are learning English as an additional language and need institutional linguistic support. Given the sheer number and growth of linguistic minority students in the K–12 pipeline, we would hope that this population is a rapidly growing presence in higher education as well. Yet there is a curious void in our knowledge about linguistic minority students' placement and participation in college. To date, work on linguistic minority students' educational achievement has focused primarily on high school graduation. In stark contrast to the voluminous body of research on college-going in other underrepresented students such as ethnic minorities and low-income students, there has been no tradition of counting or analyzing linguistic minority students' transitions to and success in higher education.

In this edited volume, we intend to start such a tradition. These 14 chapters represent state-of-the-art knowledge on an emerging field of inquiry: linguistic minority students' college-going. As these chapters indicate, many questions need to be answered: What chances do linguistic minority students in the United States stand of accessing and completing a college education? What factors inhibit or foster their college-going aspirations? How do they navigate the system? What services and programs are available for linguistic minority students who want to go to college? And, in what ways are their experiences similar to and different from those of monolingual English-speaking students? By bringing together this scholarship, our goals are to identify what we know so far and to articulate a research agenda that will advance knowledge and have a real impact on policy on linguistic minority students' higher education opportunities.

The focus of this volume is on college access and persistence for linguistic minority students cast broadly. While these studies consider the well-explored issue of students' language proficiency and its impact on college education, they also explore a variety of factors that are increasingly the focus of research and policy on college-going in other underrepresented groups. This volume therefore takes on race/ethnicity, gender, age, socioeconomic status, parental education and expectations. It also addresses structural factors in schooling including tracking, segregation of English learners from English-fluent peers, availability and support of institutional personnel, collegiate student identity and campus climate.

Some of the studies featured in this volume report statistical analyses of large-scale data. These are important because it is hard numbers that drive policy decisions; yet as these studies make clear, we currently lack adequate national- and state-level information on linguistic minority students' college access, performance, and graduation. Other chapters in the volume feature in-depth qualitative studies that zoom in on a small number of linguistic minority students in their specific settings. These studies are equally important since they illuminate complex interactions between structural factors and individual linguistic minority students' agency, and highlight the dynamics of college-going as a process. In addition, four chapters (Kanno & Grosik; Varghese; Fuentes; Shapiro) focus on one major public university that we call Northern Green University. By gathering in one place several papers that examine one university's policy and practice with linguistic minority students and the students' experiences within the institution, this volume offers an in-depth look at one institution's way of "dealing with" linguistic diversity, which we feel is rather typical of many four-year institutions in the United States.

This volume consists of three parts: (1) college preparation in high school, (2) access to college, and (3) college experiences and persistence. After an introductory chapter outlining the rationale and goals for this volume, Part 1, *College Preparation in High School*, features four chapters on college preparation in high school. These chapters examine the kinds of academic and social preparation that need to be in place in high school and barriers that prevent linguistic minority students, especially English learners, from accessing such preparation. Part 2, *Access to College*, illuminates students' process of making transitions to college. The four chapters in this section address issues such as the profile of linguistic minority students who have access to two-year and four-year colleges, and to selective and less selective four-year institutions; how students themselves negotiate the high school to college transition process; and what their initial experiences are like once they are admitted. Part 3, *College Experiences and Persistence*, consisting of five chapters, investigates what it takes, on the part of both the institution and the student, for linguistic minority students to stay in college and earn their degrees. Of particular note in this section are examinations of policies in postsecondary institutions that prevent linguistic minority students from accessing key information and from accruing necessary cultural capital. Equally important are explorations of how individual students, despite such challenges, exercise agency to navigate the system and ultimately achieve their goals.

Intended Audiences

Numerous stakeholders at different levels of schooling and in many disciplines influence linguistic minority students' chances for college education. This volume is thus necessarily and intentionally interdisciplinary, and we believe it will be of interest to a broad audience. The research contained here has clear relevance to K–12 teachers, counselors, administrators, and policy makers who work with linguistic minority students and who wish to gain greater perspective on the sorts of academic preparation and coursework in high school necessary to ensure college success and on aspects of college applications with which linguistic minority students are most likely to need assistance. We also invite higher education educators, administrators, counselors, policy makers, and researchers to participate in the research dialog we begin with this book. We believe that it is paramount for all of us in higher education to realize that linguistic minority students are already in our midst. As such, we strongly believe that it is *everyone's* business in higher education to meet the educational needs of this population, not simply those who work in the English as a second language (ESL) department. On the other hand, because many linguistic minority students are English learners, we believe it is also important for ESL teachers, first-year writing program instructors, and applied linguists to understand that the linguistic support they provide to English learners is framed in a larger context in which a number of factors, and not just language proficiency, contribute to linguistic minorities' overall educational opportunities.

Acknowledgments

First of all, we would like to thank the contributors of this volume for their enthusiasm and commitment to this project. This area of inquiry is so new that we were initially worried that we might not find enough contributors to assemble a volume. We were thus delighted to have found 20 likeminded researchers who are just as passionate about sending linguistic minority students to college. Naomi Silverman, our editor at Routledge, trusted our vision of the book from the beginning ("*Of course*, we'll do the book," she said) and kept us on track. As one can guess from the number of times her name has appeared in the acknowledgments of applied linguistics books, Naomi is one of the movers and shakers of our field, and it is always a privilege to work with her.

1

LINGUISTIC MINORITY STUDENTS GO TO COLLEGE

Introduction

Yasuko Kanno and Linda Harklau

For immigrants and their families who come to the United States in search of a better life and a better education, earning a college degree is often a dream come true. At the same time, in the context of the current U.S. knowledge economy, a college degree is no longer simply an aspiration to espouse; rather, it has become an increasingly necessary qualification for securing and maintaining a middle-class job and lifestyle. A college degree makes a tremendous difference in one's earning power. In 2010, full-time workers with bachelor's degrees on average earned 74% more than high school graduates (Carnevale & Rose, 2011). By 2018 it is estimated that 63% of new job openings will require at least some level of postsecondary education (PSE) (Carnevale, Smith, & Strohl, 2010). A college education also begets further on-the-job training; College graduates are 70% more likely to receive continuing formal training from their employers than high school graduates (Carnevale et al., 2010), giving them further advantages in terms of earnings and marketable skills and knowledge.

It is hardly surprising, then, that current higher education research and policy initiatives have focused on creating greater access to PSE and increasing the number of college graduates (Bowen, Chingos, & McPherson, 2009; College Board, 2010; Lumina Foundation, 2010; Southern Regional Education Board, 2010). The best known of such initiatives is President Obama's proposal to increase community college graduates by 5 million by 2020 (Obama, 2009). In this volume we contend that no such effort is likely to be successful without adequate consideration of *linguistic minority (LM) students*.[1] These students, also variously termed *language minority students* or *non-English language background (NELB) student*, speak a language other than English at home. They constitute the fastest growing demographic subgroup in the U.S. educational system. In the last three decades (1980–2009), the proportion of LM children in the school-age population (ages 5 to 17) has jumped from 10% to 21% (National Center for Education Statistics, 2011, p. 162). Given their rapidly growing presence in the U.S. student population, if we are serious about increasing college graduation rates, we need to make concerted efforts to facilitate LM students' pathways to and through college. Yet, in reality, apart from the linguistic challenges faced by the subset of LM students who are still learning English in college, we know very little as yet about LM students' preparation for college or their experiences with college choice, college enrollment, and persistence.

This volume, then, aims to fill this gap by offering a collection of 13 papers, each of which examines a different facet of LM students' college-going. Focusing on first-generation immigrants and children of immigrants, the volume showcases new research on LM students' preparation for, access to, and persistence in college by examining a variety of factors and circumstances that influence the process and outcome. Just as important, by bringing together this scholarship, we hope to help establish a new area of inquiry and articulate a clear research agenda that will make the presence of LM students in higher education more visible and help expand college opportunities for this population.

In introducing a collection of work on LM students and college-going, it is important to make explicit two assumptions underlying this volume. First, LM students are by definition identified by a distinct linguistic characteristic (i.e., they speak a nondominant language at home). However, we conceptualize LM students as a demographic group not only defined by language but also by a set of other, often co-occurring, characteristics as well as encompassing a great deal of heterogeneity within. An analogy with racial minority students may help illustrate our point. Deil-Amen and Turley (2007) point out that although the Black-White achievement gap has long been documented, few sociologists attribute the difference to race per se; rather, most believe that the difference is due to socially and historically constructed factors around racial difference and inequality including "the home environment, parental education, school quality, and teachers' perceptions, expectations, and behaviors" (p. 2329). Likewise, although we believe that in the case of LM students, language proficiency does affect students' college access and success, we also suggest that linguistic differences are by no means the only factor at play. Rather, a variety of commonly shared characteristics among LM students must also be taken into account such as low socioeconomic status, non-college-educated parents, low teacher expectations, enrollment in resource-poor schools, and low tracking in high school (Bennici & Strang, 1995; *Education Week*, 2009; Genesee & Gándara, 1999).

Second, it is also important to specify that linguistic minority students are not all English learners (ELs).[2] LM students includes the entire set of multilingual individuals who speak a non-English language at home; ELs are a subset of LM students whose academic English proficiency has not yet developed sufficiently to benefit from the regular English-medium instruction. Although these two terms are often erroneously conflated, they are, most emphatically, not the same. Many LM students are native or highly proficient speakers of English. It is common for LM students, especially among second-generation immigrant students, to be more dominant in English than in their home language.[3] To assume that all LM students are somehow less than fully proficient in English is a highly reductive deficit orientation that ignores the complex linguistic landscape of the United States. In the context of research on LM students' college-going in particular, it is important to distinguish LM students who are proficient in English and those who are ELs because, as we will see shortly, these two subgroups of LM students tend to show different patterns of college access and persistence.

LM Students' College Access and Success: Falling through the Cracks of Disciplinary Boundaries

In K–12 education contexts, much has been written about the academic performance of LM students, especially ELs (e.g., Callahan, 2005; Collier, 1987; Cummins, 2000, 2001; Thomas & Collier, 1997, 2002; Valenzuela, Fuller, & Vasquez Heilig, 2006). Developing the English academic language and literacy skills necessary to perform at grade-level is a protracted process that can take 4 to 7 years (Cummins, 1981; Hakuta, Butler, & Witt, 2000). This means that even students who arrive in the United States at the beginning of middle school may still be at a disadvantage linguistically compared to monolingual English-speaking peers by the time they graduate from high school (Harklau, 1998). Thomas and Collier (1997, 2002) point out that ELs in secondary school face the double challenge of catching up to their monolingual peers in English while simultaneously dealing with increasingly demanding academic material in a language they have not yet mastered. It is thus not surprising that most ELs do not catch up by the end of high school. Thomas and Collier's extensive study (1997, 2002) found that ELs who received one to two years of initial ESL pullout instruction—the most typical form of ESL support in U.S. schools— finished high school on average at the 10th percentile of academic achievement. While those receiving a substantial amount of instruction in their first language (L1) fared better, recent laws and educational policies have made such programs rare, particularly at the secondary level (Crawford, 2006; Menken, 2008; Wiley & Wright, 2004; Wright, 2007). Other studies have likewise found ELs in secondary education to be at risk academically in terms of grade promotion, high school graduation, and performance on standardized achievement examinations (Chudowsky, Kober, Gayler, & Hamilton, 2002; Solórzano, 2008; Valenzuela et al., 2006). Structural factors affecting the academic performance of LM students have been reported as well: LM students typically are concentrated in low-achieving, resource-poor urban schools where student-to-teacher ratios are high (Fry, 2008).

In contrast to the considerable attention paid to LM students' academic performance at the K–12 level, research on this population's college access and degree attainment is scant. LM students' college-going has arguably fallen through the cracks of a disciplinary division of labor. On one hand, educational sociologists and higher education policy analysts studying college-going in underrepresented populations generally employ demographic categories that do not recognize LM status. Instead, literature in this area has focused on "traditionally underrepresented" groups in higher education including racial and ethnic minorities (Deil-Amen & Turley, 2007; Kao & Thompson, 2003), low income students (Bowen, Kurzwell, & Tobin, 2005; McDonough, 1997; Walpole, 2007), first-generation college students (Nuñez & Cuccaro-Alamin, 1998; Pascarella, Pierson, Wolniak, & Terenzini, 2004), and undocumented immigrants (Contreras, 2009; Morales, Herrerra, & Murry, 2009). Educational sociologists and policy makers have shown a particularly keen interest in Latino students' educational trajectories given the rapid growth of the Latino population in the United States and the persistent underachievement of Latino students (e.g., Arbona & Nora, 2007; Auerbach, 2004; Callahan, 2008; Gándara & Contreras, 2009; Nuñez, 2009; Percy Calaff, 2008; Swail, Cabrera, Lee, & Williams, 2005). Yet researchers studying Latino students' college access and success have rarely considered the influence of linguistic minority status. For instance, Swail and colleagues (2005), who offer an otherwise comprehensive analysis of factors contributing to Latino students' college pathways, make only brief mention of linguistic background—and even then, not as a factor directly influencing students' degree attainment but as an indirect factor affecting remedial coursetaking in college. In all, then, LM status remains an almost invisible variable in most of the sociological and policy literature on underrepresented groups in higher education.

In college composition and second language (L2) writing studies, on the other hand, students' LM status has been a defining variable for inquiry. Research and policy-making in this area have centered on LM student experience in first year composition, ESL composition, and writing across the curriculum programs and requirements that are in place at virtually every PSE institution in the United States. However, by virtue of its disciplinary grounding, research and policy in this field have tended to limit themselves to the effects of students' multilingualism on college writing experiences and performance while not addressing broader issues of LM college access and persistence. Nevertheless, researchers such as Leki (2007) who have conducted extensive studies of LM students' college experiences have questioned this exclusive focus on writing, suggesting that writing researchers are "exaggerating the role of writing in the lives of L2 undergraduate students and in their intellectual and academic development" (p. 283). Observing that in her research, "the academic lives I heard about in these interviews and saw in class observations could not be reduced to issues of academic literacy" (p. 283), Leki instead finds that developing satisfying "socioacademic" relationships with peers and educators was students' first priority in college and was crucial to their college success.

In all, then, LM students and their college-going experiences are currently ill-served by disciplinary divisions in higher education research that either fail to recognize LM status as a significant variable at all or alternatively define LM collegiate experiences in terms of language to the exclusion of other aspects of their postsecondary careers.

What We Know So Far

Although research on LM students' college-going is still in its infancy, existing research nonetheless provides a kernel of understanding of the factors contributing to their college preparation, access, and persistence.

How Many LM Students Go to College?

An important prerequisite for further research in this area is to ascertain exactly how many LM students actually attend PSE. There is surprisingly little information in this regard. To our knowledge, only three studies have attempted to offer nation-wide estimates of the number of LM students attending college. In one study, Klein, Bugarin, Beltranena, and McArthur (2004) analyzed the Current Population Survey from 1999 and found that only 14% of 18- to 24-year-olds who "spoke English with difficulty" were enrolled in PSE institutions compared with 37% monolingual English speakers and 38% of LM young adults who "spoke English very well" (Table 12, p. 25). In a more recent study, Kanno and Cromley (2011) analyzed the National Education Longitudinal Study of 1988 (NELS:88). They report that only 18% of ELs advanced to four-year institutions directly from high school compared with 43% of English monolingual students and 38% of English-proficient LM students. The graduation rates showed a similar pattern: 12% of ELs, 25% of English-proficient LM students, and 32% of English monolinguals attained bachelor's degrees within 8 years of their high school graduation. Kanno and Cromley also found that roughly half of ELs never participated in any type of PSE.

In a third study, Nuñez and Sparks (this volume) drew upon the Beginning Postsecondary Students Longitudinal Study of 2004 (BPS:04) to analyze the characteristics of LM students who are already enrolled in U.S. colleges. They found that 11% of all first-time, first-year students in 2003–04 were LM students. Sixty-one percent of LM students, as opposed to 56% of monolingual English-speaking students, were enrolled in two-year colleges, confirming the widespread perception that many LM students start their PSE career at community colleges (Almon, this volume; Bunch & Endris, this volume). Nuñez and Sparks also found that LM students in PSE tend to come from lower income backgrounds than monolingual students and have slightly lower levels of academic preparation.

Taken collectively, this set of studies emphasize that LM students are already a major presence in PSE institutions in the United States. Existing data also confirms impressionistic accounts that LM students are more likely to opt for community colleges as a point of entry into PSE than their English monolingual peers. These studies also show that ELs lag far behind their more English proficient peers both in access and graduation rates. However, English-proficient LM students' patterns of college access and attainment appear to be more similar to those of monolingual-English-speaking students than those of ELs.

Poor Collegiate Preparation in High School

An obvious question to ask then is why ELs lag so much behind their English-proficient LM peers. The tendency so far has been to attribute ELs' under-achievement solely to limited English proficiency. As Gándara and Rumberger (2009) point out, "The policy discussion about educational needs of immigrant students is usually limited to remedying their lack of English" (p. 763). However, one clear theme emerging from the latest research is that there is a host of factors besides limited English proficiency contributing to ELs' lack of access to PSE. One such factor is access to college-preparatory coursework in high school. Research has shown that solid academic preparation in high school is a key predictor of both access to four-year colleges and the attainment of a bachelor's degree (Adelman, 2006; Cabrera & La Nasa, 2001). Yet it is precisely this access to high-level courses that ELs are often denied. ELs tend to be placed in low-level, non-college-bound streams (Callahan & Shifrer, this volume). In a study of a large, rural California school, Callahan (2005) found that only 2% of ELs completed the set of courses that would make them eligible for four-year college admission.

In a similar vein, Mosqueda (this volume) examined Asian and Latino LM students' opportunity to take high-level math courses and its impact on their math achievement using the Education Longitudinal Study of 2002 (ELS:2002). The sequential nature of math courses has made them a particularly useful proxy indicator for the overall academic intensity of a students' high school coursework. Unsurprisingly, taking higher-level math courses was strongly correlated with higher levels of achievement. However, Mosqueda also found that LM students benefitted more from taking advanced-level math courses than non-LM students. Asian LM students benefitted more than Latino LM students in terms of gains in math achievement tests. Thus, Mosqueda's findings offer an intriguing implication that access to advanced math coursework has differential effects on the achievement of different group of students.

The Impact of Low SES

Extant research also makes it abundantly clear that the lack of financial resources severely constrains LM students' college choice and college engagement. Statistics suggest that LM students are more likely to come from a low-income family than monolingual English-speaking students (*Education Week*, 2009; Klein et al., 2004), and many studies over several decades have demonstrated the profound impact of SES on students' college access and persistence (e.g., Bowen et al., 2005; Hearn, 1984; Karen, 2002; McDonough, 1997; Walpole, 2007). Low-income LM students often accept as a given that their option is limited to public colleges within a commuting distance from home (Kanno & Grosik, this volume). Coming from families with limited knowledge of the U.S. higher education system, immigrant students may be unaware of financial assistance available to them or be unable to navigate the bureaucracy and paperwork associated with college financial aid (Kanno & Grosik, this volume). Limited SES may also strain a family's budget for college tuition and create difficult choices for students and their families, particularly if students' legal status and eligibility for in-state tuition are at issue (Harklau, this volume).

Low SES also affects LM students' persistence in college. Nuñez and Sparks (this volume) show that LM students are overrepresented in the lowest income quartile at U.S. PSE institutions. At selective four-year institutions, for instance, 37% of LM students came from the lowest income quartile compared with only 13% of non-LM students, suggesting that LM students are likely to find it more challenging to secure enough funding to persist through a four-year degree. At the community college level too, many LM students seem to drop out for financial reasons. Almon's study of a community college on the East Coast (this volume) found that although ELs achieved a higher GPA than the college mean, their graduation rate was lower than that of the college as a whole. Based on interviews with students, Almon (2010) concluded that lack of financial resources was one of the main reasons for ELs' college attrition. Clearly further research and policy attention are needed on this aspect of LM college-going.

Agency

While most of what we know about LM student experiences with college-going focuses on obstacles and disadvantages, at the same time we have perhaps not paid enough attention to how successful LM students work to overcome these obstacles and disadvantages. Unlike other levels of education, college is not compulsory; enrollment requires the exercise of individual choice and agency. A strong sense of agency is clearly a crucial factor in many LM students' college access and attainment. Relying on varying theoretical frameworks, three chapters in this volume (Harklau and McClanahan; Varghese; Fuentes) illustrate the role of LM student agency. These case studies show the powerful effects of possessing a strong and unquestioning self-image as a college-bound student. Actions they took, such as seeking the help of a sports coach or a guidance counselor, applying for scholarships, or making strategic choices about college majors and courses, helped them reach and persist through college. These case studies provide a powerful testimony that LM students' individual agency does make a difference in shaping their college education.

Nonetheless, it is important to emphasize that students' individual agency cannot be separated from the structural conditions that surround them (Harklau & McClanahan, this volume; Kanno, Varghese, & Fuentes, 2011). That is, given America's highly valued ideology of "pulling yourself up by your bootstraps," it is too easy to attribute LM students' successes simply to individual immigrant resilience and determination. However, a careful examination of these success stories reveals that students who exercise agency effectively do so by marshaling all the social, cultural, and/or economic capital at their disposal. Put another way, students must have a foundation of family, school, and/or community support in place in order to develop the college-going expectations, as well as a solid sense of their own academic acumen and goals, that are the basis of exerting agency (Kanno et al., 2011; Zarate, Sáenz, & Oseguera, 2011). In all, we need more research on how LM students exercise agency and overcome obstacles to college enrollment and success. It is also important to examine student agency in tandem with structural conditions under which students negotiate college access and participation.

The Positive Impact of Intervention Programs

College outreach and intervention programs for students from underrepresented groups are not plentiful (Gándara with Bial, 2001), and programs that specifically aim to increase LM students' participation in college are almost non-existent (Mayer, this volume). Three chapters in this volume examine institutional efforts to facilitate LM students' college-going. Mayer provides a case study of an International Baccalaureate (IB) program at one California high school serving LM students that features an open-access policy (i.e., any student who wishes to participate in the program may do so). She finds that when given a chance to take high-level academic coursework, many LM students rise to the challenge and use the program as a springboard to reach college. Mayer shows, however, that certain conditions must be met in the program order to ensure students' success, such as a curriculum that reflects the value of bilingualism and a strong sense of community.

The validation of students' L1 is also underscored in Holmes, Fanning, Morales, Espinoza, and Herrera's analysis (this volume) of the BESITOS (Bilingual/Bicultural Education Students Interacting To Obtain Success) program at a midwestern university. Designed to encourage LM students to become public school teachers, the BESITOS program places a strong emphasis on the bilingualism-as-a-resource orientation (Ruíz, 1984). Holmes et al.'s data suggest that when Latina/o students are included in a safe community that affirms their cultural and linguistic heritage, they come to perceive their own bilingualism and struggles as resources they can use to help educate LM children.

Rodríguez (this volume) reports on how Texas' Top Ten Percent Plan affects LM student college participation. The policy guarantees admission to any public university in Texas to students who graduate in the 10% of their high school class. Rodríguez reports that due to the highly segregated nature of schools in Texas, many high-achieving LM students nevertheless graduate from high schools without a level of collegiate preparation that would make them competitive for slots at the state's highly selective top-tier universities. Although the Top Ten Percent Plan does not specifically target LM students, Rodríguez's analysis shows that it has had substantial positive effects on LM college enrollment by identifying the highest-achieving students against peers at the same school rather than at the statewide level. Nearly half of the top 10% English/ Spanish bilingual students who enroll in four-year colleges do in fact enroll at Texas' top two flagship universities.

These studies, however, also point out the limits of intervention programs. For instance, because of its open-access policy, attrition in the IB program studied by Mayer was higher than 50%. Likewise, Rodríguez shows that only 63% of Latino Top 10% students who enrolled in Texas universities graduated within 6 years: an unacceptably low rate given that they were all top 10% of their graduating class when they entered university. In all, then, these studies suggest that while intervention programs enable some underprivileged LM students to achieve success that they otherwise would not, widening access by itself does not alter the underlying structural conditions that lead to LM student academic underpreparation and thus is also likely to result in high attrition rates. This may in turn compromise stakeholders' and the public's perception of such programs' efficacy.

Language Requirements in College

Perhaps the best explored issue in research on LM students' college persistence to date has been language requirements in college. Many LM students who attend college—both community colleges and four-year schools—are required to take remedial ESL or basic writing courses, adding a layer of challenge to LM students' college success. Over 15 years ago, Williams (1995), in a survey of 78 U.S. universities, found that the vast majority had ESL courses for students who fell short of institutionally-defined English proficiency standards. Approximately three quarters of these universities required ELs to complete ESL courses before they were allowed to enroll in further requirements for first-year writing programs. Despite a 2001 position statement by the Conference on College Composition and Communication (CCCC Committee on Second Language Writing, 2001) calling for first-year writing program instructors and administrators to address the needs of L2 writers in the context of the regular writing classes, separate, remedial ESL requirements prior to enrolling in first-year writing programs remains extremely common.

While many community colleges have an "open-door" policy on the face of it, in fact they often restrict LM students' access to courses that count towards degree requirements until they complete various English placement tests, coursework, and exit tests. In a study of placement practices at community colleges in California, Bunch and Endris (this volume) find that LM students seldom receive guidance regarding whether they should be classified as ELs or as fluent English speakers. They find that this high-stakes placement decision may be made somewhat arbitrarily but is very consequential for the type and amount of courses and exit tests that LM students must take before they can proceed to completing degree requirements. Consequently, once inside the community college, LM students may find themselves "tracked" into nonacademic streams—very much like their low-level tracking in high school—without adequate information on how to navigate the community college system.

Studies have often noted that LM students find English requirements in college frustrating and demoralizing. For example, Shapiro (this volume) finds that language requirements at one university exacerbate LM students' feeling of alienation at college by labeling them as "deficient" and blocking them from registering for other courses until they have registered for remedial courses. Students who are required to take such courses are more likely to perceive these courses as punitive, as "hoops" to be jumped through rather than as a needed or valued form of academic assistance. However, it may be not the institutional identification as ELs per se that alienates students, but rather *how* such identification is institutionalized. Kanno and Grosik's (this volume) examination of two institutions' ESL policies indicates that when ESL instruction is incorporated into the regular first-year writing program and ELs are given the same number of credits for an ESL section as for a non-ESL section, EL students are more receptive to receiving help in a separate context from non-EL students. Even when given a choice, many ELs in Kanno and Grosik's study opted to take the ESL section of the first-year writing course, believing that they were getting a "better deal" for the same amount of tuition, with a smaller class size, more hands-on instruction, and instructors trained in L2 writing. In other words, when additional ESL linguistic support is incorporated into the regular undergraduate curriculum rather than instituted as separate remedial coursework, EL students seem much more open to accepting institutional support.

What We Have Yet to Learn

Thus far, we have outlined our collective knowledge base on LM students' college preparation, access, and persistence. However, we are only at the beginning stage of inquiry in this area, and we still have an enormous amount to learn if we are to help expand college opportunities for LM students. By way of conclusion, in this final section we raise several critical questions that we believe further research needs to address.

First, we see a significant need to identify which contributing factors play the greatest roles in LM students' college access and persistence. Existing research on college-going in the general population and among underrepresented groups has identified some key predictors such as race and ethnicity (Deil-Amen & Turley, 2007; Kao & Thompson, 2003), family income (Bowen et al., 2005; Engle & Lynch, 2009; Walpole, 2007), academic coursework in high school (Adelman, 2006; Cabrera & La Nasa, 2001), parental education level (Nuñez & Cuccaro-Alamin, 1998), and parental involvement (Kim & Schneider, 2005; Perna & Titus, 2005). Although it is highly likely that many of the same variables also shape LM students' college access and graduation, at the same time it is quite possible that their relative importance and interactions among them is somewhat unique for LM students. Nuñez and Sparks's analysis (this volume) revealed that many of the variables that were significant in predicting where non-LM students enrolled failed to predict where LM students enrolled in college. In other words, a different set of dynamics may be at play in LM students' college-going than in the general higher education population. If so, determining the set of factors that are most significant in shaping LM students' college-going could help us to develop better targeted college recruitment and retention efforts for these students.

Second, we currently know too little about what role families play in LM students' college-going. In general, we know that both parental education level and parental involvement positively impact students' access to college (Kim & Schneider, 2005; Nuñez & Cuccaro-Alamin, 1998; Perna & Titus, 2005). We also have scattered studies of positive familial influence on LM student academic achievement (e.g., Antrop-González, Vélez, & Garrett, 2008; Plunkett & Bámaca-Gómez, 2003). However, the dynamics of immigration may create unique familial dynamics for LM students' college expectations. We know, for example, that U.S.-born college-educated parents can help their children navigate high school course-taking and college choice based on their own experience. But we know less about what happens when students' parents are college-educated, but educated abroad so that they lack specific knowledge of American PSE. We also know that LM students come disproportionately from families with non-college-educated parents and may not receive the same level of "college knowledge" (Roderick, Nagaoka, Coca, & Moeller, 2008) from their parents as do non-LM students with college-educated parents. However, we do not know enough yet about possible compensatory factors in immigrant families that may make up for this lack. For instance, LM students may inherit a strong sense of immigrant optimism and a drive to succeed from their immigrant parents (Kao & Tienda, 1995). Even parental economic struggles may be a source of inspiration for LM students to pursue college education (Moll, Amanti, Neff, & González, 1992). We also know that children in immigrant families often take on adultlike mentoring and helping roles (Harklau & McClanahan, this volume), and yet we know too little about the role of siblings in LM students' college enrollment. Thus, families' role in LM students' college-going is a rich, complex area we need to explore.

Third, as explained earlier, we know that the community college serves as a critical point of entry into higher education for many LM students. Community college transfer rates have been the subject of longstanding concern in higher education since only about half of students in the United States who first attend a community college with the intention of ultimately earning a bachelor's degree in fact transfer to a four-year institution (Handel, 2011; National Center for Education Statistics, 2003). But we know very little about how LM students fare in transferring from community colleges to four-year institutions. Anecdotally, we know that many LM students enroll in a community college with a plan to transfer to a four-year college later. But we have almost no information on how many LM students attend community colleges with the intention of transfer, nor on how many of these students in fact transfer to four-year colleges. Considering the complex course and program placements that they negotiate in community colleges (Bunch & Endris, this volume) and the fact that LM students on average enter community colleges with less academic preparation than non-LM students (Nuñez & Sparks, this volume), we can speculate that the transfer rate for LM students is even lower than it is for the general population. If this is the case, it requires urgent policy attention. However, more information and research is needed to determine the exact numbers and extent of the problem, as well as to ascertain what dynamics and processes are at work in LM students' transfer from community colleges to four-year institutions.

Finally, we have very little research or policy analysis on how best to support LM students in college to promote retention and college graduation. Thus far, it seems that the only support provided to LM students has been English courses for ELs. The assumption seems to be that improving ELs' English skills is all that is required to level the playing field (Gándara & Rumberger, 2009). What the emerging body of research has shown, if nothing else, is that challenges facing LM students in college are much more complex and multifaceted. Academic literacy, although indisputably important, is only part of the issue. A much more comprehensive *educational* policy is needed, with an eye towards LM students' persistence and graduation, rather than simply supporting their academic literacy development. At the very least, we urge PSE institutions to identify LM students in their midst and to track their academic performance and persistence. Although most institutions have a way to identify LM students (or at least ELs for the purpose of ESL placement), few institutions use that information to track their academic progress the way they routinely do for other groups of underrepresented students such as racial/ethnic minority and low-income students. As Engle and Lynch (2009) argue, "Experience suggests that students who are not counted won't count when decisions are made and priorities are set" (p. 7). Indeed, a major part of the problem of facilitating LM students' persistence in college is that few institutions, if any, have been documenting that information.

We repeat: 21% of the K–12 school population and 11% of the college population are already linguistic minorities. These figures are only likely to increase in the future. Politicians and policy-makers continue to reiterate the vital need for the United States to produce more college graduates in order to maintain its global competitiveness (see e.g., Obama, 2009). It seems that a clearly identifiable group of students who account for more than 20% of the entire school population must be given due consideration if we are serious about increasing the number of degree holders in the United States. The magnitude of the numbers alone would suggest that we as a nation cannot afford to be complacent about the educational attainment of this segment of the student population.

Notes

1. In this edited volume, we use the term *linguistic minority* students following the term used by the United Nations (United Nations General Assembly, 1992).
2. Linguistic minority students who are currently learning academic English also have several commonly used names such as *English learners, English language learners, English as a second language students,* and *bilingual/multilingual students. English language learners (ELLs)* tend to have a strong K–12 connotation while *English as a second language (ESL) students* is more often used in postsecondary settings. *Bilingual/multilingual students,* the term we personally feel is the most accurate and fairest description of this population, is unfortunately the least often used and has little psychological reality for students and educators on the ground. In this volume, we have chosen to use the term *English Learners (ELs)* as a term that can most easily bridge across the K–12 settings and the college settings.
3. For example, according to Rumbaut's (2009) research, in the Greater Los Angeles area, 83.5% of second-generation immigrants reported growing up speaking a non-English language at home, and yet 73.4% of them also said that they prefer to speak English only at home.

References

Adelman, C. (2006). *The toolbox revisited: Paths to degree completion from high school through college.* Washington, DC: U.S. Department of Education, Office of Educational Research and Involvement.

Almon, P. C. (2010). *English language learner engagement and retention in a community college setting.* Unpublished doctoral dissertation,Temple University, Philadelphia, PA.

Antrop-González, R., Vélez, W., & Garrett, T. (2008). Examining familial-based academic success factors in urban high school students: The case of Puerto Rican female high achievers. *Marriage and Family Review, 43*(1/2), 140–163.

Arbona, C., & Nora, A. (2007). The influence of academic and environmental factors on Hispanic degree attainment. *Review of Higher Education, 30*(3), 247–269.

Auerbach, S. (2004). Engaging Latino parents in supporting college pathways: Lessons from a college access program. *Journal of Hispanic Higher Education, 3*(2), 125–145.

Bennici, F. J., & Strang, W. E. (1995). *An analysis of language minority and limited English proficient students from NELS:88* Washington DC: Office of Bilingual Education and Minority Language Affairs, U.S. Department of Education.

Bowen, W. G., Chingos, M. M., & McPherson, M. S. (2009). *Crossing the finish line: Completing college at America's public universities*. Princeton, NJ: Princeton University Press.

Bowen, W. G., Kurzwell, M. A., & Tobin, E. M. (2005). *Equity and excellence in American higher education*. Charlottesville: University of Virginia Press.

Cabrera, A. F., & La Nasa, S., M. (2001). On the path to college: Three critical tasks facing America's disadvantaged. *Research in Higher Education, 42*(2), 119–149.

Callahan, R. M. (2005). Tracking and high school English learners: Limiting opportunity to learn. *American Educational Research Journal, 42*(2), 305–328.

Callahan, R. M. (2008). Latino language-minority college going: Adolescent boys' language use and girls' social integration. *Bilingual Research Journal, 31*, 175–200.

Carnevale, A. P., & Rose, S. J. (2011). *The undereducated American*. Retrieved from Center on Education and the Workforce, Georgetown University website: http://www9.georgetown.edu/grad/gppi/hpi/cew/pdfs/undereducatedamerican.pdf

Carnevale, A. P., Smith, N., & Strohl, J. (2010). *Help wanted: Projections of jobs and education requirements through 2018*. Retrieved from Center on Education and the Workforce, Georgetown University website: http://www9.georgetown.edu/grad/gppi/hpi/cew/pdfs/FullReport.pdf

CCCC Committee on Second Language Writing. (2001). *CCCC statement on second language writing and writers*. Retrieved from http://www.ncte.org/cccc/resources/positions/secondlangwriting

Chudowsky, N., Kober, N., Gayler, K. S., & Hamilton, M. (2002). State high school exit exams: A baseline report. Washington, DC: Center on Education Policy.

College Board. (2010). *The college completion agenda*. Retrieved from College Board website: http://completionagenda.collegeboard.org

Collier, V. P. (1987). Age and rate of acquisition of second language for academic purposes. *TESOL Quarterly, 21*(4), 617–641.

Contreras, F. (2009). Sin papeles y rompiendo barreras: Latino students and the challenges of persiting in college. *Harvard Educational Review, 79*(4), 610–631.

Crawford, J. (2006). *The decline of bilingual education: How to reverse a troubling trend*. Retrieved from http://users.rcn.com/crawj/langpol/Crawford_Decline_of_BE.pdf

Cummins, J. (1981). Age on arrival and immigrant second language learning in Canada: A reassessment. *Applied Linguistics, 11*(2), 132–149.

Cummins, J. (2000). *Language, power and pedagogy*. Clevedon, England: Multilingual Matters.

Cummins, J. (2001). *Negotiating identities: Education for empowerment in a diverse society* (2nd ed.). Los Angeles, CA: California Association for Bilingual Education.

Deil-Amen, R., & Turley, R. L. (2007). A review of the transition to college literature in sociology. *Teachers College Record, 109*(10), 2324–2366.

Education Week. (2009, January). A distinctive population. *Quality Counts 2009: Portraits of a Population, How English Language-Learners Are Putting Schools to the Test*, 15.

Engle, J., & Lynch, M. (2009). *Charting a necessary path: The baseline report of Access to Success Initiative*. Washington, DC: NASH/The Education Trust.

Fry, R. (2008). *The role of schools in the English language learner achievement gap*. Retrieved from Pew Hispanic Center website: http://pewhispanic.org/files/reports/89.pdf

Gándara, P., with Bial, D. for the National Postsecondary Education Cooperative Access Working Group. (2001). *Paving the way to postsecondary education: K-12 intervention programs for underrepresented youth* (NCES 2001-205). Retrieved from: http://nces.ed.gov/pubs2001/2001205.pdf

Gándara, P., & Contreras, F. (2009). *The Latino education crisis: the consequences of failed social policies*. Cambridge, MA: Harvard University Press.

Gándara, P., & Rumberger, R. W. (2009). Immigration, language, and education: How does language policy structure opportunity? *Teachers College Record, 111*(3), 750–782.

Gándara, P., & Contreras, F. (2009). *The Latino education crisis: the consequences of failed social policies*. Cambridge, MA: Harvard University Press.

Genesee, F., & Gándara, P. (1999). Bilingual education programs: A cross-national perspective. *Journal of Social Issues, 55*(4), 665–685.

Hakuta, K., Butler, Y. G., & Witt, D. (2000). *How long does it take English learners to attain proficiency?* (Policy Report No. 2000-1). Santa Barbara: University of California Linguistic Minority Research Institute.

Handel, S. J. (2011). *Improving student transfer from community colleges to four-year institutions—The perspective of leaders from baccalaureate-granting institutions.* Retrieved from College Board Advocacy and Policy Center website: http://advocacy.collegeboard.org/sites/default/files/11b3193transpartweb110712.pdf

Harklau, L. (1998). Newcomers in U.S. higher education: Questions of access and equity. *Educational Policy, 12*(6), 634–658.

Hearn, J. C. (1984). The relative roles of academic, ascribed, and socioeconomic characteristics in college destinations. *Sociology of Education, 57*(1), 22–30.

Kanno, Y., & Cromley, J. (2011, March). *English language learners' college access and attainment: A national level analysis.* Paper presented at the American Association for Applied Linguistics, Chicago, IL.

Kanno, Y., Varghese, M. M., & Fuentes, R. (2011). *Agency and structure in immigrant English language learners' access to four-year college.* Manuscript submitted for publication.

Kao, G., & Thompson, J. S. (2003). Racial and ethnic stratification in educational achievement and attainment. *Annual Review of Sociology, 29*, 417–442.

Kao, G., & Tienda, M. (1995). Optimism and achievement: The educational performance of immigrant youth. *Social Science Quarterly, 76*(1), 1–19.

Karen, D. (2002). Changes in access to higher education in the United States 1980–1992. *Sociology of Education, 75*, 191–210.

Kim, D. H., & Schneider, B. (2005). Social capital in action: Alignment of parental support in adolescents' transition to postsecondary education. *Social Forces, 84*(2), 1181–1206.

Klein, S., Bugarin, R., Beltranena, R., & McArthur, E. (2004). *Language minorities and their educational and labor market indicators: Recent trends* (NCES 2004-009). Retrieved from National Center for Educational Statistics website: http://nces.ed.gov/pubs2004/2004009.pdf

Leki, I. (2007). *Undergraduates in a second language: Challenges and complexities of academic literacy development.* Mahwah, NJ: Erlbaum.

Lumina Foundation. (2010). *Lumina's big goal: To increase the proportion of Americans with high-quality degrees and credentials to 60 percent by the year 2025.* Retrieved from http://www.luminafoundation.org/goal_2025

McDonough, P. M. (1997). *Choosing colleges: How social class and schools structure opportunity.* Albany: State University of New York Press.

Menken, K. (2008). *English learners left behind: Standardized testing as language policy.* Clevedon, England: Multilingual Matters.

Moll, L. C., Amanti, C., Neff, D., & González, N. (1992). Funds of knowledge for teaching: Using qualitative approach to connect homes and classrooms. *Theory into Practice, 31*(2), 49–58.

Morales, A., Herrerra, S., & Murry, K. (2009). Navigating the waves of social and political capriciousness: Inspiring perspectives from DREAM-eligible immigrant students. *Journal of Hispanic Higher Education.* Advance online publication retrieved from http://jhh.sagepub.com/

National Center for Education Statistics. (2003). *The condition of education 2003.* Retrieved from http://nces.ed.gov/pubs2003/2003067.pdf

National Center for Education Statistics. (2011). *The condition of education 2011.* Retrieved from http://nces.ed.gov/pubs2011/2011033.pdf

Nuñez, A.-M. (2009). Latino students' transitions to college: A social and intercultural capital perspective. *Harvard Educational Review, 79*(1), 22–48.

Nuñez, A.-M., & Cuccaro-Alamin, S. (1998). *First-generation students: Undergraduates whose parents never enrolled in postsecondary education.* Retrieved from National Center for Education Statistics website: http://nces.ed.gov/pubs98/98082.pdf

Obama, B. (2009). *Remarks by the President on the American Graduation Initiative.* Retrieved from the White House website: http://www.whitehouse.gov/the_press_office/Remarks-by-the-President-on-the-American-Graduation-Initiative-in-Warren-MI/

Pascarella, E. T., Pierson, C. T., Wolniak, G. C., & Terenzini, P. T. (2004). First-generation college students: Additional evidence on college experiences and outcomes. *The Journal of Higher Education, 75*(3), 249–284.

Percy Calaff, K. (2008). Latino students' journeys toward college. *Bilingual Research Journal, 31,* 201–225.

Perna, L. W., & Titus, M. A. (2005). The relationship between parental involvement as social capital and college enrollment: An examination of racial/ethnic group differences. *Journal of Higher Education, 76*(5), 485–518.

Plunkett, S. W., & Bámaca-Gómez, M. Y. (2003). The relationship between parenting, acculturation, and adolescent academics in Mexican-origin immigrant families in Los Angeles. *Hispanic Journal of Behavioral Sciences, 25,* 222–239.

Roderick, M., Nagaoka, J., Coca, B., & Moeller, E. (2008). *From high school to the future: Potholes on the road to college.* Retrieved from Consortium on Chicago School Research at the University of Chicago website: http://ccsr.uchicago.edu/downloads/1835ccsr_potholes_summary.pdf

Ruíz, R. (1984). Orientations in language planning. *NABE Journal, 8*(2), 15–34.

Rumbaut, R. G. (2009). A language graveyard?: The evolution of language competencies, preferences and use among young adult children of immigrants. In T. G. Wiley, J. S. Lee, & R. W. Rumberger (Eds.), *The education of language minority immigrants in the United States* (pp. 35–71). Bristol, England: Multilingual Matters.

Solórzano, R. W. (2008). High stakes testing: Issues, implications, and remedies for English language learners. *Review of Educational Research, 78*(2), 260–329.

Southern Regional Education Board. (2010). *No time to waste: Policy recommendations for increasing college completion.* Retrieved from http://publications.sreb.org/2010/10E10_No_Time_to_Waste.pdf

Swail, W. S., Cabrera, A. F., Lee, C., & Williams, A. (2005). *Pathways to the bachelor's degree for Latino students. Latino Students & the Educational Pipeline, Part III.* Retrieved from ERIC database (ED499873)

Thomas, W. P., & Collier, V. P. (1997). *School effectiveness for language minority students.* NCBE Resource Collection Series, No. 9. Retrieved from ERIC database. (ED436087)

Thomas, W. P., & Collier, V. P. (2002). Accelerated schooling for all students: Research findings on education in multilingual communities. In S. Shaw (Ed.), *Intercultural education in European classrooms: Intercultural education partnership* (pp. 15–35). Stoke-on-Trent, England: Trentham.

United Nations General Assembly. (1992). *Declaration on the rights of persons belonging to national or ethnic, religious and linguistic minorities.* Retrieved from United Nations website: http://www.un.org/documents/ga/res/47/a47r135.htm

Valenzuela, A., Fuller, E. J., & Vasquez Heilig, J. (2006). The disappearance of high school English language learners from Texas high schools. *Williams Review, 1,* 166–200.

Walpole, M. (2007). Economically and educationally challenged students in higher education: Access to outcomes. *ASHE Higher Education Report, 33*(3), 1–113.

Wiley, T. G., & Wright, W. (2004). Against the undertow: Language-minority education policy and politics in the "age of accountability." *Educational Policy, 18*(1), 142–168.

Williams, J. (1995). ESL composition program administration in the United States. *Journal of Second Language Writing, 4*(2), 157–179.

Wright, W. (2007). Heritage language programs in the era of English-only and No Child Left Behind. *Heritage Language Journal, 5*(1), 1–26.

Zarate, M. E., Sáenz, V. B., & Oseguera, L. (2011). Supporting the participation and success of Chicanos in higher education. In R. R. Valencia (Ed.), *Chicano School failure and success: Past, present, and future* (3rd ed., pp. 120–140). New York: Routledge.

PART I

College Preparation in High School

2

HIGH SCHOOL ESL PLACEMENT

Practice, Policy, and Effects on Achievement

Rebecca M. Callahan and Dara R. Shifrer

Tension: Prioritizing Language Acquisition or Academic Content

English Learners (ELs)[1] in U.S. high schools, i.e., linguistic minority students placed in English as a Second Language (ESL) coursework, must simultaneously master both English and the content areas in order to graduate and successfully enter the postsecondary sphere. While ESL coursework generally focuses on language development, content area coursework can be modified to address language learning needs as well (Chamot & O'Malley, 1996; Echevarria, Vogt, & Short, 2007). However, EL achievement levels, as illustrated throughout this volume, are a source of concern for educators, researchers, and policy makers alike. The intersection of English proficiency and academic stratification lies at the crux of the EL achievement dilemma. ELs not only demonstrate lower levels of achievement than native English speakers but often perform at lower levels compared to their mainstreamed linguistic minority peers. Thus, compared to other linguistic minority students, it is not entirely clear whether adolescent ELs' achievement is due to differences in English proficiency, other characteristics correlated with academic achievement (e.g., socioeconomic status [SES], student behaviors, and race/ethnicity), other academic experiences influenced by identification as EL (e.g., student–teacher relationships, opportunities to learn), or other unmeasured factors.

The *Lau* decision (*Lau v. Nichols*, 1974) mandated that schools ensure access to an equitable education for students learning English. While a variety of linguistic support services, such as primary language support and maintenance, dual-immersion, and transitional bilingual education, as well as ESL instruction are often considered, the majority of high school ELs experience language-based ESL coursework separate from academic content area instruction (Zehler, Fleischman, Hopstock, Stephenson, Pendzick, & Sapru, 2003). Since *Lau* (1974), educational policy regarding ELs has focused on the acquisition of English, some might argue, to the detriment of ELs' overall academic preparation (Callahan, 2005; Gándara, 2002). For instance, the most widespread policy response in American schools, ESL placement, prioritizes language acquisition over content area mastery. However, movement out of ESL and reclassification[2] as "fluent English proficient" require content area mastery (Linquanti, 2001; Ragan & Lesaux, 2006). This chapter investigates the critical juncture between language and educational policy with respect to ELs' high school academic experiences. Many schools, districts, and states focus on high school graduation as a primary goal for ELs; this chapter is founded in the argument that a shift in focus away from high school graduation and towards college preparation may improve ELs' academic well-being and future prospects.

Over the past several years, the first author has pursued a research agenda focused on the academic preparation experienced by adolescent ELs in ESL settings in order to get to the root of the "EL achievement gap." This chapter will synthesize findings from five of these studies, both single- and co-authored, which address different facets of the EL educational experience during high school. These five studies use a range of datasets to attempt to discern the nuanced relationship of ELs' high school experiences and their academic outcomes. The present synthesis draws on findings from all five studies, as well as related literature, to conclude with a set of recommendations that address current EL educational policy.

Describing the Studies: Data and Method

Shifting away from a classroom perspective to explore broad patterns of achievement, the studies reviewed in this chapter draw from school- and national-level data to explore the association between language proficiency and ELs' high school academic preparation. Table 2.1 lists the five studies in the order they will be covered. We open this chapter with findings from the first and most recent study, offering a descriptive overview comparing ELs' end of high school course-taking outcomes to those of their peers not placed in ESL, both linguistic minority and native English speakers. Given these patterns of preparation, results from the second study are then interrogated to illustrate the tension between academic preparation via course placement and English proficiency among one high school's entire EL population. Findings from the third and fourth studies are then synthesized to describe variation in the effects of ESL placement on academic achievement by generational status, school context, and race/ethnicity. Finally, results from the fifth study are presented; this final study investigated the association between ESL placement and academic achieve-

TABLE 2.1 List of Studies Synthesized in Order of Review

	Authors	Year	Title	Journal
1	Callahan, Rebecca Shifrer, Dara	2011	English learners' secondary course-taking: Equitable academic access?	Manuscript Under Review
2	Callahan, Rebecca	2005	Tracking and high school English Learners: Limiting opportunity to learn.	*American Educational Research Journal*
3	Callahan, Rebecca Wilkinson, Lindsey Muller, Chandra	2009	ESL placement and schools: Effects on immigrant achievement	*Educational Policy*
4	Callahan, Rebecca Wilkinson, Lindsey Muller, Chandra Frisco, Michele	2008	School context and the effect of ESL placement on Mexican-origin adolescents' achievement	*Social Science Quarterly*
5	Callahan, Rebecca Wilkinson, Lindsey Muller, Chandra	2010	Academic achievement and course-taking among language minority youth in U.S. Schools: Effects of ESL placement	*Educational Evaluation and Policy Analysis*

ment, while taking into account the factors that are not only associated with EL identification, but also with academic achievement.

Four of the five studies utilized nationally representative, longitudinal data; the fifth used locally collected student data. As a whole, all five studies address distinct factors shaping high school EL achievement from a variety of theoretical perspectives. Following the synthesis and discussion of the cumulative findings and drawing from the relevant literature, this chapter concludes with recommendations for policy and practice focused on preparing ELs for entry into higher education.

The EL Achievement Gap: Courses Completed by the End of High School

Little doubt exists that high school age ELs perform at lower levels than their native English speaking peers (Freeman, Freeman, & Mercuri, 2002; Ruiz-de-Velasco & Fix, 2000), but relatively little research compares the academic performance of ELs to other linguistic minority students not placed in ESL. This comparison establishes differences in the academic outcomes of students with somewhat comparable linguistic histories, but different educational experiences (ESL vs. no ESL), and thus begins to explore how ESL placement may shape students' academic progress. The first study we present (Callahan & Shifrer, 2011) illustrates the gap in academic preparation, as measured by end of high school course completion, between ELs[3] (e.g., linguistic minorities in ESL), linguistic minorities not in ESL, and native English speakers.

Students' postsecondary trajectories—college and, subsequently, employment—are in part dependent upon the courses they completed by the end of high school. Completion of Algebra II by the end of high school is a strong predictor of college-going, and completion of Chemistry is generally recognized as a minimal requirement for admission to a four-year postsecondary institution (Adelman, 2006). Because of the strong association between course-taking and college-going, differences in students' placement patterns are perceived to reflect the sorting mechanisms that occur within schools. Indeed, academic stratification is often reflective of social stratification in the larger society (Oakes, 1985). Of all the academic content areas—science, social science, English, and mathematics—mathematics is easily the most highly stratified, with progression through the subject dependent upon completion of prerequisite courses (Riegle-Crumb & Grodsky, 2010). Science coursework is also stratified, but not quite as rigidly; if anything, advanced science course-taking depends upon the completion of mathematics prerequisites. Students placed in low-level math or science at the beginning of high school may have little opportunity to complete more than the basic graduation requirements (Algebra I, Biology) prior to their senior year (Adelman, 2006). Low levels of content area course-taking suggest limited academic preparation and curricular exposure.

This first study used student and high school transcript data from the Education Longitudinal Study of 2002 (ELS:2002) to illustrate course-taking patterns based on language status and ESL placement. The study focused on the contrast between the courses that are required for high school graduation as opposed to college admission (Callahan & Shifrer, 2011). Our analyses relied on a previously developed coding schema characterizing the different courses required for basic high school graduation and admission to a noncompetitive 4-year college (Shettle et al., 2007). Figure 2.1 illustrates the proportions of ELs

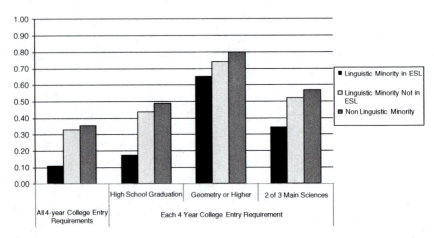

FIGURE 2.1 High school course-raking by linguistic status: Contrasting basic graduation and college preparation

(linguistic minority students placed in ESL), mainstreamed linguistic minority students, and native English speakers who completed (a) the overall college preparatory curriculum, (b) basic high school graduation requirements, (c) college preparatory math, and (d) college preparatory science.

Beginning with basic high school graduation requirements, we find that fewer than one in five ELs complete these, compared to nearly half of their peers not placed in ESL. A similar, although larger, gap is evident with the composite whole of the college preparatory curriculum, completed by only 11% of high school ELs compared to a third or more of their respective peers. While nearly two-thirds of ELs complete college preparatory math course-taking, barely one-third take coursework in two of the three main sciences, in contrast to over half of each peer group. These differences in college preparatory course-taking help to identify content-based forces contributing to the EL achievement gap in our stratified secondary system.

The largest cross-group gap occurs with the completion of basic high school graduation requirements, suggesting that the vast majority of ELs leave high school poorly prepared for the workforce, much less college. However, important policy implications emerge once we consider content area college preparatory enrollment as well. The relatively small gap in math course-taking may reflect the hierarchical nature of math course-taking, as well as math's firm foothold as a high school graduation requirement. In contrast, the larger science course-taking gap may reflect the perception of science as an advanced elective. Elective coursework that is not required for graduation, but beneficial in the college admissions process, may be considered an unaffordable luxury for students placed in ESL. The stratification of academic preparation we highlight here may reflect educators' and counselors' prioritization of high school graduation requirements and linguistic support services (e.g., ESL placement) for EL students.

Although ESL programs are designed to develop English proficiency, we ask whether a narrow focus on language alone in some programs may inadvertently result in the exclusion of academic content. Given that exit from ESL programs requires not just proficiency in English, but also grade and age appropriate academic competence (Ragan & Lesaux, 2006), a pedagogical bias toward language could preclude ELs' access to academic content compared to their mainstreamed peers. The patterns illustrated here though do not indicate whether they are due to differences in English proficiency, to other individual characteristics of EL students also associated with academic achievement, or to the educational experiences of EL students. It may be that the course-taking trajectories of ELs languish as a result of placement in lower level academic coursework while they are learning English, especially in subjects that are more hierarchically organized, like science and math. Taking high-level coursework may be dependent upon exiting ESL, but exiting ESL is dependent upon content mastery (Linquanti, 2001; Mahoney & MacSwan, 2005; Ragan & Lesaux, 2006), trapping EL students in a cycle of lesser educational opportunities.

The proceeding sections will synthesize results from the four remaining studies, all attempting to parse out language skills, other student characteristics, and educational experiences from the effect of ESL placement. The final three studies specifically explore whether the differences in academic preparation by ESL placement remain after generational status, school context, length of residence in the United States, academic history, and language proficiency, among other variables, are taken into account.

English Learner Achievement: Individual and School Predictors

There is a dearth of research that goes beyond descriptive analyses to account for the influence of differences in English proficiency and other important covariates of both ESL placement and academic achievement. Because the group of linguistic minority students who are in ESL may differ systematically from those who are not, it is impossible to determine whether academic achievement among EL students is attributable to ESL placement or to students' distinctive qualities unless the analysis accounts for a multitude of factors simultaneously. In other words, ELs may possess certain sociodemographic characteristics which distinguish them even from other linguistic minorities (Abedi & Gándara, 2006). Research exploring ELs' schooling must take into account the host of individual- and school-level characteristics that are also associated with achievement. Racial/ethnic identity (Bankston & Zhou, 2002; Kao & Tienda, 1995; Padilla & Gonzalez, 2001) and SES (Lew, 2004; Portes & Fernandez-Kelly, 2008) are both associated with overall patterns of adolescent achievement, as is immigrant generational status (Fuligni, 1997; Kalogrides, 2009; Rumbaut & Portes, 2001).

School composition and context (Cosentino de Cohen, Deterding, & Clewell, 2005; Gándara, Rumberger, Maxwell-Jolly, & Callahan, 2003; Louie & Holdaway, 2009) also play a role in shaping the academic outcomes of all adolescents; ELs may attend schools that are largely different from those attended by students who are not in ESL. For instance, ELs are more likely to come from poor neighborhoods, have parents with relatively low levels of education, attend high poverty schools, and be taught by uncredentialed teachers (Gándara et al., 2003; Schwartz & Steifel, 2004), all factors negatively associated with academic performance. The fact that numerous factors are associated with both adolescent achievement *and* ESL placement complicates the quest to understand EL achievement. To ascertain whether any portion of the EL achievement gap may be attributable to ESL placement, research must control on any number of covarying factors—those factors which predict both ESL placement *and* adolescents' academic achievement.

Language and Academic Preparation

The second study we present explored the influence of English proficiency and academic preparation on the academic outcomes of ELs in one northern California high school (Callahan, 2005). Because ELs are defined in part by their position on the English learning continuum, the role of English proficiency in their academic outcomes warrants special attention. By definition, ELs must develop English proficiency alongside content area mastery; however, learning English need not preclude the development of content area knowledge.

Although formal tracks arguably no longer exist within the secondary school system (Lucas & Berends, 2002), curricular distinctions between courses that meet basic high school graduation and college preparatory requirements ensure stratification in student preparation. Inevitably, some students will leave high school with low levels of academic preparation and few postsecondary options outside of manual labor and service-sector work, a potential consequence of the course-taking patterns evidenced in the first study. Because of stratification within schools, the effect of English proficiency must be isolated from that of track placement when exploring EL academic achievement in order to understand the disparities in course-taking achievement presented in the first study. While the second study predicted positive academic outcomes with both English proficiency level and college preparatory enrollment in the regression models, college preparatory enrollment was significantly associated with more outcomes than English proficiency among EL students. Net of other controls, college preparatory placement was positively associated with math test scores, GPA, and credits toward graduation, while English proficiency had no association with these outcomes. In contrast—again net of other student characteristics—English proficiency was positively associated solely with reading and language arts test scores, the only two language-based outcomes in the study. Ultimately, for these ELs, college preparatory enrollment mattered most for academic achievement, with higher level courses resulting in better academic outcomes for ELs of a comparable English proficiency level.

During the course of the second study, several distinctions between recent immigrants who had just entered ESL and long-term ELs became clear. The long-term ELs, having been in U.S. schools since the early elementary grades, demonstrated higher levels of English proficiency than the recent immigrants, levels comparable to those of native English speakers. Despite this English proficiency "advantage," the long-term ELs earned significantly lower GPAs and standardized math test scores, and significantly fewer credits towards graduation than their recent immigrant counterparts. The depressed academic achievement of long-term ELs ultimately restricted their eligibility for reclassification, or exit from ESL. On the aggregate, the data demonstrate an inverse relationship between English proficiency and academic achievement, with higher levels of English proficiency associated with lower levels of academic achievement.

This negative association was driven primarily by the poor grades and low test scores of the long-term ELs, suggesting that English proficiency may not be the primary factor shaping continued ESL enrollment as well as academic progression. Other factors, such as academic stratification, SES, generational status, and school context need to be considered.

Even before *Lau*, the acquisition of English has been central in the education of immigrant linguistic minority youth (Tyack, 1974). Although recent immigrants might be relatively less English proficient than long-term ELs, they tend to outperform the latter, largely second-generation group, suggesting a recent immigrant advantage (Callahan, 2005; Kao & Tienda, 1995). The inverse relationship between English proficiency and achievement suggests that long-term ELs' academic performance may be a product of the instruction received in the U.S. school system, and specifically within the ESL context. However, without careful attention paid to selection effects, i.e., the influence of systematic differences in SES, generational status, and school context among recent immigrants and long-term ELs, it is difficult to ascertain the true roots of their achievement patterns. In sum, other qualities of the EL student and her schooling experiences may contribute more to her academic outcomes than English proficiency.

Estimating the Effects of ESL Placement: Studies 3, 4, and 5

While the previous two studies explored the associations between language proficiency, academic preparation, and EL achievement, this section will synthesize results from the three remaining studies. In one way or another, each of these studies estimates the effects of ESL placement while accounting for the qualities of the student and school that may be associated with both the placement itself and the outcomes under consideration. Here, we explored the effects of ESL placement as an indicator of academic stratification, the variable itself derived from student transcript course titles.

Arguably, if schools, districts, and states are focused on the highest achievement possible among ELs, there should be no difference in course-taking patterns by ESL placement, net of English language proficiency, race/ethnicity, and other important covariates. However, a negative effect of ESL placement on students' course-taking net of controls would suggest that educators and institutions focus on the low bar of graduation for high school ELs, rather than the highest achievement possible.

In order to separate out the effect of placement in ESL coursework from that of prior achievement, one must control on a variety of covarying factors. In addition to English proficiency, factors that shape *both* adolescent achievement and a student's likelihood of ESL placement include, but are not limited to, parent education level, SES, years in U.S. schools, age upon arrival, and reading test scores. In order to account for these factors, the three remaining studies utilized propensity score matching (PSM). PSM is a modeling technique which allows the researcher to take a number of potential covariates of both ESL placement and academic achievement into account. As a result, the researcher can argue with relative certainty that the one difference between any two "matched" individuals in the sample is, in fact, the treatment: in this case, ESL placement. PSM allowed the research teams in these three studies to come as close as possible to an experimental design while using survey data. We were able to essentially "compare" any two immigrant linguistic minority students (the target population for ESL services) who were similar on a wealth of background and contextual characteristics, with the exception being that one experienced ESL placement during high school while the other did not. These studies allowed us to explore the effects of ESL placement during high school, net of numerous other confounding factors, on immigrant linguistic minority students.

The third and fourth studies used survey data from the National Longitudinal Study of Adolescent Health (Add Health), and its companion high school transcript study, the Adolescent Health and Academic Achievement (AHAA) (Muller et al., 2007), to explore variation in the estimated effects of ESL placement with respect to school context and individuals' sociocultural characteristics (Callahan, Wilkinson, & Muller, 2008; Callahan, Wilkinson, Muller, & Frisco, 2009). The fifth and final study analyzed ELS:2002 data to illustrate the estimated effects of ESL placement on immigrant linguistic minority students' college preparatory course-taking and achievement according to how well a student conforms to educators' expected EL profile (recent immigrant with relatively low levels of English proficiency and reading test scores) (Callahan, Wilkinson, & Muller, 2010). Drawing from multiple datasets fortifies the EL achievement findings from the first two studies. Likewise, the use of nationally representative data highlights broad trends in the academic preparation and achievement of high school ELs as they plan to enter into young adulthood.

School Context and Generational Status

While adolescent achievement certainly varies with individual characteristics, findings from the third and fourth studies suggested that the proportion of immigrant, linguistic minority adolescents in a given school influenced the achievement and attainment of these same students. The multivariate models employed in the third study suggest, net of other student characteristics, a negative estimated effect of ESL placement on achievement among first generation students (the most recent immigrants) in low immigrant-concentration schools, and a null or positive effect on achievement among the second generation in high immigrant-concentration schools (Callahan et al., 2009). Specifically, we found significant negative estimated effects of ESL placement among the most recent immigrants on Algebra II and Chemistry completion and overall college preparation[4] in low immigrant-concentration schools.

In contrast, results indicated a significant positive estimated effect of ESL placement on these same outcomes among second generation youth in high immigrant concentration schools (Callahan et al., 2009). The variation in the effect of ESL placement speaks to the interaction of individual characteristics (length of residence, prior schooling, generational status) with contextual factors (school composition).

Segmented assimilation theory (Rumbaut & Portes, 2001) suggests that immigrant adolescents' trajectories result from an interaction of individual characteristics and school and community contexts. The third study results presented above suggested that the estimated effect of ESL placement depends upon the interaction between generational status and school context. High immigrant-concentration schools may provide greater numbers of like-minded peers and more teachers who are attuned to the linguistic and academic needs of immigrant, linguistic minority adolescents. However, the second generation findings might best be taken with a bit of caution. Educated entirely in U.S. schools, second generation students' presence in high school ESL coursework itself raises concerns. A critical mass of co-ethnic, first generation peers imbued with "immigrant optimism" and drive (Kao & Tienda, 1995) may bolster second generation students' social capital, facilitating social integration and academic achievement (Ream, 2005; Riegle-Crumb & Callahan, 2009). First generation students would not be expected to benefit from the presence of a strong co-ethnic network as they themselves embody the critical characteristics associated with achievement. However, second generation students, somewhat more removed from the immigrant ethic and optimism, might be expected to experience a boost to achievement when in the presence of driven peers. Alternately, in schools where immigrant, linguistic minority youth comprise a small minority, ELs may find themselves socially and academically isolated, resulting in depressed levels of academic achievement as demonstrated by first generation students in low concentration schools in this work and in others.

Race/Ethnicity: Mexican-Origin Students and ESL Placement

Models in the fourth study built upon prior research exploring the interaction of individual sociocultural characteristics and context among Mexican-origin linguistic minority youth (Crosnoe, Lopez-Gonzalez, & Muller, 2004; Ream, 2003). Here, we sought to explore whether similar effects of ESL placement held among the largest group of immigrant adolescents, Mexican-origin youth, a racial/ethnic group with lower levels of academic performance overall regardless of EL identification (Gibson, Gándara, & Koyama, 2004). Results again suggested a negative estimated effect of ESL placement on first generation Mexican-origin students' math and science course-taking and grades in low immigrant concentration schools, and a positive estimated effect for second generation Mexican-origin youth in high immigrant-concentration schools

(Callahan et al., 2008). Combined, findings from these two studies suggest that the school context matters in combination with individual characteristics to determine the net effect of placement in ESL. To further explore these associations, we move to a study designed to interrogate the relationship between EL identification and linguistic minority achievement.

Fitting the EL Profile: Recent Immigrants and Long-Term ELs

Findings from the second, third, and fourth studies all speak to variation in EL achievement based on length of residence, highlighting the difficulties inherent in meeting the needs of the academically and linguistically heterogeneous adolescent EL population (Freeman, Freeman, & Mercuri, 2002; Olsen, 2010; Ruiz-de-Velasco & Fix, 2000). The tension between the linguistic and academic needs of the high school EL population speaks to the need to address individual characteristics in program design, implementation, and evaluation. While English acquisition is, of course, critical for academic success, the results of these studies call attention to the primacy of academic development in the scholastic endeavors of ESL students. In fact, an emphasis on English acquisition over academic development may lie at the root of the perceived ELL achievement gap (Callahan & Gándara, 2004).

The fifth and final study utilized the nationally representative sample of adolescents in ELS:2002 to further tease apart the effect of ESL placement on achievement depending upon an individual student's likelihood of placement in ESL (Callahan et al., 2010). Here, we stratified students based on length of residence and other factors shaping their likelihood of being placed in ESL coursework. Due to the academic competency required to exit ESL programs (Linquanti, 2001) we observe an overrepresentation of long-term ELs at the high school level (Callahan, 2005; Olsen, 2010); more often than not, these long-term ELs fit less well to the programs designed to immerse (recent immigrant) students in English and in American culture.

Among the students most likely to fit educators' expected EL profile (recent immigrants with relatively low levels of English proficiency), we found ESL placement to have a significant positive estimated effect on students' math test scores and math enrollment, and null effects in all other college preparatory areas. However, for the majority of linguistic minority youth placed in ESL who fit the traditional EL profile less well, placement in ESL resulted in negative estimated effects on math, science, and social science enrollment, as well as grades and math test scores (Callahan et al., 2010). These results hold net of English proficiency and other factors associated with both ESL placement and achievement. The negative estimated effects of ESL placement among those who fit the EL profile less well echo the significantly lower levels of achievement found among long-term ELs in the second study (Callahan, 2005). Findings from this final study highlight the distinctions between recent immigrants and long-term ELs, suggesting a need to focus on the academic needs of the bulk of high school ELs.

Discussion and Conclusions

While some adolescent ELs do in fact exit the secondary system well-prepared for entry into a postsecondary institution, results highlighted through this series of studies indicate that linguistic minority students on the whole leave high schools woefully underprepared to enter into higher education. The first and second studies illustrated the gap in academic preparation experienced by ELs, compared to their mainstreamed language minority and native English speaking peers. The third, fourth, and fifth studies simultaneously took additional individual and educational characteristics into account. Collectively, these studies demonstrated that the academic achievement of ELs remains significantly behind that of comparable linguistic minority students not placed in ESL, suggesting that they leave U.S. high schools lacking the academic preparation necessary to enter, much less compete in higher education.

Together, findings from this series of studies highlight the need for educators to be aware of four key issues. First, the cumulative effect of long-term placement in language-based ESL coursework merits considerable empirical and pedagogical attention. Second, the disconnect between ESL placement entry (linguistic) and exit (academic) criteria (Linquanti, 2001; Ragan & Lesaux, 2006) may exacerbate the EL achievement gap if ESL programs focus on the criteria for entrance (the need to learn English) rather than the criteria for exit (the need to demonstrate academic competency). Third, the struggle to balance ELs' English development and their content area mastery is magnified as the high school curriculum separates into one of basic skills and another of college preparation. The current programmatic focus on English acquisition may serve select ELs, namely recent immigrants, while precluding integration into and exposure to a rigorous academic curriculum. Fourth, certain structural and staffing constraints inherent to the secondary school system may work to limit ELs' academic exposure through the bureaucracy of schooling.

Long-term ELs

The negative estimated effects of ESL placement among long-term ELs in contrast to the perceived benefits of ESL placement among recent immigrants suggests that retention in ESL programs may ultimately atrophy linguistic minority students' academic development. Linguistic support programs designed for ELs may unintentionally limit their access to the rigorous academic curriculum required for high school graduation, admission into college, and, ironically, even successful transition from ESL programs into college preparatory coursework. It may be that ESL programs focus on language at the expense of academic mastery, which is counterproductive to students' academic development and educational opportunities.

ESL Entry and Exit Criteria: A Focus on Language

Alternately, identification as an EL and subsequent ESL placement may trigger scheduling and gate-keeping mechanisms which (albeit even indirectly) limit educational opportunities. Academic gate-keeping may actually stem from a desire to protect the EL and facilitate her schooling. EL status may unwittingly suggest to educators that a student is not eligible for placement in certain (e.g., college preparatory) coursework (Harklau, 1994; Kanno & Grosik, this volume). Well-intentioned educators who may want to ease the burden for ELs struggling to master both the language and academic content may expect less of their charges. Second, despite pedagogically driven research suggesting that the most efficient path to developing academic English proficiency is through content area instruction (Chamot & O'Malley, 1996; Crandall, Jaramillo, Olsen, & Peyton, 2002; Janzen, 2008; Olsen, 2010), educators may still tend to simplify ELs' coursework. The "pobrecito" syndrome (Mohr, 2004), thought to occur as early as the elementary grades, describes educators' efforts to "simplify" the math, science, and social science content that ELs must cover in the course of a school year. Content area simplification arguably limits ELs academic exposure.

A Focus on Academic Content

Even in programs designed to highlight the importance of accessing academic content for ELs, the theory purported in the optimal pedagogical models is not always carried out in the classroom. High school content courses labeled "sheltered" and "SDAIE," may cover less content and proceed at a slower pace than non-EL focused coursework (Dabach, 2011; Olsen, 1997; Valdés, 2001). While researchers and educators involved in the development of the sheltered approach to teaching (Chamot & O'Malley, 1996; Crandall, Jaramillo, Olsen, & Peyton, 2002; Echevarria, Short, & Powers, 2006; Echevarria et al., 2007) clearly do not advocate watering down the curriculum, teacher practitioners attempting to simplify their students' academic lives may in fact do so, as suggested in the literature (Ek, 2009; Harklau, 1999; Minicucci & Olsen, 1993). EL status, when interpreted by practitioners as an indicator that a student requires "protection" against academic struggle, might limit academic exposure, causing them to fall behind their peers not placed in ESL. In fact, the literature on "critical caring" (Antrop-González & De Jesús, 2006) clarifies that the positive teacher-student relationships often reported by linguistic minority youth may not actually coincide with teachers' holding students to high academic standards (Gibson & Hidalgo, 2009). Ream (2003) documents this process particularly well with Mexican-origin youth, many of whom are linguistic minorities, finding that students reported positive relationships with teachers who permit them to nap in class and expect little from them academically.

Bureaucracy of Schooling: (Un)intentional Barriers

At the school level, in an attempt to remain in compliance with policy designed to protect ELs, educators may attempt to ensure that ELs are placed *only* with teachers who have ESL training or certification[5] (Dabach, 2011). In theory, such policy should ensure the provision of the best pedagogical practices for ELs in their content area coursework; in practice, however, it may actually limit the course options available to ELs. For example, California Education Code Section 44253.1 indicates that all ELs must be placed with an EL certified teacher for instructional purposes; however, not all teachers currently hold (nor are required to hold) EL certification. While it is true that ELs must simulta-neously master both the language and the content, if none of a given school's Chemistry teachers have ESL certification, then ELs in that school will not be eligible to take Chemistry. Instead, they are limited to either the sheltered or SDAIE version of science offered, or no science at all.

Finally, another possible explanation for this phenomenon addresses stratifi-cation among teachers. Often AP, honors, and advanced courses are perceived as desirable courses to teach, comprised of an elite group of highly motivated students (Gamoran, 1992). High status courses are rewarded to the most expe-rienced teachers (Finley, 1984), often leaving the students with the greatest needs to the most inexperienced, and often noncertified teachers (Gándara et al., 2003). If experienced teachers do teach a less desirable course, they may be the most resistant to adapting their instruction to diverse learner needs, and, as the most senior staff members, often feel the least need to comply with certification recommendations. In fact Dabach (2011) found that often the most experienced teachers would use their clout to ensure that they were not assigned to teach EL classes. Educational policies designed to protect and sup-port ELs as they progress through the K–12 system must be carefully monitored to ensure they do, in fact, facilitate rather than impede academic integration and achievement. Language policies such as *Lau* (1974) and NCLB's inclu-sion of ELs in federal accountability measures (U.S. Department of Education, 2001) are in theory intended to ensure equitable educational access and oppor-tunities; however, these findings suggest that in practice, the converse may hold true. Careful evaluation of long-term retention in ESL programs, EL entry and exit criteria, and the focus on academic development within ESL programs may help to shift the focus from English acquisition to academic preparation for ELs.

Implications for Policy and Practice

Conventional wisdom might suggest that adolescent ELs must lack English proficiency and as a result, graduation from high school seems to be a reasonable, even laudable goal. In reality, research has found that adolescent ELs span the English proficiency spectrum, with many highly English proficient students struggling not because of lack of fluency, but rather due to limited academic preparation and content area exposure during early schooling, arguably while placed in ESL programs (Callahan, 2005; Ruiz-de-Velasco & Fix, 2000). Over half (59%) of high school ELs in California have been in U.S. schools for 6 years or more; in addition, in a third of districts, the proportion of long-term ELs exceeds 75% (Olsen, 2010). As the synthesis of results from this series of studies indicates, extended placement in ESL coursework does little to improve ELs' academic development; in fact, findings suggest a ceiling effect, with the most recent arrivals experiencing the lion's share of the benefit, while more English proficient students languish academically (Callahan et al., 2010). Ultimately, English proficiency is only one small piece of the puzzle. As findings from these studies suggest, academic preparation will likely be the lynchpin by which to measure ELs' academic and professional integration as young adults.

The tension between language and content, between English proficiency and academic development undergirds the way we as a society address the academic and linguistic needs of our growing high school EL population. Improving ELs' academic preparation will require a shift away from language proficiency alone and towards content-area mastery, away from high school graduation towards postsecondary preparation, and away from basic skills towards college readiness. Given that prior research recommends English acquisition through content area instruction (e.g., Chamot & O'Malley, 1996, Janzen, 2008), a shift from discrete, language-based ESL instruction to integrated content-based language learning will begin the complex process of content area exposure and mastery for ELs. With research suggesting that academic English proficiency requires 5 to 7 years to develop, the existence of large numbers of long-term ELs further points to the ineffectiveness of the present ESL program paradigm. Perhaps most critically, this theoretical shift will require that as a field, we move from identifying ELs by their language (or interpreted lack thereof) to identifying them as students first; students who happen to be learning English as they develop mathematic, scientific, and civic competencies for their transition into young adulthood.

Acknowledgment

This research was supported by a grant from the American Educational Research Association which receives funds for its "AERA Grants Program" from the National Science Foundation and the National Center for Education Statistics of the Institute of Education Sciences (U.S. Department of Education) under NSF Grant #DRL-0634035. Opinions reflect those of the author(s) and do not necessarily reflect those of the granting agencies.

Notes

1. Limited English proficient (LEP) status is a federal (U.S. Department of Education) term used to indicate a nonnative English speaker in need of language support services. LEP status is determined largely at the local (school or district) level. Many states and schools use the term *English learner* (EL) or *English language learner* (ELL) rather than LEP. For the sake of efficiency, and to ensure consistency, this chapter will use the term *EL* to identify linguistic minority students placed in ESL coursework in high school.
2. Reclassification, or redesignation, is the movement of a student out of EL status, to the label fluent English proficient. In most states, reclassification occurs upon satisfactory evidence of English language proficiency as well as grade-level academic achievement most often measured by standardized test scores and classroom grades. (See Linquanti, 2001; Ragan & Lesaux, 2006, for more in-depth discussion of the issues regarding reclassification.)
3. For the sake of brevity, clarity, and consistency, We use the term *EL* to indicate a language minority student placed in ESL coursework in high school. There may be students in these datasets identified as ELs but not placed in ESL coursework, however the empirical foci rest largely on ESL placement. As a result, we refer only to linguistic minority respondents in ESL coursework in high school as *EL*.
4. College preparation was measured by a sum of the basic 4-year college entry requirements: Chemistry, Algebra II, 4 years of English, 4 years of social sciences, and 3 years of foreign language, ranging from 0 to 5, with 1 point awarded for completion of each of the preceding categories.
5. California Education Code Section 44253.1 reads, "For [ELs] to have access to quality education, their special needs must be met by teachers who have essential skills and knowledge related to English language development, specially designed content instruction delivered in English, and content instruction delivered in the pupils' primary languages."

References

Abedi, J., & Gándara, P. (2006). Performance of English language learners as a subgroup in large-scale assessment: Interaction of research and policy. *Educational Measurement: Issues and Practice, 25*(4), 36–46.

Adelman, C. (2006). *The toolbox revisited: Paths to degree completion from high school through college.* Washington, DC: U.S. Department of Education.

Antrop-González, R., & De Jesús, A. (2006). Toward a theory of *critical care* in urban small school reform: Examining structures and pedagogies of caring in two *Latino* community-based schools. *International Journal of Qualitative Studies in Education, 19*(4), 409–433.

Bankston, C. L., & Zhou, M. (2002). Social capital and immigrant children's achievement. In B. Fuller & E. Hannum (Eds.), *Schooling and social capital in diverse cultures* (pp. 13–39). Amsterdam: JAI.

Callahan, R. M. (2005). Tracking and high school English learners: Limiting opportunity to learn. *American Educational Research Journal, 42*(2), 305–328.

Callahan, R. M., & Gándara, P. C. (2004). On nobody's agenda: Improving English language learners' access to higher education. In M. Sadowski (Ed.), *Immigrant and second language students: Lessons from research and best practice* (pp. 107–127). Cambridge, MA: Harvard Education Press.

Callahan, R. M., & Shifrer, D. (2011). *English learners' secondary course-taking: Equitable academic access?* Manuscript submitted for publication.

Callahan, R. M., Wilkinson, L., & Muller, C. (2008). School context and the effect of ESL placement on Mexican-origin adolescents' achievement. *Social Science Quarterly, 89*(1), 177–198.

Callahan, R. M., Wilkinson, L., & Muller, C. (2010). Academic achievement and course-taking among language minority youth in U.S. Schools: Effects of ESL placement. *Educational Evaluation and Policy Analysis, 32*(1), 84–117.

Callahan, R. M., Wilkinson, L., Muller, C., & Frisco, M. L. (2009). ESL placement and schools: Effects on immigrant achievement. *Educational Policy, 23*(2), 355–384.

Chamot, A. U., & O'Malley, J. M. (1996). The cognitive academic language learning approach: A model for linguistically diverse classrooms. *The Elementary School Journal, 96*(3), 259–273.

Cosentino de Cohen, C., Deterding, N., & Clewell, B. C. (2005). *Who's left behind? Immigrant children in high- and low-LEP schools.* Washington, D.C.: Urban Institute.

Crandall, J., Jaramillo, A., Olsen, L., & Peyton, J. K. (2002). *Using cognitive strategies to develop English language and literacy.* Retrieved from Center for Applied Linguistics website: http://www.cal.org/resources/digest/0205crandall.html

Crosnoe, R., Lopez-Gonzalez, L., & Muller, C. (2004). Immigration from Mexico into the math/science pipeline in American education. *Social Science Quarterly, 85*(5), 1208–1226.

Dabach, D. B. (2011). Teachers as agents of reception: An analysis of teacher preference for immigrant-origin second language learners. *The New Educator, 7*(1), 66–86.

Echevarria, J., Short, D. J., & Powers, K. (2006). School reform and standards-based education: A model for English language learners. *The Journal of Educational Research, 99*(4), 195–211.

Echevarria, J., Vogt, M. J., & Short, D. J. (2007). *Making content comprehensible for English learners: The SIOP model* (3rd ed.). Boston: Allyn & Bacon.

Ek, L. D. (2009). Language and literacy in the pentecostal church and the public high school: A case study of a Mexican ESL student. *The High School Journal, 92*(2), 1–13.

Finley, M. K. (1984). Teachers and tracking in a comprehensive high school. *Sociology of Education, 57*(4), 233–243.

Freeman, Y. S., Freeman, D. E., & Mercuri, S. (2002). *Closing the achievement gap: How to reach limited-formal-schooling and long-term English learners.* Portsmouth, NH: Heinemann.

Fuligni, A. J. (1997). The academic achievement of adolescents from immigrant families: The roles of family background, attitudes, and behavior. *Child Development, 68*(2), 351–363.

Gamoran, A. (1992). Access to excellence: Assignment to honors English classes in the transition from middle to high school. *Educational Evaluation and Policy Analysis, 14,* 185–204.

Gándara, P. C. (2002). Learning English in California: Guideposts for the nation. In M. M. Suárez-Orozco & M. Páez (Eds.), *Latinos: Remaking America* (pp. 339–358). Berkeley: University of California Press.

Gándara, P. C., Rumberger, R. W., Maxwell-Jolly, J., & Callahan, R. M. (2003). English learners in California schools: Unequal resources, unequal outcomes. *Education Policy Analysis Archives, 11*(36). Retrieved from http://epaa.asu.edu/epaa/v11n36/v11n36.pdf

Gibson, M. A., Gándara, P., & Koyama, J. P. (Eds.). (2004). *School connections: U.S. Mexican youth, peers and school achievement.* New York: Teachers College Press.

Gibson, M. A., & Hidalgo, N. (2009). Bridges to success in high school for migrant youth. *Teachers College Record, 111*(3), 683–711.

Harklau, L. (1994). Tracking and linguistic minority students: Consequences of ability grouping for second language learners. *Linguistics and Education, 6,* 217–244.

Harklau, L. (1999). The ESL learning environment in secondary school. In C. J. Faltis & P. Wolfe (Eds.), *So much to say: Adolescents, bilingualism and ESL in the secondary school* (pp. 42–60). New York: Teachers College Press.

Janzen, J. (2008). Teaching English language learners in the content areas. *Review of Educational Research, 78*(4), 1010–1038.

Kalogrides, D. (2009). Generational status and academic achievement among Latino high school students: Evaluating the segmented assimilation theory. *Sociological Perspectives, 52*(2), 159–183.

Kao, G., & Tienda, M. (1995). Optimism and achievement: The educational performance of immigrant youth. *Social Science Quarterly, 76*(1), 1–19.

Lau v. Nichols, 414 U.S. 563 (1974).

Lew, J. (2004). The "Other" Story of model minorities: Korean American high school dropouts in an urban context. *Anthropology & Education Quarterly, 35*(3), 303–323.

Linquanti, R. (2001). *The redesignation dilemma: Challenges and choices in fostering meaningful accountability for English learners*. Retrieved from WestEd website: http://www.wested.org/online_pubs/redesignation.pdf

Louie, V., & Holdaway, J. (2009). Catholic schools and immigrant students: A new generation. *Teachers College Record, 111*(3), 783–816.

Lucas, S. R., & Berends, M. (2002). Sociodemographic diversity, correlated achievement, and de facto tracking. *Sociology of Education, 75*(4), 328–348.

Mahoney, K. S., & MacSwan, J. (2005). Reexamining identification and reclassification of English language learners: A critical discussion of select state practices. *Bilingual Research Journal, 29*(1), 31–42.

Minicucci, C., & Olsen, L. (1993). Caught unawares: California secondary schools confront the immigrant student challenge. *Multicultural Education, 1*(2), 16–19.

Mohr, K. A. J. (2004). English as an accelerated language: A call to action for reading teachers. *The Reading Teacher, 58*(1), 18–26.

Muller, C., Pearson, J., Riegle-Crumb, C., Harris-Requejo, J., Frank, K. A., Schiller, K. S., et al. (2007). *Wave III education data: Design and implementation of the Adolescent Health and Academic Achievement study*. Chapel Hill: Carolina Population Center, University of North Carolina at Chapel Hill.

Oakes, J. (1985). *Keeping track: How schools structure inequality*. New Haven, CT: Yale University Press.

Olsen, L. (1997). *Made in America: Immigrant students in our public schools*. New York: The New Press.

Olsen, L. (2010). *Reparable harm: Fulfilling the unkept promise of educational opportunity for California's long term English learners*. Retrieved from California Together website: http://www.californiatogether.org/reports/

Padilla, A. M., & Gonzalez, R. (2001). Academic performance of immigrant and U.S.-born Mexican heritage students: Effects of schooling in Mexico and bilingual/English language instruction. *American Educational Research Journal, 38*(3), 727–742.

Portes, A., & Fernandez-Kelly, P. (2008). No margin for error: Educational and occupational achievement among disadvantaged children of immigrants. *The Annals of the American Academy of Political and Social Science, 620*(1), 12–36.

Ragan, A., & Lesaux, N. (2006). Federal, state, and district level English language learner program entry and exit requirements: Effects on the education of language minority students. *Education Policy Analysis Archives, 14*(20), 1–29. Retrieved from http://epaa.asu.edu/epaa/v14n20/v14n20.pdf

Ream, R. K. (2003). Counterfeit social capital and Mexican-American underachievement. *Educational Evaluation and Policy Analysis, 25*(3), 237–262.

Ream, R. K. (2005). Toward understanding how social capital mediates the impact of mobility on Mexican-American achievement. *Social Forces, 84*(1), 201–224.

Riegle-Crumb, C., & Callahan, R. M. (2009). Exploring the academic benefits of friendship ties for *Latino* boys and girls. *Social Science Quarterly, 90*(3), 611–631.

Riegle-Crumb, C., & Grodsky, E. (2010). Racial-ethnic differences at the intersection of math course-taking and achievement. *Sociology of Education, 83*(3), 248–270.

Ruiz-de-Velasco, J., & Fix, M. (2000). *Overlooked and underserved: Immigrant students in U.S. Secondary schools*. Washington, DC: The Urban Institute.

Rumbaut, R. G., & Portes, A. (2001). *Ethnicities: Children of immigrants in America*. Berkeley: University of California Press.

Schwartz, A. E., & Steifel, L. (2004). Immigrants and the distribution of resources within an urban school district. *Educational Evaluation and Policy Analysis, 26*(4), 303–327.

Shettle, C., Roey, S., Mordica, J., Perkins, R., Nord, C., Teodorovic, J., et al. (2007). *The nation's report card: America's high school graduates*. Washington, DC: U.S. Department of Education, National Center for Education Statistics.

Tyack, D. B. (1974). *The one best system: A history of American urban education*. Cambridge, MA: Harvard University Press.

Valdés, G. (2001). *Learning and not learning English: Latino students in American schools.* New York: Teachers College Press.

Zehler, A., Fleischman, H. L., Hopstock, P. J., Stephenson, T. G., Pendzick, M. L., & Sapru, S. (2003). *Descriptive study of services to LEP students and LEP students with disabilities.* Retrieved from National Clearinghouse for English Language Acqusition (NCELA) website: http://www.ncela.gwu.edu/files/rcd/BE021195/policy_report.pdf

3

LINGUISTIC MINORITY STUDENTS' OPPORTUNITIES TO LEARN HIGH SCHOOL MATHEMATICS

Eduardo Mosqueda

The number of linguistic minority (LM) students in the United States has grown substantially in the past few decades. Recent data show that in 2008 nearly 10.9 million 5- to 17-year-olds (21% of the national total) spoke a language other than English at home (National Center for Education Statistics, 2010). Although over 450 of the world's languages are represented in U.S. schools, nearly 80% of all LM students speak Spanish at home (Téllez, 2010). The overwhelming majority of the Spanish-speaking students are Latinos; most are of Mexican descent (Kindler, 2002). Students from LM backgrounds are typically foreign-born immigrants or the U.S.-born children of immigrants. LM students thus represent a wide variety of linguistic backgrounds and span from emergent to proficient English skills and are often classified by schools as English learners (ELs). LMs are also often unfamiliar with the school system in the United States. LM students are more likely to live in poverty, attend dysfunctional schools, and begin school well behind in the content knowledge their language majority counterparts possess (Abedi & Gándara, 2006; Ruiz-de-Velasco & Fix, 2000). Consequently, recent research has focused on how schools can improve the academic achievement of LM students to help improve their postsecondary school prospects, particularly to improve their chances of attending college.

One strand in this research has found that institutional barriers in schools hinder the academic preparation of LM students. Much of this work illuminates the ways in which access to rigorous content courses is often constrained by the low levels of English proficiency of many LM students (Gándara, 1999; Gándara & Contreras, 2009; Gándara, Rumberger, Maxwell-Jolly, & Callahan, 2003; Harklau, 1994a; Olsen, 1995) as well as the institutional designation of Limited English Proficiency (LEP) (Callahan, Wilkinson, & Muller, 2010; Callahan, Wilkinson, Muller, & Frisco, 2009). Mathematics courses in particular are gatekeepers, and limited access to rigorous mathematical content can severely impede high school mathematics preparation and subsequent opportunities to attend college for all students (Adelman, 2006).

LM students' limited access to mathematics gate-keeping courses is an important area of inquiry in the educational integration of LMs in high school given the chronic and disproportionately lower achievement outcomes of LM students, particularly those with low levels of English proficiency, on standardized tests relative to non-LMs (Abedi & Lord, 2000; Secada, 1992; Tate, 1997). Additionally, widely cited large-scale studies of the LM children of immigrants in U.S. schools have not carefully considered the effects of course-taking on the educational outcomes of these students. For instance, while Portes and Rumbaut (2001) have made important contributions to our understanding of what accounts for segmented assimilation patterns among ethnic groups in the United States, they do not take into account how academic tracking, or differential access to rigorous courses accounts for some of the variation in academic achievement among the Latino and Asian students in their research. Not accounting for the effects of strong explanatory predictors such as course-taking on the academic achievement of LM immigrant students can lead one to overemphasize the effects of other factors such as ethnicity, immigrant generational status, and culture in explaining achievement discrepancies. Although recent studies demonstrate that course-taking patterns are strong predictors of LM student achievement (Callahan, 2005; Callahan et al., 2010; Callahan et al., 2009; Wang & Goldschmidt, 1999), they have not closely examined differences the course-taking patterns of LM students of different ethnicities, particularly in the area of mathematics.

The purpose of this chapter is to examine whether LM status and access to rigorous courses in the high school mathematics college preparatory sequence (which include Algebra 1, Geometry, Algebra 2, Pre-Calculus, and Calculus) differentially influence the mathematics assessment scores of Asian and Latino students at the end of their high school years. If institutional mechanisms such as course-taking have a larger negative effect on the achievement of Latino LMs compared to Asian LMs, particularly in advanced mathematics courses, it would suggest that students' ethnicity, in addition to language background, play an important role in institutional decisions about the mathematics course placements of LMs. A focus on differences in mathematics course-taking and their relation to Asian LM and Latino LM student achievement outcomes can provide a useful means for the identification of critical and contrasting factors as well as revealing possible sources of divergent educational performance. Such an analysis can also point to potential strategies and approaches to examine institutional sources of variation in LM student performance.

The analysis reported in this chapter is based on Asian and Latino ethnic groups in the United States and does not disaggregate among their respective subgroups (e.g., Mexican- or Vietnamese-descent LM students). Although it is generally important to disaggregate among Asian and Latino subgroups, this study highlights what we can learn from achievement patterns of both groups in the aggregate; that is, although not all Asian nor Latino subgroups are academically successful, the achievement patterns of panethnic groups can yield important findings.

This quantitative study analyzes the first and second waves of data from the Education Longitudinal Study of 2002 (ELS:2002) using Hierarchical Linear Models (HLM) to examine the relationship between LM status, course-taking, and mathematics achievement. The study tests whether these effects differ among Asian and Latino non-LM and LM students at the end of their senior year of high school. This inquiry is guided by the following research questions:

1. Is there a relationship between course-taking and mathematics achievement among Latino and Asian LM and non-LM high school seniors in U.S. schools?
2. Does the effect of course-taking on mathematics achievement differ between Latino LM and Asian LM high school seniors in U.S. schools?

Asian and Latino Student Achievement and Demographic Trends

Recent achievement trends in a report based on multiple sources of data collected by the National Center for Education Statistics (NCES) reflect the enduring disparate patterns in U.S. educational attainment outcomes. Asian students, on average, outperform all other racial and ethnic groups (including Whites and Latinos) on multiple mathematics assessments. For instance, a higher percentage of Asian students scored at or above the "Proficient" level on the National Assessment of Educational Progress (NAEP) than did 4th and 8th graders of all other racial and ethnic groups (Aud, Fox, & KewalRamani, 2010). Among 2005 high school graduates, a lower proportion of Latinos completed courses in the college preparatory sequence than students of all other racial and ethnic groups (Aud et al., 2010). Asian students not only took more rigorous mathematics courses but also had the highest number of college credit and eligibility exam test-takers, and also had the highest mathematics mean on the Advanced Placement (AP) exam, and on both college entrance exams, the SAT and the ACT (Aud et al., 2010).

Although popular explanations for the higher Asian student achievement relative to all other U.S. racial and ethnic groups tend to solely emphasize Asian "culture" and specifically point to Confucian values that promote academic achievement (Caplan, Choy, & Whitmore, 1991; Zhou, 1997), researchers have argued that the higher academic achievement of some nonnative-born Asians can also be explained by the immigrant selectivity. That is, because large numbers of Asian immigrants have high pre-immigration SES, they are better positioned to integrate into more privileged segments of U.S. society in comparison to more economically disadvantaged immigrants from Latin American countries (Feliciano 2006; Rong & Grant, 1992; Zhou & Kim, 2006). Zhou and Kim (2006) have argued that "ethnicity cannot be simplified into a proxy for culture because it encompasses not only values and behavioral patterns, but also group-specific social structures that may be contingent upon circumstances prior to and after immigration" (p. 2).

Demographic trends reported by Aud et al. (2010) reflect patterns of Latino students' SES disadvantages relative to more advantaged Asian students. In 2007, nearly three times the number of Latinos were living in poverty compared to Asian students, 27% to 11% respectively. In elementary schools, a snapshot of fourth graders in 2009 reveals that 34% of Asian students relative to 77% of Latino students were eligible for free or reduced-price lunch. In 2008, a nearly five times the percentage of Asian children (51%) had a mother with at least a bachelor's degree compared to 11% of Latinos and 36% of Whites. However, the proportion of LM students is similar between Latinos and Asians. In 2007, about 64% of Asian and 69% of Latino elementary and secondary school students spoke a language other than English at home, and of these, 17% of Asian and 18% of Latinos were not proficient English speakers.

Latino students in U.S. schools, in contrast to Asian students, do not fare well academically. Researchers have expressed a deep concern over the future academic and subsequent job prospects of Latino students because of their persistent and disproportionate rates of academic failure (Gándara & Contreras, 2009; Portes & Macleod, 1996; Rumberger & Larson, 1998; Valencia, 2002). For example, as a result of a recent study on Mexican-origin immigrants—the largest Latino sub-group—researchers warn that they are in danger of becoming the next "underclass" due to their disturbingly low academic achievement and their extraordinarily high school dropout rates (Lopez & Stanton-Salazar, 2001; Portes & Rumbaut, 2001).

English Proficiency and LM Student Achievement

Research shows that the varying levels of English proficiency of LM students play an important role in learning mathematics, specifically because of the complexity of rigorous secondary school mathematics content (August & Hakuta, 1997; Khisty, 1995). As a complex register of words, expressions, and meanings (Cuevas, 1984; Secada, 1992), mathematics is a language (or, more specifically, a dialect) that appropriates everyday English words and phrases (Cuevas, 1984; Garrison & Mora, 1999; Gutiérrez, 2002). For instance, the language of mathematics has specialized meanings for words and phrases such as "horizontal," "vertical," "subtract," "difference," "equivalence," and "inverse," to name a few. LM students must learn these mathematical terms as well as the everyday conversational and academic meanings they encounter in their English-language arts courses (Ron, 1999). Wong Fillmore (2007) found that when a student has not learned the academic language used in mathematics courses and in instructional texts, they will "need help learning it or they will find language to be an insuperable barrier to learning" (p. 337).

LM Students and Course-Taking Patterns

Research shows a strong link between mathematics course-taking patterns and both higher standardized test scores (Callahan, 2005; Mosqueda, 2010; Wang & Goldschmidt, 1999) and future educational opportunities (Pelavin & Kane, 1990). Studies have shown that secondary school students who completed mathematics courses beyond Algebra 2 (e.g., Trigonometry, Pre-Calculus, and Calculus) were twice as likely to earn a college degree compared to those who only took Algebra 2 and below (Adelman, 2006). Access to mathematics courses, such as algebra and other more challenging gatekeeper courses, also play an important role in structuring the academic success and failure of LM students (Gándara et al., 2003; Olsen 1995). Research has shown that both Asian LM students (Harklau, 1994a, 1994b) and Latino LM students (Callahan, 2005; Mosqueda, 2010; Olsen, 1995) are likely to be placed in low-level courses as a result of their lower levels of English proficiency or their LEP designation. The limited access to rigorous content courses can undermine the potential academic achievement of LM students.

Research shows that Asian students take more mathematics courses compared to Latino students, but also the mathematics courses taken by Asian students are often of a higher quality (Smith, 1995; Wang & Goldschmidt, 1999). Although higher proportions of Latinos take disproportionately fewer courses in the college preparatory mathematics sequence, this study investigates differences between LM students and non–LM students. In the next section I discuss the study parameters that are used to analyze the relationship between course-taking patterns and the mathematics achievement of Asian and Latino LM and non–LM students.

Method

The data for this study are drawn from the first and second wave of the ELS:2002, a large nationally representative dataset provided by the National Center for Education Statistics (NCES). The base-year and first follow-up studies will ultimately provide policy-relevant trend data about critical transitions experienced by a national probability sample of students as they proceed through high school and into college or their careers (Ingels, Pratt, Rogers, Siegel, & Stutts, 2004). The ELS dataset is comprised of a longitudinal sample of students who were in the 10th grade in 2002 and in 12th grade in 2004. The complete ELS sample includes 15,362 students from a random sample of 752 public, Catholic, and other private schools. The dataset contains assessments of students in reading and mathematics performance in addition to measures of important student, family, teacher, classroom, and school characteristics. It also contains information on students' immigrant status, language proficiency, and course-taking. It is especially suited for the present study because both Latinos and Asians were intentionally oversampled.

This analysis was based on the first follow-up (2004) sub-sample (unweighted) of 4,100 immigrants and U.S.-born Asian and Latinos present in the ELS data-set. The sample is further divided into 2,440 Latinos and 1,660 Asian students. Statistical power analyses (Light, Singer, & Willett, 1990) suggest that this sample size provides power sufficient (.90) to detect small effects at the typical levels of statistical significance ($\alpha = 0.05$).

Variables in the Models

Outcome Variable. Twelfth grade mathematics achievement (MTH_ACH_{ij}) represented an IRT (Item Response Theory) scaled score (recoded from F1TXMSTD), which provides a norm-referenced measurement of achievement relative to the population of high school seniors in 2004 (Ingels et al., 2004) for each student *i* in school *j*. The ELS assessment itself contained items in arithmetic, algebra, geometry, data/probability, and advanced topics (Ingels et al., 2004). These scores were standardized to a mean of 50 and a standard deviation of 10 in the *full* ELS sample (Ingels et al., 2004). The mean test scores for the sub-sample of Latinos is 45.7 with a standard deviation of 9.6 points, and for Asians, the mean test score is 53.5 with a standard deviation of 9.8 points on the ELS assessment. IRT scaled scores were used because they simplify the interpretation of the impact of predictors on the outcome. A one-point difference associated with the outcome variable equals one item correct on the ELS assessment. For a more detailed description of all of the variables included in this analysis see Table 3.1.

Question Predictor. The first primary question predictors is the dummy variable LM_{ij}, which is used to distinguish between LM and non-LM students (1 = LM, 0 = non-LM). About 50.5% of the students in this sample reported being LM students. LM status was coded from F1STLANG, a survey question that asked students, "Is English your native language (the first language you learned to speak when you were a child)" (Ingels et al., 2004).[1]

The second primary question predictor is $HIGHMATH_{ij}$ and indicates the highest mathematics course taken by the end of each student's senior year of high school. Given that high school mathematics courses are typically taken in sequence, this variable is treated as an interval scale (0 = no math taken, 1 = pre-algebra or basic math, 2 = algebra I, 3 = geometry, 4 = algebra II, and 5 = trigonometry, pre-calculus, or calculus).

Additionally, in order to differentiate among the level of English proficiency of LM students, the cross-product LMij *ENGPROFij is used. ENGPROFij

TABLE 3.1 Data and Coding of All Variables

Variable	ELS 02-04	Definition	Notes/Coding
Student Background			
SES	F1SES1	Standardized Composite measure that includes Family Income, Parent Education and Occupational Status	Ranges from -1.98 to 1.79
FEMALE	F1SEX	Students Gender	1 = Female, 0 = Male
Immigration Status			
FIRSTGEN	BYP17/23	Indicates whether both the student and both parents are foreign born.	1 = yes, 0 = no
SECGEN	BYP17/23	Indicates whether the student is US-born while at least one parent is foreign born.	1 = yes, 0 = no
THIRDGEN	BYP17/23	Indicates whether both the student and parents are US-born.	1 = yes, 0 = no
Teacher Preparation			
MTHMAJOR	BYM31A	Indicates whether each student's mathematics teacher has a bachelor's degree in mathematics or a math related field.	1 = yes, 0 = no
MTHCERT	BYTM29	Indicates whether each student's mathematics teacher is certified.	1 = yes, 0 = no
School Context Measures			
PCTLUNCH	F1SCFLP	This is a proxy for school SES and measured by the percentage of 10th grade students that are eligible for free or reduced lunch in the school.	1= 0 - 5%, 2 = 6-10%, 3 = 11- 20%, 4 = 21 - 30%, 5 = 21- 30%, 6 = 51- 75%, 7 = 76- 100%,
PUBLIC	BYSCTRL	Indicates whether the school is public, or Catholic or other type of private.	1= public 0= Catholic or Private
English Proficiency			
LM	F1HOMLNG	Indicates whether the student is a non-native English speaker or a native English speaker.	1 = LM, 0 = Non-LM
ENGPROF	BYS70A BYS70B BYS70C BYS70D	This is a weighted composite of the self-reported level of English proficiency of each respondent, and is based on their ability to understand, speak, read and write English.	Ranges from 3 to 8.

Variable	ELS 02-04	Definition	Notes/Coding
Course-Taking			
HIMATH	F1HIMATH	Indicates the highest mathematics course taken by each respondent by the end of their senior year of high school.	0 = No Math, 1 = Pre Alg., or general math, 2 = Algebra I, 3 = Geometry, 4 = Algebra II, 5 = Trig., Pre-Calc., Calc.

is a composite that ranges from 3 to 8 (low to high), based on each student's self-reported level of English proficiency.[2] This weighted composite score is constituted from students' responses to four ordinal dimensions of self-reported English proficiency that include how well students: "understand spoken English," "speak English," "read English," and "write English."[3] For each of these dimensions of English proficiency, students provided one of following ordinal responses: "Very well," "Well," "Not well," or "Not at all." Table 3.1 provides a list of all of the predictors in this analysis along with descriptive data for each variable disaggregated by Asian and Latino LM and native-English-speaking students. The descriptive statistics of all the variables in this analysis are disaggregated by Asian and Latino students and displayed in Table 3.2.

Control Predictors. The analysis includes a series of control predictors in order to account for individual background and school context variation that may impact the outcomes, and to assess the potential impact of selectivity bias. These controls include individual-level gender, SES, parental education, and each immigrant student's prior level of education in their native country. At level 2, included are a set of controls for selected aggregate measures of the school context such as whether the school is public or private, and the percentage of low-income within each school. The number of students within each school that qualify for free or reduced-price lunch is used as a proxy for poverty.

Missing Data and Sample Weights

Multiple imputation was used to replace missing data in the ELS survey (Rubin 1987). This procedure (PROC MI) in the SAS statistical software package replaces missing values with randomly generated values from the sample distributions of the variables in the analysis. Regression models were fit separately in each of the five imputed datasets, and the results were averaged and corrected for the inclusion of the random variation in each of the imputed datasets. The ELS student-level panel weights (F1QWT)[4] and school-level weights (BYSCHWT) were applied to the analysis according to the guidelines provided for the HLM software (Raudenbush & Bryk, 2002).

TABLE 3.2 Descriptive Statistics Disaggregated by Native and Non-native English Speaking Asians and Latinos

Variable	Asian		Latino	
	LM Mean	Non-LM Mean	LM Mean	Non-LM Mean
Student Characteristics				
Socioeconomic Status	-0.15	0.33	-0.59	-0.15
Females (vs. Males)	49.50	46.9	0.53	0.48
Immigration Status				
First Generation	0.41	0.18	0.35	0.03
Second Generation	0.35	0.37	0.34	0.14
Third Generation	0.24	0.45	0.32	0.83
English Proficiency				
Level of Eng. Proficiency	6.98	--	6.92	--
Teacher Background Preparation				
Math Major	0.58	0.49	0.49	0.51
Certified	0.74	0.71	0.67	0.72
Course–Taking Patterns				
Highest Math Course Taken by 12th Gr.	4.35	4.32	3.63	3.76
Mathematics Performance				
Math Test Scores	53.41	53.45	43.6	46.6

Data Analysis

Using Hierarchical Linear Models (HLM), the following four fitted multilevel models were evaluated in which the mathematics achievement of Latino relative to Asian students is modeled as a function of the control and question predictors. Multi-level modeling is well suited for this analysis as it can account for the clustering of students within schools. The first fitted model (Model 1) is the null or unconditional model that contains no predictors, and estimates the average mathematics achievement for the sub-sample of Latino 12th graders in the ELS dataset. The second fitted model (Model 2) is the baseline control model, and includes all of the individual-level and school-level control predictors. The third model (Model 3) adds the key question predictors and presents the main effect on mathematics performance of the LM students compared to native-English-speaking Asian and Latino students in addition to the relationship with the highest mathematics course taken by their senior year of high school. The fourth and final fitted model (Model 4) presents the main and interaction effects among Latino and Asian students, LM status, and the highest mathematics course taken by their senior year of high school.

Findings

To address the first research question, multilevel Model 3 was fit (in Table 3.3) to examine the main effects of the primary question predictors that include

TABLE 3.3 Final Estimated Hierarchical Linear Models of the Predictors of the 12th-Grade Mathematics Achievement

Fixed Effects	Model 1	Model 2	Model 3	Model 4
Intercept	51.87***	51.75***	51.42***	50.19***
Student Characteristics				
Latino (ref=Asian)		−5.62***	−4.57***	−3.08***
Socioeconomic Status		3.21***	2.29***	2.31***
Female (ref=Male)		−0.59	−0.92~	−0.97*
Immigration Status				
First Generation (ref=Third gen.)		−0.37	−0.05	−0.30
Second Generation (ref=Third gen.)		1.67*	1.03~	1.31*
English Proficiency				
LM (ref=Non-LM)		−4.18***	−3.34***	−6.70***
Level of Eng. Proficiency (of LMs)		0.62***	0.49***	0.47***
Teacher Background Preparation				
Math Major		1.97***	1.04***	1.06*
Certified		0.64	0.74	0.73
School Context Features				
10th Gr. Pct. Free Lunch		−1.45***	−1.58***	−1.58***
Public School (ref=Catholic & Private)		0.46	0.19	0.19
Course-Taking Patterns				
Highest Math Course Taken by 12th Gr.			3.03***	2.57***
Interaction Effects				
High Math X LM				1.29***
High Math X LM X Latino				−0.58*
Random Effects				
Within Schools ($\tau 00$)	36.12	18.37	22.75	19.67
Between Schools ($\sigma 2$)	70.24	61.72	51.10	51.36
Chi-square	2669.67***	1888.87***	2313.30***	2132.30***

~ p< .10. * p< .05; ** p < .01. *** p<.001.

ethnicity (Latino compared to Asian), LM status (compared to non-LM), and the highest mathematics course taken by the end of high school. The analysis in Model 3 revealed that Latino students perform nearly 46% of a standard deviation ($\beta = -4.57$) below the mean performance of Asian students on the ELS:2002 assessment. LM students also perform nearly 33% of a standard deviation ($\beta = -3.34$) below the mathematics achievement of native English speakers, on average. And most importantly, every additional higher level course taken in the high school mathematics sequence by the of 12th grade is associated with a positive difference of 3 points on the ELS assessment in 2004, a difference that equals 33% of a standard deviation. The cumulative effect of these measures can be academically devastating for LM students, but more so for Latino LMs. For example, the predicted score of a Latino LM student who did not take any math courses beyond pre-algebra 1 will be about one full standard deviation below the mean of Asian LM student achievement on the ELS:2002 assessment.

Relative to course-taking, English proficiency is a lesser yet important predictor of LM mathematics achievement. The results show that English proficiency has a small yet statistically significant effect on LM student mathematics achievement. A one unit positive change in the level of English proficiency is associated with a higher test score of about one half (0.49) of a test score point on the ELS: 2002 assessment.

To address the second research question and examine the joint effect of LM status between Asian and Latino students and their course-taking patterns, I fit Model 4. This analysis revealed statistically significant interactions between the variables for ethnicity, LM status, and highest mathematics course taken by the 12th grade. This suggests that the impact of ethnicity and LM status differed as a function of mathematics course-taking. Given the nature of interaction terms, one cannot interpret these coefficients alone. Rather, they must be interpreted in conjunction with the main effects of each question predictor. The results from Model 4 show that LM students benefit more from taking advanced level mathematics courses than non-LM students. However, the analysis also shows that the benefit to LMs for taking higher-level mathematics courses is higher for Asians than for Latino students. More specifically, the results show that Asian LM students scored much higher from taking advanced mathematics courses than Latino LM students that took similar advanced courses. For every course in the mathematics college sequence that Asian students take, their predicted score is associated with a positive difference of 3.85 additional points on their ELS assessment, a difference of nearly 40% of a standard deviation. For Latino students, the difference in tests scores associated with taking an additional course in the college preparatory mathematics sequence is only 3.27 points on the ELS assessment, a difference of 33% of a standard deviation. Due to the complexity of interpreting statistical interactions, these findings were represented visually in Figure 3.1, holding all control predictors constant at their respective means. The chart in Figure 3.1 shows that among high school

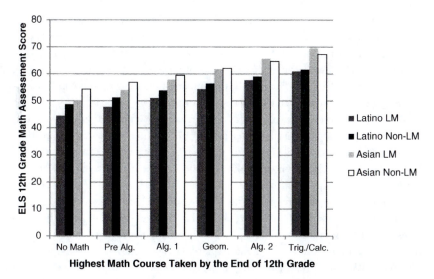

FIGURE 3.1 Interaction effects bar chart of mathematics performance on the ELS Assessment of Asian and Latino native and nonnative English speakers and their mathematics course-taking.

seniors whose highest mathematics course was below Algebra 1, Asian and Latino LM students' mathematics scores lag behind non-LMs. The chart in Figure 3.1 also shows the differential effect of course-taking on mathematics achievement among Asian and Latino high school seniors whose highest mathematics score by the end of 12th grade was above Algebra 2. Asian LM students whose highest mathematics course was geometry reach parity with and surpass their non-LM peers in more advanced mathematics courses. However, only Latino LMs that took a course in Trigonometry or above nearly reached parity with Latino non-LMs in similar courses. Another important finding shows that the level of English proficiency of LM students remained a strong predictor of mathematics achievement. A one unit positive change in the level of English proficiency was associated with a higher test score of about one half (0.47) of a test score point on the ELS 12th grade assessment, a difference of 5% of a standard deviation for every unit difference in the level of English proficiency of individual students.

Discussion

The main goal of this study was to examine differences in high school course-taking and mathematics achievement between Asian LM and Latino LM students and their non-LM co-ethnic peers. The findings suggest that LM students benefit more from having taken advanced mathematics courses by the end of their senior year of high school in terms of their mathematics achievement. Latino LMs are disadvantaged relative to their non-LM co-ethnics. However, the findings also revealed that the effect of course-taking on LM student mathematics achievement differs between Asian and Latino students. The results show that Asian LMs benefit much more than Latino LMs from having taken advanced mathematics courses by the end of their senior year of high school, even after controlling for background characteristics, their mathematics teachers' preparation, and selected school context measures.

Based on previous research, it was not surprising to find that both Asian LM and non-LM students scored higher on the ELS mathematics assessment than Latino LM and non-LMs. However, the results of this study reveal that Asian LM high school seniors whose highest mathematics course by the end of 12th grade was above Algebra 2, *surpassed* the scores of their non-LM Asian counterparts. In fact, these students were the highest achievers in this study.

Latino LM students do not fare as well as Asian LM students. The relationship between course-taking and mathematics achievement for Latino LMs reveals disparities in their mathematics achievement relative to non-LM Latinos, Asian LMs and non-LMs. Latino LM students whose highest mathematics course by the end of high school was Trigonometry, Pre-Calculus, or Calculus, only nearly reach parity with Latino non-LMs. This finding is consistent with the extant literature that has documented the pervasively low achievement of Latinos, particularly for LM students (Gándara & Contreras, 2009; Gándara et al., 2003; Mosqueda, 2010; Valdés, 1998, 2001; Valenzuela, 1999).

This study's findings also show that having a lower self-assessment of English proficiency has a negative effect on the mathematics achievement of both Asian and Latino LMs. This finding is consistent with the aforementioned literature which has found that LM students with lower levels of English proficiency who take low-level mathematics courses underperform compared to their English speaking peers in advanced-level courses (Callahan, 2005; Mosqueda, 2010; Wang & Goldschmidt, 1999).

Conclusion

These findings suggest that in the case of Latino LM students and Asian LM students, limiting access to course work can curtail their chances for college participation. Because the consequences for missing out on advanced mathematics courses are so great, schools must be vigilant in providing appropriate linguistic supports to maximize the achievement of LM students in college preparatory courses. In addition, the common practice of requiring LM students' to gain full English proficiency before they are allowed into rigorous mathematics content courses must be reconsidered. Rather than delaying opportunities to learn college preparatory mathematics content, LM students require accelerated mathematics courses that integrate explicit scaffolding of the academic language of mathematic into the instruction of rigorous content. The traditional institutional practice of maintaining LM students in low-level courses ensures that they will remain at the lowest rungs of mathematics achievement.

Moreover, explaining the achievement differences in mathematics test scores among Asian and Latino students solely in terms of individual characteristics such as "culture" can lead to inappropriate and unfair conclusions. Rather than blaming Latino LMs for not performing at the level of Asian LMs, it may be more productive to understand the extent to which providing linguistic supports in rigorous mathematics courses can minimize the enduring disparities between Asian and Latino students.

This study also has some important implications for future research on LM student achievement and course-taking. First, future research is needed to investigate the relation between LM student achievement and course-taking among the Asian and Latino student subgroups. Second, given that English proficiency was also found to be an important and statistically significant predictor of mathematics achievement, future research should investigate whether the differential impact of course-taking on LM status reported in this study varies further as a function of the level of English Proficiency of LM students. In other words, it may be possible that the effect of LM status on mathematics achievement may be lower for LMs with emergent levels of English proficiency. Lastly, recent research has begun to illuminate the complex ways in which LM students in college are often denied access to college-credit-bearing courses because of their English as a second language (ESL) designation (Bunch & Endris, this volume; Kanno & Varghese, 2010). A longitudinal study that is able to examine both course-taking patterns through the end of high school and through the end of college can help illuminate the extent to which institutional inequities that disproportionately affect the academic achievement of LMs in high school are also being reproduced in similar or more complex ways for the LMs that are able to overcome the odds against them and complete college.

Acknowledgments

The research reported in this article was generously supported by the University of California Language Minority Research Institute (UC LMRI). I wish to thank Yasuko Kanno, Linda Harklau, Kip Téllez, George Bunch, Saul I. Maldonado, and Israel Lazo for their helpful feedback on this chapter. The opinions expressed in this article are the author's and do not necessarily reflect the views of the supporting agency.

Notes

1. Although LM students in the general sense of the word can be native or nonnative speakers of English, in ELS:2002 LM students are by definition nonnative speakers. The F1STLANG question asks, "Is English your native language (the first language you earned to speak when you were a child)?" Students who answered "yes" to this question were instructed to skip the next three questions on home language use and English proficiency. Only those who identified themselves as nonnative speakers of English were instructed to answer the subsequent language questions. Thus, the way these language-background questions were phrased in

the ELS BY survey does not allow for the possibility that native speakers of English may also speak another language at home.

2. Widely cited large-scale sociological studies of immigrants using similar types of datasets have used these same self-reported English proficiency measures and find that they are relatively reliable measures of language skills (Portes & Rumbaut, 2001).

3. The principal components analysis routine in STATA yielded the following weighted composite equation: ENG_PROF = .486*UNDERSTAND + .511*SPEAK + .510*READ + .492*WRITE. This single construct of English proficiency captured 68% of the variance in the four English proficiency subscales.

4. The questionnaire weight (for F1) applies to all first follow-up respondents.

References

Abedi, J., & Gándara, P. (2006). Performance of English language learners as a subgroup in large-scale assessment: Interaction of research and policy. *Educational Measurement Issues and Practice, 25*, 36–46.

Abedi, J., & Lord, C. (2000). The language factor in mathematics. *Applied Measurement in Education, 14*, 219–234.

Adelman, C. (2006). *The toolbox revisited: Paths to degree completion from high school through college.* Washington, DC: U.S. Department of Education.

Aud, S., Fox, M., & KewalRamani, A. (2010). *Status and trends in the education of racial and ethnic groups* (NCES 2010-015). U.S. Department of Education, National Center for Education Statistics. Washington, DC: U.S. Government Printing Office.

August, D., & Hakuta, K. (1997). *Improving schooling for language-minority children: A research agenda.* Washington, DC: National Research Council, Institute of Medicine, National Academy Press.

Callahan, R. (2005). Tracking and high school English learners: Limiting opportunity to learn. *American Educational Research Journal, 42*, 305–328.

Callahan, R. M., Wilkinson, L., & Muller, C. (2010). Academic achievement and course taking among language minority youth in U.S. schools: Effects of ESL placement. *Educational valuation and Policy Analysis, 32*(1), 84–117.

Callahan, R. M., Wilkinson, L., Muller, C., & Frisco, M. (2009). ESL placement and schools: Effects on immigrant achievement. *Educational Policy, 23*(2), 355–384.

Caplan, N., Choy, M. H., & Whitmore, J. K. (1991). *Children of the boat people: A study of educational success.* Ann Arbor: University of Michigan Press.

Cuevas, G. (1984). Mathematics learning in English as a second language. *Journal for Research in Mathematics Education, 15*, 134–144.

Feliciano, C. (2006). Beyond family: The influence of premigration group status on the educational expectations of immigrants' children. *Sociology of Education, 79*, 281–303.

Gándara, P. (1999). Staying in the race: The challenge for Chicanos in higher education. In J. F. Moreno (Ed.), *The elusive quest for equality: 150 years of Chicano/Chicana education* (pp. 169–196). Cambridge, MA: Harvard Educational Review.

Gándara, P. C., & Contreras, F. (2009). *The Latino education crisis: The consequences of failed social policies.* Cambridge, MA: Harvard University Press.

Gándara, P., Rumberger, R. W., Maxwell-Jolly, J., & Callahan, R. (2003). English language learners in California Schools: Unequal resources, unequal chances. *Education Policy Analysis Archives, 11*(36). Retrieved from http://epaa.asu.edu/epaa?v11n36

Garrison, L., & Mora, J. K. (1999). Adapting mathematics instruction for English language learners: The language concept. In L. Ortiz-Franco, N. G. Hernandez, & Y. De La Cruz (Eds.), *Changing the faces of mathematics: Perspectives on Latinos* (pp. 35–48). Reston, VA: National Council of Teachers of Mathematics.

Gutiérrez, R. (2002). Beyond essentialism: The complexity of language in teaching mathematics to Latina/o students. *American Educational Research Journal, 39*, 1047–1088.

Harklau, L. (1994a). "Jumping tracks": How language-minority students negotiate evaluations of ability. *Anthropology & Education Quarterly, 25*, 347–363.

Harklau, L. (1994b). Tracking and linguistic minority students: Consequences of ability grouping for second language learners. *Linguistics and Education, 6*, 217–244.

Ingels, S. J., Pratt, D. J., Rogers, J. E., Siegel, P. H., & Stutts, E. S. (2004). *Education longitudinal study of 2002: Base year data file user's manual.* Washington, DC: U.S. Department of Education, National Center for Education Statistics.

Kanno, Y., & Varghese, M. M. (2010). Immigrant and refugee ESL students' challenges to accessing four-year college education: From language policy to education policy. *Journal of Language, Identity, and Education, 9*(5), 310–328.

Khisty, L. (1995). Making inequality: Issues of language and meanings in mathematics teaching with Hispanic students. In W. G. Secada, E. Fennema, & L. B. Adajian (Eds.), *New directions for equity in mathematics education* (pp. 279–298). Cambridge, UK: Cambridge University Press.

Kindler, A. L. (2002). *Survey of the states' limited English proficient students and available educational programs and services.* Washington, DC: Office of English Language Acquisition, Language Enhancement and Academic Achievement for Limited English Proficient Students.

Light, R., Singer, J. D., & Willett, J. B. (1990). *By design: Planning research in higher education.* Cambridge, MA: Harvard University Press.

Lopez, D., & Stanton-Salazar, R. (2001). Mexican Americans: A second generation at risk. In R. Rumbaut & A. Portes (Eds.), *Ethnicities: Children of Immigrants in America* (pp. 57–90). Berkeley: University of California Press.

Mosqueda, E. (2010). Compounding inequalities: English proficiency and tracking and their relation to mathematics performance among Latina/o secondary school youth. *Journal of Urban Mathematics Education, 3*(1), 57–81.

National Center for Education Statistics. (2010). *The condition of education 2010.* Indicator 5: Language minority school-age children. Washington, DC: U.S. Department of Education. Retrieved from http://nces.ed.gov/programs/coe/2010/section1/indicator05.asp

Olsen, L. (1995). School restructuring and the needs of immigrant students. In W. A. Cornelius & R. G. Rumbaut (Eds.), *California's immigrant children: Theory, research, and implications for educational policy* (pp. 209–231). San Diego: Center for U.S.-Mexican Studies, University of California.

Pelavin, S. H., & Kane, M. 1990. *Changing the odds: Factors increasing access to college.* New York: The College Board.

Portes, A., & MacLeod, D. (1996). Educational progress of children of immigrants: The roles of class, ethnicity, and school context. *Sociology of Education, 69*, 255–275.

Portes, A., & Rumbaut, R. G. (2001). *Legacies: The story of the immigrant second generation.* Berkeley, CA: University Press and Russell Sage.

Raudenbush, S. W., & Bryk, A. S. (2002). *Hierarchical linear models: Applications and data analysis methods* (2nd ed.). Newbury Park, CA: Sage.

Ron, P. (1999). Spanish-English language issues in the mathematics classroom. In L. Ortiz-Franco, N. G. Hernandez, & Y. De La Cruz (Eds.), *Changing the faces of mathematics: Perspectives on Latinos* (pp. 22–33). Reston, VA: National Council of Teachers of Mathematics.

Rong, X. L., & Grant, L. (1992). Ethnicity, generation, and school attainment of Asians, Hispanics, and non-Hispanic Whites. *The Sociology Quarterly, 33*(4), 625–636.

Rubin, D. B. (1987). *Multiple imputation for nonresponse in surveys.* New York: Wiley.

Ruiz-de-Velasco, J., & Fix, M. (2000). *Overlooked and underserved: Immigrant students in U.S. secondary schools.* Washington, DC: Urban Institute.

Rumberger, R. W., & Larson, K. A. (1998). Toward explaining differences in educational achievement among Mexican American language-minority students. *Sociology of Education, 71*, 69–93.

Secada, W. G. (1992). Race, ethnicity, social class, language, and achievement in mathematics. In D. A. Grouws (Ed.), *Handbook of research on mathematics teaching and learning* (pp. 623–660). New York: McMillan.

Smith, T. M. (1995). *The educational progress of Hispanic students.* Washington DC: U.S. Department of Education, Office of Educational Research and Improvement (NCES 95–767).

Tate, W. F. (1997). Race-ethnicity, SES, gender, and language proficiency trends in mathematics achievement: An update. *Journal for Research in Mathematics Education, 28,* 652–679.

Téllez, K. (2010). *Teaching English learners: Fostering language and the democratic experience.* Boulder, CO: Paradigm.

Valdés, G. (1998). The world outside and inside schools: Language and immigrant children. *Educational Researcher, 27*(6), 4–18.

Valdés, G. (2001). *Learning and not learning English: Latino students in American schools.* New York: Teachers College Press.

Valencia, R. R. (2002). *Chicano school failure and success: Past, present, and future* (2nd ed.). New York: Routledge/Falmer.

Valenzuela, A. (1999). *Subtractive schooling: U.S.-Mexican youth and the politics of caring.* Albany: New York State University Press.

Wang, J., & Goldschmidt, P. (1999). Opportunity to learn, language proficiency, and immigrant status effects on mathematics achievement. *Journal of Educational Research, 93*(2), 101–111.

Wong Fillmore, L. (2007). English learners and mathematics learning: Language issues to consider. In A. H. Schoenfeld (Ed.), *Assessing mathematical proficiency* (pp. 333–344). Cambridge, MA: Cambridge University Press.

Zhou, M. (1997). Growing up American: The challenge confronting immigrant children and the children of immigrants. *Annual Review of Sociology, 23,* 63–95.

Zhou, M., & Kim, S. S. (2006). Community forces, social capital, and educational achievement: The case of supplementary education in the Chinese and Korean immigrant communities. *Harvard Educational Review, 76*(1), 1–29.

4

PAVING THE WAY TO COLLEGE

An Analysis of an International Baccalaureate Diploma Program Serving Immigrant Students in California

Anysia P. Mayer

> Even though I stopped going to the pull-out ESL program in third grade, when I got to college I still felt my writing wasn't that good. I did really well on the SAT in math but I did below average in reading and writing. But, the reason I made it all the way through college was because of the IB [International Baccalaureate] program. It taught me to persevere. I figured if I could do IB, I could do anything.
>
> *(Interview, Vietnamese, female, first-year pharmacy student, Jefferson IB alumna)*

While schools in the United States like to label students who arrive at school from homes where English is not spoken as English learners (ELs), then remove the label after students receive a passing score on a standardized test, the challenges these students face as they move through the educational pipeline last even after the label of EL is wiped from their educational profile (Suarez-Orozco, Suarez-Orozco, & Todorova, 2007). There are multiple points of data to suggest the experience communicated by the quote above is not hers alone; it is shared by students throughout the United States. For example, while the vast majority of White youth graduate from high school and continue their education beyond the secondary level, 18% of Latino students dropped out of high school in 2009 (Gándara & Contreras, 2009). Also, 37% of bachelor degrees earned in the United States in 2009 went to White students while only 12% went to Latino students (Gándara & Contreras, 2009). Although high school graduation and college-going rates have risen slightly among Southeast Asians and Latinos between 1997 and 2007, low educational attainment continues to be a critical issue for Southeast Asians and Latinos born outside the United States (Aud, Fox, & KewalRamani, 2010). There are multiple factors in the lives of many ethnic minority immigrant children that contribute to discrepancies between their academic performance and that of their more privileged White classmates. While the families of immigrant youth from Southeast Asia and Mexico have a rich linguistic and cultural heritage, they do not have access to the types of social and cultural capital and educational and community socioeconomic status within their family that can be easily exchanged for additional resources in the U.S. economy (Grant & Sleeter, 2011). These factors often translate to low educational attainment for immigrant youth (Aud et al., 2010; Bic & Lee, 2007; Gándara & Contreras, 2009; Lee, 2001). Immigrant students face additional challenges as they enter and seek to participate in U.S. schools; these include immigration status (Passel, 2005); racial ethnic stereotyping (Steele, 1997); access to qualified teachers (Gándara & Contreras, 2009); and limited access to academically rigorous, developmentally appropriate content courses (Callahan, Wilkinson, & Muller, 2010).

Limited English proficiency is often cited as the biggest educational challenge for immigrant students (Gandara & Rumberger, 2009). Some research estimates it takes 7 to 10 years of learning English for ELs to be able to perform cognitively demanding tasks in English on par with their monolingual-English peers (Thomas & Collier, 2002). In practice, however, ELs typically exit ESL programs after 3 years (August & Hakuta, 1997; Parrish et al., 2006). The structure of academic programs—the myth that ELs only need English language development in particular—limits these children's access to academic content knowledge while they are designated as ELs (Callahan & Shifrer, this volume; Callahan, Wilkinson, & Muller, 2010; Gándara, Rumberger, Maxwell-Jolly, & Callahan, 2003).

Not all ethnic minority children are poor or disadvantaged, nor do all perform below expected levels of achievement. In fact, some perform at exceptionally high levels (Valdés, 2003). However, their likelihood of academic success is lower than average. Even top achievers among minority youth experience an achievement gap. For example, the top fifth of Latino students in 2004 had a mean SAT score in math of 588 ($SD = 52$) while for the top fifth of African Americans the mean SAT score in math was 560 (55). In contrast, the top fifth of White students had a mean score of 664 (47) and the top fifth of Asian students had a mean score of 732 (39) (Gándara, 2006; Gándara & Contreras, 2009). While recent College Board data suggest a trend towards greater parity among examinees of all racial and ethnic groups, an analysis of advanced placement (AP) courses offered in urban, rural, and suburban high schools suggests an opportunity gap continues to exist. Large urban and small rural schools serving the nation's students of color and our least economically advantaged students still offer the fewest AP courses. Fifty-seven percent of suburban schools offer four or more AP courses compared to 38% of urban schools. Even more troubling is data that suggest that among urban schools offering multiple AP courses, African American and Latino students are the majority population, but White and Asian students are the majority in AP courses in those schools (Handwerk, Tognatta, Coley, & Gitomer, 2008).

Providing High Quality, College-Prep Opportunities for Immigrant Students: Research-Based Practice

Numerous intervention programs have been designed to supplement formal schooling in order to break the cycle of underachievement and to identify and nurture talent among linguistic minority (LM) immigrant children. These efforts are supported by both public and private entities and they exist along the entire developmental continuum from preschool through high school. In this section, however, I focus on research findings on programs at the secondary level. There is research to suggest that thoughtfully designed and well-implemented EL programs can promote the academic achievement of LM students to very high levels (DeJong 2004; Morales & Aldana, 2010). Aguirre and Hernandez (2002) evaluated Project GOTCHA (Galaxies of Thinking and Creative Heights of Achievements), a program designed to serve gifted and talented K–12 English learners. Funded by the Academic Excellence Program of the Office of Bilingual Education and Minority Language Affairs, the program represents a major innovation in gifted education because of its comprehensive nature. The program's four components (student identification, teacher professional development, curriculum and instruction, and parent workshops) were all specifically designed to serve gifted EL students. While the program has only been implemented in 20 elementary schools and 6 middle schools, schools that have adopted this program all saw gains in student achievement. Given the number of EL students in states like California, perhaps the biggest impact a program like GOTCHA will have is in the shift in paradigm: "Students do not need to be proficient in English to be identified as gifted" (p. 209). Other researchers have reported positive findings for small-scale implementations of programs specifically designed to improve identification of and the success of gifted minority students, such as Project Synergy (Borland & Wright, 1994), Project EXCITE (Olszewski-Kubilius, Lee, Ngoi, & Ngoi, 2004; Olszewski-Kubilius, 2006), and the Project Based Approach (Hertzog, 2005). Notably, these studies all document significant shifts in teacher expectations and attitudes towards the academic abilities of minority students. Each study also provides some evidence that program participants made some academic progress as evidenced by performance on standardized test. These studies' major weaknesses are that they report on very small numbers of students, fewer than 100 in each case, and pre-post data on student achievement are not available for students in any of the studies.

Looking across these studies, one can identify five best practices of programs that promote high academic achievement for LM students (Figueroa & Ruiz, 1999; Goldenberg & Coleman, 2010; Lucas, Henze, & Donato, 1990; Valdés, 2003; Walqui, 2000). These five attributes are:

1. Staff members value students' language and culture and demonstrate it by learning about students' cultures and languages themselves. Staff also encourage students to demonstrate and maintain a heritage language;
2. Staff members demonstrate high academic expectations for students by offering culturally relevant, college prep coursework and scaffolding the college application process for both students and their parents;
3. Staff members offer social and academic supports for students through tutoring and extra-curricular experiences;
4. Staff members provide meaningful settings for parents to interact with students in classes, learn about postsecondary schools, and communicate with staff in their native language; and
5. The program has the full support of its school district, which facilitates the operation the program across grade levels by aligning resources and by providing multiple opportunities for professional development related to the needs of LM students.

In all, research suggests the importance of positive attitudes and high expectations among teachers, program counselors, and principals to the success of students in the program. It also points out the critical importance of the support of the school district.

International Baccalaureate Diploma Programs: A Potential Model Program for LM Students

Founded in 1968 in Geneva, Switzerland, the International Baccalaureate Organization (IBO) originally served the needs of highly mobile international students in Europe and South America. Today, the IBO has authorized 2,668 schools worldwide in 137 countries and offers a Primary Years, Middle Years, and Diploma Programs to over 725,000 students aged 3 to 19. In the United States there are 1,258 authorized IB schools. In 2010, 40,646 11th- and 12th-grade students took diploma candidate exams, of whom 55% self-identified as White, 14% as Asian/Pacific Islander, 9% as Black/Non-Hispanic, and 8% as Hispanic (13% did not identify their ethnicity). A small group of 481 students (1.2%) identified themselves as limited English proficient. Eleven percent reported qualifying for free or reduced-priced lunch. The overarching goals of the curriculum are for students to gain both depth and breadth in each area of knowledge, for students to think critically about how all six areas of knowledge (described below) fit together and become engaged global citizens (IBO, 2005). IBO's mission is to develop students who respect identity, understand differences, tolerate ambiguity, serve the community, and take an individual role in creating a more peaceful world.

While International Baccalaureate Diploma Program courses are often compared to the College Board's AP courses, IB programs differ in important ways. The IB Diploma Program (IBDP) is a comprehensive 2-year curriculum that is both vertically and horizontally aligned to promote students' critical thinking skills and deep content knowledge development. For example, the IBDP includes an Extended Essay requirement that is similar to the Capstone or Senior Projects offered in some U.S. schools, a service learning requirement, and a capstone course similar to that of a college level philosophy course that guides students through epistemological traditions across academic disciplines. Becoming an authorized IB school is a multi-step process that can take up to 5 years. Buy-in from key stakeholders is an important aspect of the application process. IBO administrators attempt to weed out schools that do not appear to have allocated the necessary resources to the IB program and often deny initial applications for authorization. Perhaps the most dramatic difference between the IBO and the College Board is IBO's reliance on active and retired teachers for administrative tasks such as scoring student exams, curricular review, site visits for schools seeking authorization, and professional development courses. Each IB teacher must make a major time commitment to serve the organization in addition to their time in the classroom. The payoff for the organization is that it creates a sense of ownership among teachers and increased teachers' willingness to accept the myriad of IBO rules and regulations for the operation of programs (Mayer, 2006). The payoff for teachers is the opportunity to be recognized for excellent practice and exercise to leadership in places with very flat career ladders (Mayer, 2006).

Of particular relevance to LM students, the IBO specifically fosters linguistic diversity and multilingual education as a matter of policy. According to the IBO, "The IB is committed through its access agenda to reach students from a variety of cultural, linguistic and social backgrounds. The purpose of this policy is to provide a framework that will ensure that the IB's values and aims in relation to access and multilingualism are reflected in the organization's activities" (IBO, 2005). The organization aims to provide materials and services of comparable high quality in all the languages supported. Currently, courses and exams in the Diploma Program are available in Chinese, English, French, German, and Spanish (IBO, 2005, p. 9).

IB curriculum also supports secondary language acquisition at a very high level. From a curricular and policy perspective, the IB programs are a particularly attractive alternative for meeting the needs of ELs and supporting their bilingualism. The field of secondary EL intervention unfortunately remains fixated on a "closing the gap" approach to increasing achievement that pays relatively little attention to boosting performance at the high end of the achievement continuum (Mayer, 2008). In contrast, language instruction options in IB are such that native Spanish speakers, who make up the majority of the LM students in the United States (Gándara & Contreras, 2009), or even native Vietnamese speakers, can meet the IB Literature course requirement by taking these classes in their native language.

Method

In this chapter, I present data drawn from a 6-year ethnographic (2000–2006) case study of one International Baccalaureate Diploma Program serving LM students operating in Jefferson High School (pseudonym). I chose Jefferson from a list of 42 IB Diploma Programs at Title 1 designated schools in the United States. Jefferson High had the largest number of participants of the 6 programs in California. Jefferson is an archetype of the urban comprehensive high school in California and perhaps the nation. It is set in a residential neighborhood with relatively low property values, a few miles from the downtown area of a moderately sized industrial city of Portville. Jefferson is designated as a Title 1 school by the Department of Education. It is large, serving 3,176 students with 132 teachers on staff. It is diverse: 60% of students are Latino, 13% Asian, 12% African American, 10% White, and 5% American Indian or Alaskan Native. According to the California Department of Education (CDE) Academic Performance Index (API) report for 2005, 1,374 (43%) students were classified as economically disadvantaged. Their API score was 539 of a possible 1,000 points in 2004, ranking them among the lowest performing schools in the state.

Research Site

The International Baccalaureate Diploma Program at Jefferson High School was established in 1993 as a magnet program for Portville Unified School District in California. However, the program languished with a lack of interest and leadership until 1999 when John (a history teacher) and his wife Helen (an English teacher) were asked by Jefferson's principal to serve as co-coordinators of the program. In 1998, there were only 32 seniors eligible for the full diploma; by 2004 the number had risen to 116 seniors. John and Helen are both Stanford University graduates. John has a teaching certificate in Gifted and Talented Education, had taught at Jefferson for 30 years and was chair of the history department. Making the IB program work for the Latino, African American, Asian, and Native American students from Jefferson's attendance area became John and Helen's personal crusade. They once told me in an interview, "Doing this work remains an exciting and rewarding labor of love" (May 31, 2005).

As coordinators, John and Helen proved to be both charismatic and tenacious. Their first task was to increase the number of students participating in the IB program, which meant adopting a new admission philosophy. It is not uncommon for IB programs, like high school honors and AP classes, to serve as extensions of districts' K–8 gifted and talented programs. They therefore often maintain minimum admission criteria, such as a score in the 85% on a standardized test, according to IB administrators at the national level (Interview, IBNA Executive Officer, January 24, 2005). The IBO itself does not officially have any admission policy to the IB Diploma program and thus admission criteria are set by local coordinators. John described his admission philosophy in the following way:

> One of the main reasons for our program's recent growth is access. There are no entrance exams, no GPA requirements, and no interviews prior to taking IB courses. Any student who has the desire to enter our program may do so. We encourage students to be at or near grade level in language and math. We also emphasize the need to be self-motivated. We prefer to have students make the attempt, assess their prospects, and choose to leave the program on their own, rather than to exclude them at the outset.
>
> *(Interview, May 31, 2005)*

In the winter of 2003 the open admission process attracted 172 eighth graders from local middle schools with a wide range of GPAs. Of the incoming eighth graders, 59% had GPAs of 3.0 or higher, 35% had GPAs between 2.0–3.0, and the remainder had GPAs below 2.0. Only half of these students had completed algebra in 8th grade. Almost 43% of these students began their education in the U.S. as English learners. Approximately 50% of these students receive federal free or reduced-price lunch services. John and Helen realized that their open enrollment policy meant that students were entering the program with different levels of academic preparation. In order to ameliorate these differences, they developed several different types of scaffolds to help students acquire the academic skills. John said,

> The more things you have in place to reach more kids—teachers who are supportive and coming from their heart, a program where overall kids are excited to be there, where there are social connections—you have a chance of drawing in and keeping more and more kids.
>
> *(Interview, May 31, 2005)*

Jefferson's IB students were succeeding in an extremely rigorous academic curriculum and preparing to go to college. In 2006, 48 of the 55 diploma candidates went on to college. Over 90% of these students went on to four-year colleges; several went to very selective universities, such as the University of Chicago and University of California at Berkeley. One female student, the first person in her family to go to a four-year college, was accepted to University of California, Berkeley. A Latina female who qualified for free lunch and began school as an English learner graduated with a 4.20 GPA, and enrolled at private catholic university with a full scholarship. These are just a few of the success stories shared by IB graduates that attest to the efficacy of the IB program at Jefferson.

Under John and Helen's leadership, program staff also worked hard to make sure the program represented the diversity of students attending schools in the district: 11.4% African American, 20% Asian American (Cambodian, Hmong,

Mien, Vietnamese, and Filipino), 56% Latino, and 12% White. In academic year 2003–2004 there were 550 students, grades 9–12, participating in the program.[1] Over half of the students (n = 324) in the IB program came from families where a language other than English is spoken at home. Forty-two percent of IB students (n = 231) had entered school in the United States as English learners.

Data Collection and Analysis

I visited the school for 2 days a week from September to June, academic year (AY) 2003–2004 for a total of 76 days at the school. Data consisted of transcriptions from structured interviews with district administrators, school principals, program coordinators, counselors, and teachers (28 interviewers altogether) as well as fieldnotes and program documents. When I was not conducting formal interviews, I sat in the staff lounge or observed IB classrooms. In most cases, I was invited to observe their classes either before or after our interview. At Jefferson, the IB program had a small classroom designated as the IB office/workroom. During the days I observed at Jefferson, I spent time in the IB office and conversed informally with one or both coordinators and IB teachers. I supplemented my interviews with observations of coordinators in different settings (club meetings, recruitment fairs, PTO meetings, ninth-grade preregistration and orientation sessions) in order to gain an emic perspective of the program understanding of the culture of the school and to triangulate interview data (Creswell, 2007). As Becker, Geer, Hughes, and Strauss (1961) found in their qualitative research study of a medical school, I often found that individual's uninitiated comments were more closely related to the actions I observed and were more reliable than participants' answers to my questions during interviews. By 2006, my formal research had ended but my relationship with the program continued; I assisted the program coordinators in applying for and implementing a scholarship program for IB program graduates (2008–2009). I subsequently interacted with students who had received the scholarship via email and phone interviews as they transitioned from high school to college.

The approach to data analysis I used was described by Yin (1989) as a pattern-matching approach to data analysis. During the analysis phase, I compared aspects of the IB program to the attributes of high school programs successfully promoting the academic achievement of LM students as described by researchers (see, e.g., Figueroa & Ruiz, 1999; Goldenberg & Coleman, 2010; Lucas, 1997; Lucas, Henze, & Donato, 1990; Valdés, 2003; Walqui, 2000). The analysis examined the relationship between schools and teachers' background, job satisfaction, influences on teaching behaviors, teachers' perceptions of student participants and nonparticipants as well as the contextual aspects influencing program implementation.

Features of the IB Program at Jefferson High School: How Do They Compare with Research on Best Practices?

Staff Value Students' Language and Culture and Demonstrate It by Learning about Students' Cultures and Languages Themselves. Staff Encourage Students to Demonstrate and Maintain a Heritage Language

One third of the teachers involved in the IB program spoke Spanish, and five teachers identified themselves as Latino/a. The program only offered French and Spanish languages as second language courses (Language B); all students chose a language and pursued the same language for 4 years. Students whose home language is Spanish were encouraged to take high-level Spanish classes. Students from Asian backgrounds were not able to study their home language in the program. Two teachers, a ninth-grade Vietnamese math teacher and Jefferson High alumnus and a Spanish teacher who identified himself as Latino both talked at length during their interviews about making connections with male students and offering extra support to students who sought to make personal connections because they shared a similar cultural heritage. These teachers also said they helped students communicate with their parents by translating descriptions of program activities into the students' home language. The IB chemistry teacher, Jen, a White woman from Montana, was mentored by a Latina biology teacher shortly after she arrived at Jefferson High. During our interview she shared that her mentor encouraged her to learn Spanish and pursue her Bilingual Credential through the Portville County Office of Education so that she could help students who were not fluent in English access the college preparatory science curriculum. Jen did earn her Bilingual Credential and teaches chemistry for EL students and IB students. Five of the LM graduates mentioned Jen in their interviews. Students from Mexican, Hmong, and Vietnamese families said Jen worked hard to recruit LM students for her 2-year chemistry course. They said that Jen had a way of making them feel they could be successful in her classes. When asked how she did this, these students said that because Jen took the time to learn chemistry in Spanish, they felt she would be empathetic to their own struggles with learning English. The students also said Jen worked with many students afterschool and on weekends preparing teams for Academic Decathlon and other science completions. Students reported that the extra time spent studying science helped them do better in their IB classes and it helped them develop close relationships with Jen and with each other.

The program coordinators admitted that they would have liked to expand the number of languages offered in IB. However, it is difficult to find enough qualified bilingual teachers to meet the needs of their students. The program coordinators spoke of their successful efforts to expand the Visual/Performing Arts programs so that more students would be able to participate in those programs. While the school had been de-emphasizing such electives so that it could increase the number of remedial courses for students to pass the Exit Exam (Holme, Richards, Jimerson, & Cohen, 2010), John noted that he was able make the argument to the district that his IB students had to have arts courses in order to be eligible to earn the IB Diploma. Both coordinators shared an understanding that their students needed ways to express themselves that was not so closely tied to language. Between 2006 and 2011, the program produced four Gates Millennium Scholars who all excelled in the Visual/Performing Arts program.

Staff Demonstrate High Academic Expectations for Students by Offering Culturally Relevant College Preparatory Coursework and Scaffolding the College Application Process for Both Students and Their Parents

Cultural Relevance. The multicultural and global focus stated in the IB mission statement was evident in several places in the curriculum. The following are just a few examples gathered from Jefferson IB documents and syllabi. In a Languages and Literature course, the introduction to the course syllabus stated,

> In the view of the international nature of IB courses, this course does not limit the study of literature to the achievements of one culture or the cultures covered by any one language. In this class the study of world literature is important because it helps students to gain a global perspective. This perspective offers students the opportunity of the various ways in which cultures influence and shape life experiences common to all humanity.

Likewise, the history teachers I interviewed spoke with enthusiasm about how students' multinational backgrounds enriched their courses. One teacher, for example, said that he asked students to create family trees as a way of connecting students' own life experiences to the course material. Out of 150 students a year, he learned his class usually has only a handful from a traditional U.S. family. He went on to say that when students share their family trees with their classmates, all see how many of their classmates have experienced revolution, Communism, oppression, and economic challenges that spur migration across national borders.

Monitoring Students' Progress in Courses and College Counseling. The staff assigned to the IB program actively assist students in attaining their collegiate aspirations. They provide close monitoring of student progress through the 4-year course sequence, provide special mentoring and support activities beyond academic instruction, and are highly involved in the evaluation of student performance and citizenship. During one of my visits, a performing arts teacher stopped by the IB office to ask the coordinators for a copy of her students' grades in their other IB classes. She said she wanted to make sure they were doing well in all of their classes not just her class. A student said, "In some regular classes teachers aren't the greatest, but in IB we have teachers that genuinely care about their students and want to help them succeed" (student 55).

A single school counselor serves as the 11th- and 12th-grade IB Diploma Program counselor. She works intimately with the students and the program coordinators to assure proper student course placement and to provide them with the information and encouragement to successfully navigate the college application and admissions process. Additionally, in 2006, a counseling technician was assigned to help college-bound students complete federal student aid, college financial aid, and scholarship applications. Between 2006 and 2011, as a result of the college counseling technician's interventions with the IB students, there was a significant increase in the number and value of scholarships awarded to IB diploma candidates to between $2 and $3 million each year. In addition, students identified specific college preparatory resources that the IB program had given them access to such as presentation skills, college information, critical thinking, time management, study habits, and test taking skills. For example one student said,

> I believe the IB program will prepare me for college because of all the skills the program will offer me.... It will benefit me not only because of the material we learn but that the classes require skills such as creativity, perseverance, and hard work.
>
> *(Student 78)*

Staff Offer Social and Academic Supports for Students through Tutoring and Extra Curricular Experiences

Building a Sense of Community: Scaffolding and Tutoring. The Jefferson IB Program established a strong community of peers, mentoring, and close relationships with teachers. The program utilized a cohort model that encouraged strong peer support networks and personal connections with teachers. During an interview, one science teacher said her students often tell her that even though they are barely passing her class they do not want to be moved into the general education courses. She said that students told her she was more motivating, more entertaining, and there were more hands-on activities in her classes. Other teachers said that due to the strong sense of community among students, parents called to ask that the teacher allow their children stay in the program even though their children might be struggling. A student summed up the attitude of her IB classmates, "In [regular] classes we are interrupted by students who are not willing to learn. Instead, in IB we are in a classroom filled with students who are there for the same reason that I want to [be] there" (student 4).

John noted that the program looked to help students entering the program feel like they were in a close knit family, to feel like they were a part of something. "We want kids to want to come to school and feel good when they say, 'I'm IB.'" The coordinators began early with community building activities. Incoming freshmen participated in the "Warm-Up Week." For 5 hours a day during the "Warm-Up Week," teachers helped students have the opportunity to develop positive attitudes towards achievement and introduced to teamwork strategies. Students from grades 11 and 12 also attended and advised small groups, providing new students with additional peer mentors. Students who attended the "Warm-Up Week" said they felt more confident and better prepared starting the school year. To help support seniors, the coordinators, beginning in 2000, instituted a Senior Diploma Candidate Retreat each fall. Diploma candidates and teachers travelled outside the city to a rustic campground in the nearby foothills for 3 days to encourage teamwork, strengthen personal connections, and to build the students' capacity to achieve program completion. An IB parent described the effects that the scaffolds instituted by the program had on students:

> We feel that one thing which the IB program provides, which is very seldom accomplished in public schools, is a sense of community. This is a quality which is most often found in the home, church, or organizations and clubs, but which is quite often difficult, if not impossible, to create in a public school. Both of our children have found a close-knit support group within the Urban IB community, both with other students and with staff. This has made it easier, more fun, and more rewarding to achieve the difficult goals of the IB program. Achieving these goals has made it possible for them to better synthesize, analyze and articulate the information in the curriculum.
>
> *(IB parent, interview, February 18, 2004)*

Staff Provide Meaningful Settings for Parents to Interact with Students in Classes, Learn about Postsecondary Schools and Communicate with Staff in Their Native Language

Where the IB program had many exemplary practices, providing for parent involvement was a significant weakness. Coordinators and teachers at Jefferson did not provide opportunities for LM parents to participate in the IB program. Letters of invitation, in English, to magnet fairs and parent information sessions were sent to all eighth-grade parents by the district office. During these sessions, the coordinators spoke in English and did not make an effort to bring students or teachers to act as translators. Based on my observations of the coordinators' presentation of the IB program at the Parent Information meetings, it was apparent that they assumed that parents and students already knew whether they were planning to attend college or not. Thus, John emphasized in his presentation that the IB program's main benefit to students was increased access to college-preparatory curriculum and ability to earn college credits. In his presentation, John did not attempt to make the program attractive in any other way. From my perspective, the coordinators' message did not appropriately address the concerns of the parents in the audience. According to the 2010 census data, Portville had less than half the number of college graduates as the rest of the state; only 14.5% of Portville residents had a bachelor's degree and 41.5% of Portville's adult population's primary language was not English, suggesting most families in the parent orientations did not have much exposure to higher education. Parents' questions during the session, regarding what sort of jobs a person could get after graduating from a competitive four-year college compared to the local community college and exactly how much money they could save if their child earned college credits at high school, provided evidence that the coordinator's message could have been modified to better address parents' concerns.

Interviews with coordinators and teachers revealed that they thought that students in the program did not have much parental support at home. This view seemed to emanate from the knowledge that many parents did not have educational experiences in the United States and many had only an elementary-level education. During our discussions, coordinators would tell stories of parent interactions that followed the theme of parents having only vague notions of a better life for their children. Jen related that "Parents tell me, 'I don't want my child working the fields, I don't want them to struggle like we do.'" Jen, the bilingual teacher, described her interactions with her students' parents in the following way:

> Most of the parents I speak with are happy that they [their kids] will graduate from high school and they see it as a huge accomplishment because they [themselves] didn't graduate from high school. So going on to university, parents see that as an unattainable goal. These parents can't even imagine that happening. So the support for what it takes to get their kids to college is totally lacking.
>
> *(Interview, February, 2003)*

As I interacted with teachers in the IB program, it became apparent that teachers had a very narrow and utilitarian view of how parents could support their children at school. Unfortunately, like many other educators across the United States, these teachers' adopted dominant ideologies related to the ways immigrant families are able to support their children's education. These views significantly limited the ways teachers thought about involving parents in the program (Arzubiaga, Noguerón, & Sullivan, 2009).

While Latino/a students spoke about the importance of studying Spanish so that they could communicate with parents and grandparents who were not fluent in English, Vietnamese and Hmong students did not have the opportunity to maintain their heritage language at school. Hmong and Vietnamese students said that communicating with parents about school and program activities was a big challenge. One Hmong student said,

> I just didn't know how to describe all of the out of school activities like the IB retreats and Academic Decathlon. You know, they just didn't have experiences like that when they were growing up. I guess I was lucky that they trusted me because I got good grades. But I always felt bad that I wasn't able to tell them about what I was doing.
>
> *(Student 18)*

Successful Programs are Located in Districts that Facilitate Program Operation and Provide Adequate Resources

The deputy superintendent of the district suggested he valued the program when he said, "Some students don't pass the IB exams, however the experience, in and of itself is beneficial and rewarding. I believe that any student that goes through and completes the program benefits." However, although individual school board members and the superintendent voiced support for the IB program at Jefferson, this support did not translate into policy exemptions or the creation of policies that supported the mission of the program. Meeting NCLB graduation and testing requirements became the only district priority as the district's K–12 schools failed to meet benchmarks for 4 consecutive years. While IB teachers saw themselves as actively supporting the district's efforts to raise students' test scores and keep students from dropping out of school, teachers had a difficult time making this case to district administrators.

The coordinators' inability to make a case to the district has implications for any academic program seeking to boost LM students' preparation for college and not just remediate the lowest achieving students. Many of the negative perceptions held by educators outside the IB program related to the program's open-door application process. Taking any student who expressed interest in the program without requiring parent permission, interviews, or teacher recommendations resulted in a high attrition rate. In 2003, for example, the program accepted 172 freshmen; this number declined to 94 (54.7%) by their sophomore year, and 74 (43.0%) graduated in 2007. Other IB programs only accept students who score above the 85 percentile on standardized tests and have a rigorous application process that requires parent, teacher, and student essays (Mayer, 2006). The Jefferson coordinators believed that given the history of racial segregation in the district, it made the most sense for students to make the decision not to participate rather than have White teachers pre-judge students' abilities using measures that did not accurately "measure" what their students could accomplish. An IBO representative I interviewed shared an attitude similar to that of the Jefferson program coordinators:

You have to be careful how you interpret the results of an IB exam if your only goal is to get 5, 6, 7 on an IB exam or for every kid to get a diploma. A school can accomplish that by limiting the number of kids that you allow to take the program, by making sure that you take only the best—the best isn't the right word—only the readiest. But you start to appreciate how much this program can help all kinds of kids, then you may be gentler when the diploma rate goes down or your kids are getting 3s and 4s. Because you are aware that the distance they have traveled is more important than the destination where they have arrived.

(Interview, January 21, 2004)

While the coordinators saw their program's attrition rate as a normal consequence of their application process, district administrators who espoused a more "traditional" selective honors program model saw the high student attrition rates as a sign of failure. District representatives also believed that the IB goal of getting as many students to college as possible was at odds with district-wide goal to raise standardized tests scores of the lowest-performing students because the IB, which is an expensive program, took limited resources away from efforts to raise test scores district-wide. This disconnect between district and IB coordinators' goals was a major source of tension in the district-program relationship. This tension is apparent in the 5-year review document prepared by the coordinators for IBNA. In it they said,

The district has chosen to place its energy and emphasis on numerical indicators of student progress and matching its programs with externally imposed standards ... which do not consider the learner as an important participant in what is to be learned. The prevailing educational philosophy within the district is to focus on improving the test performance of students in the lowest third in order to raise overall school test scores.

(IB Diploma Program Evaluation, March 2005)

The statement above is one example of the Jefferson coordinators' concern that district administrators cared more about raising students' test scores than students' completion of college-preparatory courses. The Jefferson principal relayed the message he was getting from the district, "District views IB as a drain on this school's resources. District officials have indicated that they do not want to attract too many students to the diploma program as it is a burden to the school" (Interview, November 20, 2004). The principal acknowledged that he was getting pressure from the district to direct more resources towards students who had not passed the high school exit exam at the 10th grade and fewer towards the IB program. By 2009, the district had shifted all financial support away from the IB program to invest in teachers for remedial high school exit exam courses. The future of the IB program at Jefferson became uncertain.

Discussion and Policy Implications

Three of the five features researchers identified as factors related to increasing the academic performance of LM students were present in the IB Diploma Program at Jefferson: teachers valued students' heritage language; enrolled students in honors level, college-preparatory courses; and instituted academic and social supports throughout the program. While causal arguments cannot be made in case study research, it seems likely that the culturally relevant college-preparatory coursework, 4-years of language coursework, supportive relationships with teachers, and academically oriented peer culture were related to the success of students in Jefferson's IB program, in terms of college-going. The IB Diploma program may be one of the most promising academic programs on the horizon not only because of the strengths mentioned in the case study, but also because it is a program widely accepted by the mainstream educational communities. In the current policy environment where restrictive language policies are commonplace (Gándara & Hopkins, 2010), the widespread acceptance of IB programs is a way for bilingual educators to leverage rigorous, bilingual educational opportunities for students who might otherwise receive remedial English-only coursework.

Important lessons for policy makers and educators can also be learned from the two aspects of the program not present at Jefferson High: parent involvement and district support. In the current fiscal and policy environments, no local intervention program can be sustained without political support from the district (Borman, Carter, Aladjem, & Le Floch, 2004). Educators who are interested in providing access to a wide range of students, rather than just capturing those most capable at the outset, need to think about how to account for program attrition to educators outside the program at the district level. Educators interested in preparing students for college must figure out ways make their case in terms of test scores and curbing dropouts so that the value of the program can be communicated to school board administrators who under the pressures of NCLB may only be interested in raising test scores of the lowest-performing group of students. New research using district level achievement and demographic data to identify 6th and 8th graders at risk of dropping out of school could be used by program coordinators to prove to stakeholders that the students they are serving face the same "risks" as the lowest-performing students in the district (Gándara, 2006).

While teachers in the program clearly had limited perspectives of how students' families could participate in their children's education, it is encouraging that this perspective did not translate into teachers' low expectations for the students themselves (Feliciano 2006; Ruiz de Velasco, Fix, & Clewell, 2000). This finding suggests these teachers may be open to research-based strategies if provided with professional development opportunities in this area (Grant, & Sleeter, 2011; Lopez, Scribner, & Mahitivanichcha, 2001). The IB curricula's international perspectives are one way to credibly add a multicultural focus to curricula across the United States. Another potential strength of the program is its ability to accommodate students whose first language is not English. IB students whose first language is Spanish, for example, can take Spanish instead of English as their Language A1 course and then take English as their second language course. This would allow students to maintain their native language and progress in English language acquisition simultaneously. A comprehensive college-preparatory program like IB, with its accountability measures, formative and summative assessments, and professional development support may be one of the best reform options available to school districts seeking to significantly raise LM students' academic performance and boost college aspirations and readiness.

Note

1. Not all students participated in the full diploma program. Some students took only one or two IB courses. Of the 550 students, 116 seniors were eligible for a full diploma in 2004.

References

Aguirre, N., & Hernandez, N. E. (2002). Portraits of success: Programs that work. In J. A. Castellano & E. I. Diaz (Eds.), *Reaching new horizons: Gifted and talented education for culturally and linguistically diverse students* (pp. 200–219). Boston: Allyn and Bacon.

Arzubiaga, A.A., Noguerón, S., & Sullivan, A. (2009). The education of children in immigrant families. *Review of Research in Education, 33,* 246–251.

Aud, S., Fox, M., & KewalRamani, A. (2010). *Status and trends in the education of racial and ethnic groups* (NCES 2010-015). Retrieved from National Center for Education Statistics website: http://nces.ed.gov/pubs2010/2010015.pdf

August, D., & Hakuta, K. (1997). *Improving schooling for language-minority children: A research agenda.* Washington, DC: National Academy Press.

Becker, H., Geer, B., Hughes, E., & Strauss, A. (1961). *Boys in white: Student culture in medical school.* Chicago: University of Chicago Press.

Bic, N., & Lee, S. J. (2007). Complicating the image of model minority success: A review of Southeast Asian American research. *Review of Educational Research, 77,* 415–453.

Borland, J. H., & Wright, L. (1994). Identifying young, potentially gifted economically disadvantaged students. *Gifted Child Quarterly, 38,* 164–171.

Borman, K., Carter, K., Aladjem, D., & Le Floch, K. (2004). Challenges for the future of comprehensive school reform. In C. Cross (Ed.), *Putting the pieces together: Lessons from comprehensive school reform research* (pp. 109–150). Washington, DC: George Washington University Press.

Callahan, R., Wilkinson, L., Muller, C. (2010). Academic achievement and course taking among language minority youth in U.S. schools: Effects of ESL placement. *Educational Evaluation and Policy Analysis, 32*(1), 84–117.

Creswell, J. (2007). *Qualitative inquiry and research design: Choosing among five approaches.* Thousand Oakes, CA: Sage.

DeJong, E. J. (2004). After exit: Academic achievement patterns of former English language learners. *Education Policy Analysis Archives, 12*(50), 1–20.

Feliciano, C. (2006). Beyond the family: The influence of premigration group status on the educational expectations of immigrants' children. *Sociology of Education, 79,* 281–303.

Figueroa, R., & Ruiz, N. (1999). Minority underrepresentation in gifted programs: Old problems, new perspectives. In Tashakkori, A., Salvador, H., Kemper, E. (Eds.), *Readings on equal education Vol. 16. Education of Hispanics in the United States: Politics, policies and outcomes* (pp. 119–141). New York: AMS Press.

Gándara, P. (2006). *Fragile futures: Risk and vulnerability among Latino high achievers*. Princeton, NJ: Educational Testing Services.

Gándara, P., & Contreras, F. (2009). *The Latino education crisis: The consequences of failed social policies*. Cambridge, MA: Harvard Education Press.

Gándara, P., & Hopkins, M. (2010). The changing linguistic landscape of the United States. In P. Gándara & M. Hopkins (Eds.), *Forbidden language: English learners and restrictive language policies* (pp. 7–19). New York: Teachers College Press.

Gándara, P., & Rumberger, R. (2009). Immigration, language policy and education: How does language policy structure opportunity? *Teachers College Record, 111*(3), 750–782.

Gándara, P., Rumberger, R., Maxwell-Jolly, J., & Callahan, R. (2003). English learners in California schools: Unequal resources, unequal outcomes. *Education Policy Analysis Archives, 11*(36). Retrieved from http://epaa.asu.edu/epaa/v11n36/

Goldenberg, C., & Coleman, R. (2010). *Promoting academic success among English learners: A guide to research*. Thousand Oakes, CA: Corwin.

Grant, C., & Sleeter, C. (2011). *Doing multicultural education for achievement and equity*. New York: Routledge.

Handwerk, P., Tognatta, N., Coley, R., & Gitomer, D. (2008). *Access to success: Patterns of advanced placement participation in U.S. high schools*. Princeton, NJ: Educational Testing Services.

Hertzog, N. (2005). Equity and access: Creating general education classrooms responsive to potential giftedness. *Journal for the Education of the Gifted, 29*, 213–257.

Holme, J. J., Richards, M., Jimerson, J., & Cohen, R. (2010). Assessing the effects of high school exit examinations. *Review of Educational Research, 80*(4), 476–452.

International Baccalaureate Organization (IBO). (2005). *Program standards and practices*. Geneva: Author.

Lee, S. (2001). More than model minorities or dropouts: A look at Hmong American high school students. *Harvard Educational Review, 71*, 505–528.

Lopez, G., Scribner, J., & Mahitivanichcha, K. (2001). Redefining parental involvement: Lessons from high-performing migrant-impacted schools. *American Educational Research Journal, 38*, 253–288.

Lucas, T. (1997). *Into, through and beyond secondary school: Critical transitions for immigrant youths*. Washington, DC: Center for Applied Linguistics.

Lucas T., Henze, R., & Donato, R. (1990). Promoting the success of Latino language minority students: An exploratory study of six high schools. *Harvard Educational Review, 60*(1), 315–340.

Mayer, A. (2006). *Interrupting social reproduction: The implementation of an International Baccalaureate Diploma Program in an urban high school*. Unpublished doctoral dissertation. University of California, Davis.

Mayer, A. (2008). Expanding opportunities for high academic achievement: An International Baccalaureate Diploma Program in an urban high school. *Journal of Advanced Academics, 19*, 202–235.

Merickel, A., Linquanti R., Parrish, T.B., Pérez, M., Eaton. M. & Esra, P. (2003). *Effects of the implementation of Proposition 227 on the education of English learners, K–12 Year 3 Report*. Retrieved from American Institute for Research website: http://www.air.org/files/Yr_3_FinalRpt.pdf

Morales, Z., & Aldana, U. (2010). Learning in two languages: Programs with political promise. In P. Gándara & M. Hopkins (Eds.), *Forbidden language: English learners and restrictive language policies* (pp. 159–174). New York: Teachers College Press.

Olszewski-Kubilius, P. (2006). Addressing the achievement gap between minority and nonminority children: Increasing access and achievement through Project EXCITE. *Gifted Child Today, 29*, 28–37.

Olszewski-Kubilius, P., Lee, S., Ngoi, M., & Ngoi, D. (2004). Addressing the achievement gap between minority and nonminority children: By increasing access to gifted programs. *Journal for the Education of the Gifted, 28,* 127–158.

Parrish, T., Merickel, A., Pérez, M., R. Linquanti, R., Socias, M., Spain, A., et al. (2006). *Effects of the implementation of Proposition 227 on the education of English learners, K–12 findings from a fiveyear evaluation.* Retrieved from WestEd website: http://www.wested.org/online_pubs/227Reportb.pdf

Passel, J. S. (2005). *Unauthorized migrants: Numbers and characteristics. Background briefing pre- pared for task force on immigration and America's future.* Washington, DC: Pew Hispanic Center.

Ruiz de Velasco, J., Fix, M., & Clewell, B. C. (2000). *Overlooked and underserved: Immigrant students in U.S. Schools.* Washington, DC: Urban Institute.

Steele, C. (1997). A threat in the air: How stereotypes shape intellectual identity and performance. *American Psychologist, 52,* 613–629.

Suarez-Orozco, C., Suarez-Orozco, M., & Todorova, I. (2007). *Learning a new land: Immigrant students in American society.* Cambridge, MA: Harvard University Press.

Thomas, W. P., & Collier, V. P. (2002). *A national study of school effectiveness for language minority students' long-term academic achievement.* Retrieved from http://www.usc.edu/dept/education/CMMR/CollierThomasExReport.pdf

Valdés, G. (2003). *Expanding definitions of giftedness: The case of young interpreters from immigrant communities.* Mahwah, NJ: Erlbaum.

Walqui, A. (2000). *Access and engagement: Program design and instructional approaches for immigrant students in secondary school.* McHenry, IL: Delta Systems/Center for Applied Linguistics.

Yin, R. K. (1994). *Case study research: Design and methods* (2nd ed.). Thousand Oaks, CA: Sage.

5

HOW PAOLA MADE IT TO COLLEGE

A Linguistic Minority Student's Unlikely Success Story

Linda Harklau and Shelly McClanahan

Latinos/as, the fastest growing demographic group in U.S. schools, leave the educational pipeline at disproportionate rates at every stage of the educational system. Researchers cite a litany of grim statistics. While more than 75% of White students nationally earn high school diplomas, only 56% of Latinos/as do (Editorial Projects in Education Research Center, 2010). First generation immigrant Latinos/as are particularly vulnerable to dropping out (American Federation of Teachers, 2004). While the high school graduation rates for Latinas have of late surpassed those of Latinos, they nevertheless continue to have among the lowest proportions of high school graduates compared to all other racial and ethnic groups (Zambrana & Zoppi, 2002). Nearly one in five (19%) young adult Latinas in 2007 were neither in school nor in the workforce, a proportion that is rivaled only by that of young Black men (16%) (Fry, 2009).

Statistics on Latino/a college enrollment rates are even more stark. While 36% of 18- to 24-year-olds in the United States overall enroll in college, only 23% of Latinos/as do so. Latina high school graduates continue to lag behind White female graduates in college enrollment (44% to 54%) (Fry, 2009), and they are less likely to complete a four-year college degree (Ginorio & Huston, 2001). As a result, in spite of their growing prominence in the American workforce, Latinos/as earn lower than average wages and are more likely to be unemployed than other demographic groups (National Council of La Raza, 2009).

Not surprisingly, then, there has been a significant amount of attention devoted to identifying factors that impede Latinos/as' academic achievement and college enrollment. Frequently identified factors include Latinos' disproportionate enrollment in resource-poor schools with inexperienced and unqualified teachers, lack of access to high-level college preparatory coursework, families with lower than average educational backgrounds and financial resources, high family mobility and disrupted schooling, and problems with access to higher education caused by undocumented legal status (American Federation of Teachers, 2004).

While risk factors have been well studied, facilitative factors and success stories have less often been the focus. Nevertheless, a growing number of researchers (see, e.g., Gándara, 1995; Garrett, Antrop-González, & Vélez, 2010) argue that it is equally, if not more, important to study cases of academically successful students if we are to develop effective strategies for getting more Latinos/as through high school and into college. In this chapter we consider one such success story. We trace the path of one Mexican American linguistic minority student, Paola, as she found her way to college in spite of overwhelming obstacles. We use Paola's story to emphasize the importance of understanding the individual process through which factors that have been associated with college enrollment play out in the high school career of a linguistic minority student.

Method

The purpose of the study was to answer the question: What factors over time contribute to high school completion and college enrollment for academically talented Latino/a youth in one southeastern new Latino diaspora community?

The study took a longitudinal qualitative case study approach. Most work on college access has relied on large-scale demographic trends and comparisons of Latinos/as to other ethnic groups (Zarete & Gallimore, 2005). Less has focused on the process through which individual Latinas/os make the decision to attend or forego college (although see Gándara, 1995). While large-scale studies can provide broad overviews of college-going patterns, they nevertheless leave us with significant gaps in our understanding of how individual Latinas fare in the college-going decision process (Zarete & Gallimore, 2005).

Paola, the subject of this chapter, was part of a larger study of five[1] first-generation Latina/o immigrant students in one rapidly growing "new Latino diaspora" community (Hamann & Harklau, 2008; Hamann, Wortham, & Murillo, 2002). Latino/a educational experiences in new immigrant communities like this rural Piedmont Appalachian foothill setting are as yet little studied and understood. Such communities present unique features unlike those in traditional immigrant settlement areas. For one, in the space of less than two decades the Piedmont area has gone from a place with a highly stable, predominantly White population to an area with a dramatically growing Latino/a population (Kochhar, Suro, & Tafoya, 2005). Also unique is the fact that the new migrants are predominantly foreign-born (Kochhar et al., 2005). To look at college-going in this population, case studies were drawn from participants in a summer program at a local community college. The program's purpose was to identify potentially college-bound rising 8th graders from underrepresented groups and to boost their academic aspirations.

This chapter is based on 35 20- to 90-minute open-ended interviews that Harklau conducted with Paola spanning spring 2001 through spring 2005. Longitudinal case studies were chosen as the study methodology in order to create "naturalistic sagas of individual experience" (Crawford & Brunner, 1998) that are often missing from large-scale studies of Latino/a student educational outcomes. Longitudinal case study methodology has the advantage of fostering trust and confidence with informants (Harklau, 2008). Through iterative, long-term questioning, the approach builds in checks about the consistency of participants' reported experiences and perceptions. The approach also allows a unique window into on-going processes of student identity formation and school achievement. The underlying assumption in interview studies is that "Discourse, rather than other kinds of human activities or behavior, is ... the best available window into cultural understanding and the way that these are negotiated by individuals" (Quinn, 2005, p. 3).

Interviews took place during the school day, primarily in an unoccupied teacher's workroom. Paola was asked to talk about classroom routines, assignments, and grades; issues identified in the literature; and topics that had come up in interviews with other case study students. Paola often initiated her own topics as well. Interviews were audiorecorded and transcribed. To augment interview findings, students were also asked to supply samples of schoolwork. A research assistant observed and took fieldnotes on Paola's classes for two days at the beginning of the study. Harklau also kept fieldnotes on every visit she made to Paola's school over the 4½ years of the study. These visits sometimes included not only talking with Paola, but also acting as Paola's advocate in talking with her counselor, the counseling secretary, or other teachers to gain information or urge action on her behalf. Data were recursively coded in NVivo by all the authors. We take a social constructionist perspective (see, e.g., Crotty, 1998) in this chapter, which assumes that interview data are inextricably interwoven with the dynamics of interpersonal interaction (see, e.g., Kvale & Brinkman, 2009). We also assume that both Paola's and Harklau's perspectives were limited and partial.

The Case—Paola

Paola's parents were originally from Tamaulipas, Mexico. They were a transnational family with relatives on both sides of the Texas border. A wealthy aunt had sponsored Paola's mother's education, allowing her to attend some college and obtain a job as a secretary to a highly placed Mexican official. She had traveled widely in Mexico and owned her own home in Matamoros. Her first marriage had been to an American, the father of Paola's oldest sister Cate. Upon divorce, she had returned to Mexico where she remarried and had two more daughters, Angie and Paola. Paola lived in Mexico until the end of kindergarten. The family then moved to Florida where Paola's father was working as a migrant worker and mechanic. Her mother became a nanny and housekeeper. They moved frequently to follow her father's work, first arriving in Lymanton when Paola was in third grade. Her parents divorced. Alarmed by Cate's growing friendship with gang members, her mother moved the family to Brownsville, Texas, when Paola was in fifth grade. The family then returned to the Lymanton area, where she had remained since sixth grade. Paola's mother remarried and her stepfather lived with the family for most of the study. When Harklau first met her in eighth grade, Paola was interested in a career in law enforcement. She expressed particularly interest in the FBI, "because I like investigating, and finding out things, and being like [undercover] and stuff." As the years went on, and in particular as a result of getting a summer job at a church-sponsored day camp, Paola's career objectives changed to early childhood education. Throughout the study, she never wavered in her assumption that she would go to college. Against all odds she graduated from high school on time. Although Harklau's study concluded with Paola's high school graduation, Paola continued to keep in touch with her. Paola enrolled in a local community college in the fall after she graduated from high school. While she was forced to withdraw spring semester 2006 so that she and her family could save money for tuition, she returned the following fall and eventually completed an associate degree in early childhood education with hopes of being admitted to a 4-year program with teacher certification in early childhood education.

Obstacles to College-Going

A rather daunting set of obstacles stood between Paola and her college ambitions. These included disrupted schooling, unstable family income, undocumented legal status, and learning disabilities.

Disrupted Schooling

Paola's family had moved frequently to follow employment, to be closer to family, or when Paola's mother perceived local schools to be failing her children. As a result, Paola had attended five different schools in two different countries by the end of elementary school. Even though she attended the same school district in middle and high school, because of the district's rapid growth she attended two different high schools. Paola had thus faced considerable discontinuities in subject matter learning. Paola's transfer to a newly opened school in the district in 10th grade created further disruptions. While the new school was overall better resourced than others in the district, it had a rocky opening. In a state with teacher shortages, course offerings were at first a hit-and-miss affair. Students sometimes encountered shortages in required math and science courses, a scarcity of desirable electives, and inexperienced teachers. More importantly, it took the school a couple of years to develop a routine for delivering course planning and college information to students. In her senior year, Paola complained that "now they give them a lot of stuff. Like, they go to homeroom and they're always talking about their courses and what they're gonna need and all this, and like, they give them a lot of help. But they didn't give us help, back then ... And now it's too late for us."

Unstable Family Income

Related to instabilities in Paola's family life were precarious financial circumstances. Low income has also been associated with poorer academic outcomes across the board, including Latinos/as (National Women's Law Center, 2009; Roscigno, 2000). While Paola's middle school years were spent in relative prosperity with a two-income family, her mother had been the family's sole source of support for much of the rest of her life. Her mother and stepfather separated in Paola's junior year, and she anxiously reported that her mother "got laid off, or like a couple of things, and that just, but it's a little bit behind bills and now we've gotta catch up." Research suggests that the sorts of disruptive family changes like marital separations and divorces experienced in Paola's family often result in fewer familial economic resources which in turn can cause declines in academic achievement of children in single-parent families (see, e.g., Pong & Ju, 2000). Even though Paola's mother soon found another job, it took her, Cate, and Angie's salaries to make ends meet. As a result, Paola talked about taking multiple summer jobs to cover the expense of her sports, particularly a volleyball camp that was considered almost mandatory for players. The cost of college weighed heavily on Paola and her family, particularly as she came to realize her undocumented status (see below). Even early in the study, however, she expressed concern that she needed a scholarship to cover tuition, "cuz I do not want to pay for it and make my mom pay for it, cuz, like, just—that is too much to pay."

Generational and Legal Status

Nationally, Latinos/as born abroad are less likely than U.S.-born students to complete high school (Chapman, Laird, & KewalRamani, 2010). While Paola's oldest sister Cate was a U.S. citizen, Paola and her older sister Angie had been born in Mexico and were undocumented. For most of her high school career, it appeared that Paola was unaware of her legal status. In her sophomore year, she was still avidly tracking her GPA in terms of eligibility for state and federal financial aid. Finally, at the beginning of her junior year, she realized that

> I honestly don't know about the immigration thing. I just know I've been here long, and my mom says there's some things we didn't have and then there's some things that we do have that makes us here, but then there's things we don't have.

While her mother continued to tell her, "We're legal here, but we're still working that out," Paola came to understand she was undocumented. Her ineligibility for financial aid was not the worst of it. While in 2005 undocumented students could still attend public universities in Georgia,[2] they paid out of state tuition, a staggering financial burden for a family that was barely making ends meet. Because of Paola's mother's U.S. legal residency and sister's citizenship, Paola and Angie were eligible for residency but her mother had never filed the paperwork because of the legal costs. By the end of high school, Paola told Harklau that her mother had finally hired an immigration attorney but that it would take 3 to 4 years to establish residency. Paola rightfully felt that this was a very long time to wait for college. Paola's immigration status also made it difficult for her to find a good-paying job to save for tuition costs. Her legal status also prohibited her from obtaining a driver's license, leaving her to choose to either break the law by driving or have to depend utterly on her family and friends for transportation to school and work.

Learning Disabilities

Even though there were indications early on that Paola had learning disabilities, she was not tested for them until eighth grade. Under-diagnosis of learning disabilities is not uncommon among English proficient Hispanic students like Paola (Guiberson, 2009; Ortiz, Wilkinson, Robertson-Courtney, & Kushner, 2006). By the end of middle school, she was scoring 3 to 5 years below grade level on standardized tests of reading and math, and it was determined that although Paola was of above-average intelligence, she had serious learning disabilities that affected her spelling, written syntax, handwriting, and ability to read and to do math problems. Statistically, students with learning disabilities are at a severe disadvantage in even completing high school, much less enrolling in college. In states like Georgia where there are standardized high school exit examinations, they are over 20% less likely than their peers to graduate from high school (McGee, 2011), and even high school graduates are 7% less likely than average to enroll in college.

Paola's diagnosis resulted in helpful accommodations. These included special tutoring and adjunct courses where she was given extra help with work for mainstream content-area courses; study skills courses; and accommodations including using peers to assist in note-taking, extra time on tests, and oral presentation of test items. Without these accommodations, it is doubtful that Paola could have graduated from high school; even with accommodations it took her four attempts to pass the math portion of the high school graduation examination and a grueling seven attempts to pass the science section.

However, as previous research has noted (McDermott, Goldman, & Varenne, 2006; Mehan, 1993; Smardon, 2008), a diagnosis of learning disabilities can be accompanied by an institutional identity as academically less capable. In Paola's case, this label was almost as debilitating as the learning disabilities themselves. For example, at one of Paola's semi-annual Individualized Educational Plan (IEP) meetings attended by Harklau, educators talked about Paola's test scores and academic performance in the third person even though she was sitting at the table among them. Fieldnotes from the meeting noted a clinical, pathologizing tone that cast low expectations as compliments. For example, the school psychologist said something to the effect that "I've seen kids with test scores like this before, and I've got to say, what she's accomplished is just amazing!"

Moreover, because of Paola's diagnosis she was steered into courses that actually made it more difficult for her to fulfill high school graduation or college entrance requirements. For example, she was forced to take pull-out study skills courses over and over again throughout high school, eventually preventing her from accumulating elective credits needed for graduation. As a result she was forced to end her senior year with 4½ half hours per day of home and consumer sciences courses where, instead of sharpening her academic skills for college, she planned an imaginary wedding, reared an imaginary baby, and redecorated her imaginary home. More consequentially, Paola was forced to take math classes taught by special education teachers who lacked the subject matter expertise to offer a college-track course. She complained that "This is why I suck at math. 'Cause my freshman year I had the special teacher. He was NEVER there. EVER. I never learned." When Harklau asked her what they did in the class, she said, "*Little House on the Prairie*. We would watch every episode of it [laughs]." The teacher, apparently beset by constant meetings out of class, fed the class a steady diet of videos and worksheets. Likewise, in her sophomore year, Paola was coerced into taking a non-college track "Applied Problem Solving" course where the teacher "didn't teach me anything 'cause she didn't know anything about math. She was just a resource [teacher] … so it was like really, really watered-down." As a result, by the time Paola took a mainstream geometry class in her junior year, her math skills were woefully inadequate to the task. She failed Algebra II in her senior year and thus did not graduate with the prerequisites she would need to enter a public four-year college in Georgia. Finally, because her diagnosis resulted in special forms and special arrangements to take college entrance tests like the PSAT and ACT, Paola's teachers did not encourage her to take these tests. It took her and Harklau's combined persistent efforts for the better part of four months to get the counselor and special education department to arrange for her to take the ACT.

Remarkably, however, in spite of all these factors that have been identified in the literature as leading to diminished college ambitions and enrollment, Paola nevertheless did graduate from high school and embark on a college career. The question then becomes, what factors could counter this overwhelming set of obstacles to college enrollment?

Facilitative Factors in College-Going

Parental and Sibling Support for Education

Research suggests that parental (Ceja, 2006; Hurtado-Ortiz & Gauvain, 2007; Plunkett & Bámaca-Gómez, 2003) and sibling (Alfaro & Umaña-Taylor, 2010; Ceja, 2006) involvement and support have a significant influence on Latino/a adolescents' school motivation and college ambitions. Particularly influential in Paola's case was that not only was her mother relatively well educated—a factor often connected with Latino/a positive college-going decisions (Hurtado-Ortiz & Gauvain, 2007)—but also that her oldest sister Cate graduated from high school and enrolled in a nearby community college when Paola was in ninth grade. By the time Paola graduated from high school, Cate had finished her associate degree and transferred to a four-year college. As a result, she noted that the family expected that "since Cate already did it, they expect me to do it, too. Like, even better than her. Since she was the first one, I have to be even BETTER than the first." Cate's experience with college-going made her a useful source of information about college entrance requirements, tuition costs, and financial aid. Just as important as her conversance with the logistics of college enrollment was Cate's enthusiastic support of Paola's college plans. Cate was hopeful about getting her an athletic scholarship. Paola reported, "And she's so excited for me. She's like, 'You know what, if you keep doing that, we can get, like, a scholarship in sports.'" In Paola's senior year, she took the initiative to collect the names and contact information of soccer coaches at nearby colleges and provided them to Harklau. Although a sports scholarship ultimately turned out to be more elusive than they had hoped, Cate nevertheless remained instrumental in getting Paola enrolled in the same community college she had attended.

Not only was Cate in college, but she also had taken a leadership position as president of the community college's Hispanic Student Association, giving her access to considerable social capital and insider knowledge about how colleges work. Such knowledge has been linked to positive outcomes for younger siblings (Alfaro & Umaña-Taylor, 2010). In the final years of the study, she took a job in Paola's school district as a parent liaison, further developing her insights into the school system.

It is important to note, however, that while parental and sibling support may be correlated on the large-scale level with greater academic success, Cate's college success was nevertheless regarded as an anomaly in her family. Paola emphasized that she was "the only one that went to college, out of my whole family." High familial expectations ultimately did not prevent Paola's older sister Angie from failing the state high school exit examination in science, and she never received a high school diploma.

Prosperous Suburban School

Latinos/as are disproportionately educated in schools that lack resources and have poor records of academic preparation (Roscigno, 2000). Moreover, southeastern U.S. high school graduation rates as a whole are well below the national average (Chapman et al., 2010). This combination resulted in Latina high school graduation rates in Georgia that were particularly abysmal at less than 43% (Editorial Projects in Education Research Center, 2006). However, Paola was quite fortunate in that in her sophomore year her district placed her in a brand new high school built in response to a growing suburban population. This particular school was better than most in the area. For one thing, it had better facilities than any other school in the district, boasting four teacher workrooms, multiple computer labs, a two story gymnasium with an indoor track, capacious art and music spaces, and school sponsors from the local business community who had exceptionally deep pockets. The new school also attracted experienced educators from around the district.

As a result, Paola noted a higher quality of instruction than at her previous high school. In comparing the two, she saw her old school as "just bad people, bad influence, bad everything ... and over here, it's a great school, great system, great teachers." For example, she said she noticed the difference in looking at performance on statewide graduation tests, "You notice that all the people from West Creek were ... going back—had failed the test." From being at the new school, she realized that there were many things students were supposed to have learned in their freshman year that she had never heard of.

The school served a more prosperous student body as well. Paola reported that "our school is considered the preppy school and the rich school." She observed, half appalled and half fascinated, that some of the students at the school could afford to spend $300 on designer glasses or $500 on a purse. The school's Latino population mirrored this affluence. Paola estimated that over half the "Hispanic" students at her new school were Colombian-origin students who by and large came from more highly educated and more affluent backgrounds than the working-class Mexican students who predominated at other schools in the area. She reported that most of the Latinos were "school boys" who she defined as "like, you're just studying all the time, and you just want all A's, and you're just nerdy, kinda." At her previous school, she reported that "ALL of them are ... like, *cholos*, so if you're NOT *cholo*, then you look bad, but over HERE, it's different." In fact, she said that the affluent peer influence was so pervasive that

> there's this one guy who came from like *cholo* and he—you would see
> him dress up all like, all thug, and he was bad and everything. After a
> while, you see them, that they change. They're the only ones that are
> like that, so that makes them change ... cause, you know how—my
> majority rules.

For this peer group of students who were well-off and whose parents had attended college, Paola found that college-going was not considered optional. For example, she reported that "my other friend is well-off ... her family did go to college, so she has to go to college even though she's the oldest."

It is important to note, however, that while this peer group might have been a positive influence overall, it also had significant negative aspects. In particular, Paola felt very isolated as one of the few Mexican American students at the school. She complained that "none of my friends are here." Along with a wealthier, predominantly White and Colombian peer group came racism towards Mexican Americans, which she felt made peers doubt whether she could go to college. "It was like the race issue, like, 'Yah, you'll go to college. Maybe.' They still were, like, 'Su:ure.'"

Involvement in Sports

Another factor in Paola's achievement was her involvement in sports. Research suggests that involvement in athletics and other extracurricular activities is associated with increased academic performance (Flores-González, 2000) and higher rates of college enrollment. This effect is particularly pronounced in rural Latinas (Staurowsky et al., 2009). Paola was a gifted athlete who, over the course of the study, participated in volleyball, track, and both junior varsity and varsity soccer. One way that extracurricular involvement is thought to increase students' engagement with school is by fostering a disciplined and pro-school peer group (Flores-González, 2000), and this was indeed the case for Paola. She not only participated in team sports themselves, but also had a running "buddy" who was on her teams. She also dated the goalie of the boys' soccer team. She observed that many other "Hispanics" at the school were either in sports or friends with athletes. As a result, she said, "If you're in a sport, you can't do bad things. You just can't. You're not allowed, so their friends are good too, they have a good influence on them." Another advantage of sports was the opportunities it provided to develop positive mentoring relationships with teachers who served as coaches. Developing such relationships is thought to be a key mechanism through which extracurricular activities increase Latino student school retention and achievement (see, e.g., Flores-González, 2000). For example, Paola once told Harklau of a cross-country meet where one of the coaches for another school had been a former teacher of hers. She said that "he hugged me and he was encouraging me on the finish line, all like, 'Go girl!'" The strength of Paola's bonds with her teacher-coaches was indicated by the fact that they used Booster Club funds to buy her a letter jacket in her senior year when she had ordered a jacket but then could not afford to pay for it.

It is important to note, however, that sports was not always a source of positive or supportive peer influence. In Paola's senior year, she reported in growing dismay that on her volleyball team "there's lots of bickering and a lot of discussions and who's better than who." Unfortunately, she was unable to stay above the fray because "I have a boyfriend, and two of the girls like him." Her teammates turned on her, and despite the fact that she had been tapped to be the team's next setter and captain, it became so unpleasant that she eventually quit the team, joining the track team instead. Paola found the episode very distressing and for a time it affected her attitude towards school.

Religiosity

Religiosity has been shown to have a favorable effect on the academic achievement of Latino students (Antrop-González, Vélez, & Garrett, 2008; Jeynes, 2002; Muller & Ellison, 2001; Regnerus, Smith, & Fritsch, 2003). At some points during the study, Paola was heavily involved in activities in a small Protestant congregation founded by local Venezuelan immigrants. She reported that

> All week we're in church doing stuff. Mondays we'll be practicing dance choreography. Tuesday is the Bible study. Wednesday, dance, like for church dance ... And on Friday I go and practice, to play the drums. Then Saturday's a free day and then Sunday is church.

Paola's church-based activities were both goal-oriented (such the church dance team rehearsals and performances, or playing drums for the youth services) and social (she frequently went to the beach, the movies, or played volleyball with friends from church). In her sophomore year, when Paola was most heavily involved in church, she talked fondly about a friend from church, saying that "we're like kinda best friends." Like her affiliation with sports, religious involvement gave Paola access to another disciplined and goal-oriented peer group that kept her away from oppositional youth cultures (see, e.g., Antrop-González et al., 2008; Jeynes, 2002). Her peers from church included college students, providing her with more models for Latino immigrant college-going. Moreover, since her church peers were considered to be "from good families," she was allowed to stay out late and even sleep over at her best friend's house. This sort of "sponsored independence" (Reese, 2002) has been associated with academic success in Latino/a youth and families.

While religious involvement was largely a positive force in Paola's force, it is important to note that it was not unilaterally so. In particular, Paola's involvement in sports and religious activities were frequently in competition for her time and attention. For example, Paola worriedly explained in one interview that "I'm not going to the [volleyball] game cause I have to go present for the church." She incurred the ire of coaches and teammates as well as the penalty of having to sit on the sidelines for a game. On another occasion, when she chose to attend Homecoming rather than a presentation at the church, her church friends expressed their strong dismay with any activities that competed with them for her time and attention. Moreover, both sports and religious activities collectively took time away from homework and other academic pursuits, leaving Paola to complain frequently of exhaustion during the study.

Self-Efficacy

The facilitative factors in Paola's environment interacted with Paola's strong sense of self-efficacy to create positive academic outcomes in spite of the numerous obstacles standing in her way. *Self-efficacy* (see, e.g., Bandura, 1997; Pajares & Urdan, 2006)—an individual's beliefs in their own ability to produce a wanted result or level of performance—is strongly associated with academic outcomes in adolescents and young adults. Paola's strong sense of self-efficacy was indicated by her perseverance in and optimism about school even in the face of academic difficulties. For example, Paola's initial psychological report in eighth grade noted that "teachers report that Paola is a very hard-working student, has good attendance, and is self-motivated." Throughout high school, Paola's special education assessments remained unanimous in asserting that Paola was "a diligent worker who always tried her best on all work." Her sense of self-efficacy was also evident in her close and unflinching monitoring of her own academic performance and her unshakable belief that she could change poor outcomes. For example, when her class average in her junior History class fell below an 80 (B), she told Harklau, "Hopefully I have to get it—I HAVE to—not hopefully. I HAVE to get it to an 80, 'cause I cannot have 70 … I can only have one 70 in the whole year, and I already had that for Biology." In her junior year, even in the face of a demoralizing 60 (D) class average in English, she still expressed cautious optimism that she could change it: "I can bring it up though, I guess. I don't know, maybe." In fact, she did eventually bring her grade up to a 70 (C) to pass the class. Perhaps most remarkable was Paola's persistence and refusal to give up in spite of repeated failures on the math and science sections of the high school graduation examinations. Despite some understandable frustration and anxiety as well as the precedent of an older sister who never passed one of the tests, she doggedly persevered. Finally, after seeking out computer-based tutorials and National Honors Society tutors at the school library late in her senior year, she passed her final section on the seventh attempt.

Paola's strong sense of self-efficacy was particularly notable given that students with learning disabilities tend overall to have diminished senses of self-efficacy (Baird, Scott, Dearing, & Hamill, 2009). Twice a year since eighth grade she had endured IEP meetings where her abilities were cast into doubt. Nevertheless, even when given explicit opportunities to blame poor academic performance on external factors, she refused, consistently reasserting her belief in the power of her own efforts. For example, when asked if her extracurricular activities left her without enough time for studying, she rebutted, "I have enough time. It's just I don't use it wisely," conceding only that "and I come home tired, though, too." Likewise, when discussing Paola's failing grade in junior English, Harklau speculated, "Is part of it that it just doesn't match with, like, your learning disability?" Paola immediately rejected this explanation, replying, "I think it's just me, honestly ... I'm just not s—in track. I need to get in track. I'm starting to get in track. Just hard." In all, then, Paola's strong sense of self-efficacy played a key role in her eventual success in graduating from high school and college enrollment.

Nevertheless, a caution is in order should one be tempted, given the prevalent American discourses of self-made individual success and striving immigrants, to cast Paola's success as principally due to her own persistence and optimism. It is important to note that the very notion of self-efficacy comes out of social-cognitive theories of learning and personality (Bandura, 1997; Pajares & Urdan, 2006) that see individual personality and academic performance as intrinsically embedded in and growing out of contextual factors in school, family, and community. In other words, from this perspective Paola's story is not a parable of individual self-made success against all odds but rather a story of how development within and interactions with strong supports and resources in her social environment engendered Paola's strong sense of self-efficacy.

Conclusion and Implications

In many ways, Paola's case confirms previous findings regarding the factors that hinder Latino/a linguistic minority students' academic progress and college enrollment. For one, it shows how disrupted schooling works to create gaps in subject area knowledge and college entrance requirements as well masking learning difficulties. Paola's case also shows us how instabilities in family life and income create anxiety about tuition costs, particularly when they are seen as a collective family rather than individual burden. Paola's case also shows us how undocumented status exacerbates these anxieties and adds additional complications with income and transportation. It is also noteworthy that given her mother and Cate's legal status, Paola's undocumented status could have easily been remedied had the family had the financial resources to pay legal costs. Finally, the study confirms what research has long told us about how a diagnosis of learning disabilities can create an institutional identity that is at odds with academic achievement and college going.

Paola's case also provides an illustration of how factors found to be facilitative of academic success in large survey studies actually operate on the ground. For example, it shows how parental and especially sibling expectations play into students' own academic expectations. It also shows the importance of family and school social supports in the development of students' academic self-efficacy. It shows how schools with wealthier populations create better instructional environments and higher academic expectations. It shows the role of extracurricular involvement in sports and religious activities in providing Paola with academically ambitious and successful peer groups as well as adult mentors and role models.

However, Paola's case is perhaps most interesting as a pointed reminder that these previously identified and often cited factors work in ways that are not unilaterally positive or negative. For one thing, it shows that positive and negative factors are both present in any given individual student's background. This is illustrated, for example, by the fact that while Paola had one older sibling who enrolled in college and could be a role model and source of support, at the same time she also had another older sibling who never finished high school.

The study also illustrates that previously identified factors may not just facilitate or hinder Latino/a students' progress in the college pipeline but may do both simultaneously. For example, Paola's case shows that a learning disability diagnosis evokes a complex set of responses in schools. It helps a college-bound linguistic minority student with special classroom and testing conditions that can boost academic achievement. At the same time, though, it simultaneously creates an institutional identity that potentially damages students' college ambitions through placement in classes poorly suited to the college bound, low expectations and pathologizing talk to and about students, and diminished access to college entrance tests. Likewise, attending a prosperous high school afforded Paola access to better facilities, teachers, and a more academically ambitious peer group than other schools in the area. At the same time, though, being a low-income Mexican American student at a middle-class, predominantly White school exposed Paola to heightened racism and low expectations, not only from White students but also from other Latinos/as—her Colombian middle-class peers. Athletic or church involvement may provide students with more academically disciplined and ambitious peers, but at the same time it can divert students' attention and energy away from academics.

Paola's case also reminds us that the variables we associate with linguistic minority student academic success or failure can be highly unstable over time. It thus reminds us to treat with caution studies that rely on the measurement of variables at only one given point in time. For example, Paola's involvement with athletics and church activities, both associated with academic success, waxed and waned considerably over the 4 1/2 years of this study and were at times jeopardized by the savage dynamics of adolescent social relationships. Even more significant was that familial socioeconomic status, a factor that is usually thought of as relatively stable, in Paola's case varied considerably even over the course of the study, highlighting the potential lability of social class in immigrant families. It also points out the value of longitudinal work in this area.

In all, Paola's study confirms the need to look at success stories and to "deconstruct, reconstruct, and transcend" research on Latino/a schooling failures (Garrett et al., 2010) to focus rather on factors that create success. At the same time, however, it emphasizes the complexity and instability of the factors that lead to college-going in linguistic minority students over time, and the inextricable grounding of success in a particularistic matrix of family, peer, and institutional support.

Acknowledgments

The authors wish to thank Matthew B. Mendez for his invaluable assistance with transcription and data analysis for this chapter.

Notes

1. Six students were originally selected but one dropped out of the study after 1 1/2 years.
2. Regrettably, since that time Georgia has passed laws making it impossible for undocumented students to pursue higher education.

References

Alfaro, E. C., & Umaña-Taylor, A. (2010). Latino adolescents' academic motivation: The role of siblings. *Hispanic Journal of Behavioral Sciences, 32*, 549–570.

American Federation of Teachers. (2004). *Closing the achievement gap: Focus on Latino students. Policy Brief Number 17.* Washington, DC: Author. Retrieved from www.aft.org

Antrop-González, R., Vélez, W., & Garrett, T. (2008). Examining familial-based academic success factors in urban high school students: The case of Puerto Rican female high achievers. *Marriage and Family Review, 43*(1/2), 140–163.

Baird, G. L., Scott, W. D., Dearing, E., & Hamill, S. K. (2009). Cognitive self-regulation in youth with and without disabilities: Academic self-efficacy, theories of intelligence, learning vs. performance goal preferences, and effort attributions. *Journal of Social and Clinical Psychology, 28*, 881–908.

Bandura, A. (1997). *Self-efficacy: The exercise of control.* New York: W.H. Freeman.

Ceja, M. (2006). Understanding the role of parents and siblings as information sources in the college choice process of Chicana students. *Journal of College Student Development, 47*(1), 87–104.

Chapman, C., Laird, J., & KewalRamani, A. (2010). *Trends in high school dropout and completion rates in the United States: 1972–2008. A Compendium Report.* Washington, DC: National Center for Education Statistics. Retrieved from nces.ed.gov/pubs2011/2011012.pdf

Crawford, G., & Brunner, C. C. (1998). Marginalized by the web of meaning: Marion is missing. *Journal for a Just and Caring Education, 4*, 284–306.

Crotty, M. (1998). *The foundations of social research: Meaning and perspective in the research process.* Thousand Oaks, CA: Sage.

Editorial Projects in Education Research Center. (2006). *Diplomas Count. Georgia. An essential guide to graduation policy and rates.* Retrieved from www.edweek.org/ew/toc/2006/06/22/index.html

Editorial Projects in Education Research Center. (2010). *Diplomas Count 2010. Graduation by the numbers. Putting data to work for student success.* Retrieved from www.edweek.org/ew/toc/2010/06/10/index.html?intc=ml

Flores-González, N. (2000). The structuring of extracurricular opportunities and Latino student retention. *Journal of Poverty, 4*(1/2), 85–108.

Fry, R. (2009). The changing pathways of Hispanic youths into adulthood. Retrieved from the Pew Hispanic Center website: http://pewhispanic.org/reports/report.php?ReportID=114

Gándara, P. C. (1995). *Over the ivy walls: The educational mobility of low-income Chicanos.* Albany: State University of New York Press.

Garrett, T., Antrop-González, R., & Vélez, W. (2010). Examining the success factors of high-achieving Puerto Rican male high-school students. *Roeper Review, 32,* 106–115.

Ginorio, A., & Huston, M. (2001). *Si, se puede! Yes, we can. Latinas in school.* Washington, DC: American Association of University Women.

Guiberson, M. (2009). Hispanic representation in special education: Patterns and implications. *Preventing School Failure, 53*(3), 167–176.

Hamann, E. T., & Harklau, L. (2008). Education in the new Latino diaspora. In E. G. Murillo (Ed.), *Handbook of Latinos and education: Theory, research, & practice* (pp. 157–169). Mahwah, NJ: Erlbaum.

Hamann, E. T., Wortham, S., & Murillo, E. G. (2002). Education and policy in the new Latino diaspora. In S. Wortham, E. G. Murillo, & E. T. Hamann (Eds.), *Education in the new Latino diaspora: Policy and the politics of identity* (pp. 1–16). Westport, CT: Ablex.

Harklau, L. (2008). Developing qualitative longitudinal case studies of advanced language learners. In L. Ortega & H. Byrnes (Eds.), *The longitudinal study of advanced language capacities* (pp. 23–35). New York: Routledge.

Hurtado-Ortiz, M. T., & Gauvain, M. (2007). Postsecondary education among Mexican American youth: Contributions of parents, siblings, acculturation, and generational status. *Hispanic Journal of Behavioral Sciences, 29*(2), 181–191.

Jeynes, W. H. (2002). A meta-analysis of the effects of attending religious schools and religiosity on Black and Hispanic academic achievement. *Education and Urban Society, 35*(1), 27–49.

Kochhar, R., Suro, R., & Tafoya, S. (2005). *The new Latino South: The context and consequences of rapid population growth.* Washington, DC: Pew Hispanic Center. Retrieved from pewhispanic. org/reports/report.php?ReportID=50

Kvale, S., & Brinkman, S. (2009). *InterViews: Learning the craft of qualitative research interviewing.* Los Angeles: Sage.

McDermott, R., Goldman, S., & Varenne, H. (2006). The cultural work of learning disabilities. *Educational Researcher, 35*(6), 12–17.

McGee, A. (2011). Skills, standards, and disabilities: How youth with learning disabilities fare in high school and beyond. *Economics of Education Review, 30*(1), 109–129.

Mehan, H. (1993). Beneath the skin and between the ears: A case study in the politics of representation. In S. Chaiklin & J. Lave (Eds.), *Understanding practice: Perspective on activity and context* (pp. 241–268). New York: Cambridge University Press.

Muller, C., & Ellison, C. G. (2001). Religious involvement, social capital, and adolescents' academic progress: Evidence from the National Education Longitudinal Study of 1988. *Sociological Focus, 34*(2), 155–183.

National Council of La Raza. (2009). *Latino employment status, March 2009.* Retrieved from www. nclr.org/index.php/publications/latino_employment_status_march_2009/

National Women's Law Center. (2009). *Listening to Latinas: Barriers to high school graduation.* Washington, DC: National Women's Law Center and Mexican American Legal Defense and Educational Fund. Retrieved from www.nwlc.org/resource/ listening-latinas-barriers-high-school-graduation

Ortiz, A. A., Wilkinson, C. Y., Robertson-Courtney, P., & Kushner, M. I. (2006). Considerations in implementing intervention assistance teams to support English language learners. *Remedial and Special Education, 27*(1), 53–63.

Pajares, F., & Urdan, T. C. (2006). *Self-efficacy beliefs of adolescents.* Greenwich, CT: Information Age.

Plunkett, S. W., & Bámaca-Gómez, M. Y. (2003). The relationship between parenting, acculturation, and adolescent academics in Mexican-origin immigrant families in Los Angeles. *Hispanic Journal of Behavioral Sciences, 25,* 222–239.

Pong, S.-L., & Ju, D.-B. (2000). The effects of change in family structure and income on dropping out of middle and high school. *Journal of Family Issues, 21*(2), 147–169.

Quinn, N. (2005). Introduction. In N. Quinn (Ed.), *Finding culture in talk: A collection of methods* (pp. 1–34). New York: Palgrave Macmillan.

Reese, L. (2002). Parental strategies in contrasting cultural settings: Families in México and "El Norte." *Anthropology and Education Quarterly, 33*(1), 30–59.

Regnerus, M., Smith, C., & Fritsch, M. (2003). *Religion in the lives of American adolescents: A review of the literature. Report of the National Study of Youth and Religion.* Retrieved from University of North Carolina, Chapel Hill, National Study of Youth & Religion website: http://youthandreligion.org/publications/docs/litreview.pdf

Roscigno, V. J. (2000). Family/school inequality and African-American/Hispanic achievement. *Social Problems, 47*(2), 266–290.

Smardon, R. (2008). Broken brains and broken homes: The meaning of special education in an Appalachian community. *Anthropology & Education Quarterly, 39*(2), 161–180.

Staurowsky, E. J., Miller, K. E., Shakub, S., De Souza, M. J., Ducher, G., Gentner, N., … Williams, N. I. (2009). *Her life depends on it II. Sport, physical activity, and the health and well-being of American girls and women.* Retrieved from the Women's Sports Foundation website: http://www.womenssportsfoundation.org/Content/Research-Reports/Her-Life-Depends-On-It-II.aspx

Zambrana, R. E., & Zoppi, I. M. (2002). Latina students: Translating cultural wealth into social capital to improve academic success. *Journal of Ethnic and Cultural Diversity in Social Work, 11*(1/2), 33–53.

Zarete, M. E., & Gallimore, R. (2005). Gender differences in factors leading to college enrollment: A longitudinal analysis of Latina and Latino students. *Harvard Educational Review, 75*(4), 383–408.

PART II

Access to College

6

TOP 10% LINGUISTICALLY DIVERSE STUDENTS' ACCESS AND SUCCESS AT TEXAS PUBLIC UNIVERSITIES

Cristóbal Rodríguez

According to the 2010 U.S. Census, the Texas population by race is 45% White, 38% Latina/o, 12% Black, and 4% Asian. The public school population is 50.3% Hispanics, 31.2% White, 12.9 % Black, 3.4 Asian, 1.6% Two or More Races, 0.5% American Indian/Alaskan Native, and 0.1% Native Hawaiian/Other Pacific Islander (Texas Education Agency, 2011). Additionally, the Texas Education Agency (2010) reports that 17% of students enrolled in the Texas K–12 system are identified as English learners. Considering this wealth of diversity, by understanding the link between higher education experiences of diverse students and education policy, both educators and policy makers can improve their practices and improve overall access and academic success. However, prior to this implication and at the crux of this chapter, we must first grasp what lies at the intersection of top culturally/linguistically diverse students, and their access to and success in Texas higher education. This chapter uses descriptive statistics with statewide individual-level data from a state agency to present demographics, with an emphasis on linguistically diverse students in Texas. Additionally, this chapter differentiates data by regional dynamics by aggregating data by Borderland universities, top tier[1] universities, and other Texas universities. In order to highlight both access and success, this work will report a breakdown of top 10% linguistically diverse students by ethnicity, gender, economic status, college generation status, and regional diversity.

A Critical History of the Texas Top Ten Percent Plan

As a state legislative policy response in 1997 to a temporary ban on affirmative action practices on college admissions, due to legal action in *Hopwood v. State of Texas* (1996), a collaboration between Latina/o state legislators, scholars, and administrators devised a plan to provide guaranteed admissions at all Texas public universities for all Texas high school students graduating in the top 10% of their class (Texas House Bill 588, 1997; Valencia, 2008). This legislation was sponsored by the late Irma Rangel, from Kingsville, Texas, who is known as one of the most influential women in the history of the Texas legislature (Valencia, 2008). Through the collaboration with Latino administrators and scholars, Rangel's hope was to improve access beyond affirmative action. More specifically, and with controversy, this meant ensuring access across ethnicity, economic status, and across the entire state of Texas to the top tier public universities in Texas, The University of Texas at Austin and Texas A&M University.

The available and reliable statewide data in the past 8 years (1999–2008) have documented that the Top Ten Percent Plan has indeed improved access and success across ethnicity, economic status, and regional diversity, particularly at the top tier universities (Rodriguez, 2009; UT-Austin, 2008). One background factor that has contributed to the success of the Top Ten Percent Plan is the highly segregated nature of high schools in Texas. The average student of color, particularly in the case of Latina/o students in Texas, is more likely to attend a school where 90% or more of all students are both economically and ethnically alike (Orfield & Lee, 2005). By leaving academic competition at the local level, instead of at the state level, the Top Ten Percent Plan provides access to the top tier universities to students of color who come from economically depressed regions of the state. Indeed, the first-year enrollment student percentage from diverse racial backgrounds at UT-Austin increased from 35% in 1998 to 48% in 2008 (UT-Austin, 2008). In addition to improved access of top ethnic, economically and regionally diverse students, the plan has also improved academic success at the top tier universities (Alon & Tienda, 2005; Texas A&M University, 2009; UT-Austin, 2008). Specifically, when controlling for SAT and ACT scores, top 10% students outperformed non-top 10% students in GPA and graduation rates; additionally, with the increase of top 10% students at UT-Austin, the university has reduced the number of remedial course work and has increased the number of honors courses (UT-Austin, 2007, 2008). The powerful implication here is that college success is best predicted through high school GPA, over the use of standardized college entrance exams, score differences of which are often explained by differences in quality high school preparation (Tienda & Niu, 2006b).

Enrollment figures at the two flagship universities show the impact of the Top Ten Percent Plan. For example, at UT-Austin 81% of its fall-2008 first-year undergraduate enrollment consisted of top 10% students (UT-Austin, 2008). UT-Austin by far exceeds any other top tier public university in this regard. The representation of top 10% students at Texas A&M University is more modest at 47% of the fall 2008 first-year student enrollment (Texas A&M University, 2009). The impact of the Top Ten Percent Plan on the two flagship universities has drawn criticisms as well as praises. Because of the heated debate in the Texas legislature during the 2009 legislative-session regarding the plan, first-year student enrollment under the plan will be capped at 75% only at UT-Austin starting the fall of 2011 (Texas Senate Bill [SB] 175, 2009). Additionally, UT-Austin will probably face continued legal scrutiny for the use of race in their multiple-criterion admissions of non-top 10% admissions (Smith, 2010), even though the latest legal challenge lost in the Federal 5th Circuit Court (*Fisher v. UT-Austin*, 2011).

At the same time, even with the major impact of the Top Ten Percent Plan, enrollment disparity between Whites and Latina/os persists, even when controlling for varying school demographics (Tienda & Niu, 2006a). Tienda and Niu (2006a) explained, "Concentrated disadvantage rather than segregation per se is what dampens enrollment odds for minority students who attend schools with few white students" (p. 341). Even with the race-neutral policy that has created new opportunities to enroll at any public university in the state, Latina/os overall continue to have a lower likelihood than Whites of enrolling at the elite institutions of Texas (Niu, Tienda, & Cortes, 2006). Niu et al. explained, "Many qualifying students, particularly those from resource-poor high schools with low college-going traditions and members of under-represented groups, do not apply, and thus are excluded from the enrollment sample" (p. 269). This appears to be a greater issue for Latina/o students. Tienda and Niu (2006b) added that historical feeder patterns since the implementation of the Top Ten Percent Plan have not changed dramatically, explaining, "Contrary to claims proliferated in the print media, these results demonstrate that feeder high school students enjoy a substantial advantage in their access to the Texas flagships" (p. 723).

Given that the Top Ten Percent Plan's success of diversifying admissions at top tier universities is largely based on the growing segregation of high school populations in the U.S. Southwest (Orfield & Lee, 2005), can the same access and success be said specifically about top linguistically diverse students? This is particularly important, as linguistic diversity requires educational systems to acknowledge cultural dynamics beyond traditional racial and ethnic considerations (Bourdieu, 1977; Hurtado, Kurotsuchi Inkelas, Briggs, & Rhee, 1997; Lareau, 1993; MacLeod, 1987; Mallette & Cabrera, 1991; McDonough, 1997; Terenzini, Lorang, & Pascarella, 1981; Tinto, 1993). In other words, although the Top Ten Percent Plan has improved access for diverse populations at top tier universities, this chapter provides further evidence in the continued disparity in enrollment and success of diverse populations, especially linguistically diverse Latino students who grow up largely in the Texas Borderland region. Furthermore, based on this evidence and because of these disparities and differences between top tier universities and Borderland universities, this chapter draws further implications on the vital role of regional or Borderland universities.

Regional Dynamics: The Texas Borderland

The Texas Borderland, spans from El Paso, through San Antonio, and south-ward to Brownsville and Corpus Christi, and provides nine public universities to the students of this region (see Figure 6.1). Texas Borderland students live in a region that lies at an intersection of a linguistic diverse population; large Latina/o demographics; disparities in economic development, health, and edu-cation; and distance from top tier universities (Combs, 2001). In fact, if the Texas Borderland were a state in itself among all other states in the United States of America, the Borderland would rank 24th in population size (4.1 million); 3rd in the percentage of the foreign-born population (14.7%); and 1st in the percentages of population that speaks Spanish at home (57.1%), lives in poverty (26.8%), has school children in poverty (33.8%), is unemployed (7.5%), and has an adult population without a high school diploma (37.3%) (Combs,

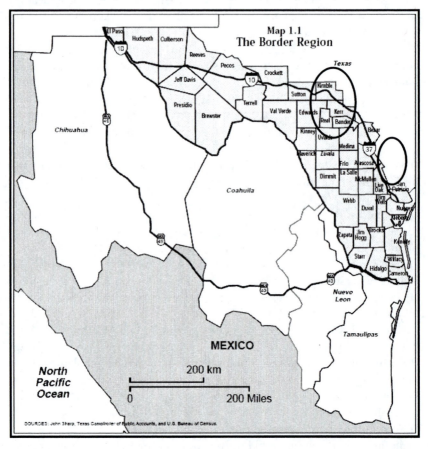

FIGURE 6.1 The Texas Borderland. Adapted from Sharp (1998). Shaded counties were used in Sharp. Circled areas are counties referenced in LULAC v. Richards (1993) but not in Sharp's report.

2001). This area, generally defined as the Texas–Mexico border region, presents not only various challenges for its residents and a history of tumultuous transnational engagements but, more importantly, a rich history of cultural diversity and linguistic transitions. However, this chapter recognizes not only the regional dynamics of Texas, particularly the rich demographics of the Texas Borderland, but also important education policy histories intersecting across this region and state politics.

In *LULAC v. Richards* (1993), lawyers argued for funding inequities in the Texas higher education funding formula. Mexican American Legal Defense and Education Fund (MALDEF) lawyers argued that the finance system was inherently discriminatory against the vast Latina/o demographics in the Borderland by underfunding public universities in the region, especially in comparing how other public universities in the state were being funded. For the most part, MALDEF lawyers identified the similar counties that would be used in a vital policy report to come. This vital policy report, Sharp's (1998) "Bordering the Future," contributed research to policy and advocacy of Texas Borderland issues. In 1997, as the Texas Comptroller of Public Accounts, John Sharp directed the Division of Research and Policy Development to assemble a research team. The result was a comprehensive report about the Texas Borderland and the multitude of issues facing this region. This report provided an array of analyses of economics, health, education, families, housing, immigration, and other vital policy issues facing this region. For the analysis in this chapter, all 45 counties mentioned in both *LULAC v. Richards* and in Sharp's report are used to identify the Texas Borderland. The public universities found in the Texas Borderland, henceforth known as the Borderland Universities, are the following nine: (a) UT–El Paso, (b) UT–Pan American, (c) UT–San Antonio, (d) UT–Brownsville, (e) Texas A&M–Kingsville, (f) Texas A&M–Corpus Christi, (g) Texas A&M–International, (h) Sul Ross State University, and (i) Sul Ross State University–Rio Grande College.

The Texas public higher education system identifies linguistically diverse students based on student-submitted information through the required Texas Common Application for all public universities. Using this identifier of students who speak Spanish or another language other than English, this chapter reports on a study focused on Texas Borderland students who access Texas public universities under the top 10% admissions plan. To further explain why regional dynamics are important in analyzing the demographics of Texas linguistic diverse higher education students, during the 2007–2008 academic year, of all Texas top 10% students who were enrolled for the first time and are bachelor's degree-seeking at a Texas public university, 12% reported that along with English they also spoke another language at home, 8% specifically identified Spanish as the other language. Of that 8% English/Spanish speaking students, 49% came from the Texas Borderland region, therefore highlighting the concentration of linguistically diverse students in this region. Of those Borderland linguistically diverse students, 42% stayed close to home and attended a Borderland public university, 44% attended one of the two top tier public universities, and the remaining attended other Texas public universities.

Regional and Cultural Dynamics of College Choice

The economic models of college access and choice assume that students ultimately make a decision based on a cost-benefit analysis (Hossler, Braxton, & Coopersmith, 1989; Hossler, Schmit, & Vesper, 1999). Yet, for many Latina/o students other considerations also play a role in their decision. Tienda and Niu (2006a) reported,

> Students enrolled at the less selective public institutions, including those students who graduate at the top of their class, consider cost, financial aid, academic support, institutional recruitment efforts, and distance to home in making their college choices, whereas those who attend one of the flagships place greater importance on academic reputation, institutional prestige, and social life.
>
> *(p. 336)*

For Latino/a students, this has been true regarding their overall college choice. A policy advocate organization based in Washington, DC, *Excelencia in Education*, commissioned a study on Hispanic Serving Institutions (HSIs) that confirmed the findings of Tienda and Niu (2006a) on Latina/o college choice:

> Latino students at HSIs prioritized college costs, proximity to where they lived, and an accessible campus as decisive factors in their college choice; Latino graduates who did not attend HSIs were more likely to prioritize financial aid, institutional prestige, and academic programs as critical factors influencing their college choice.
>
> *(Santiago, 2007, p. 3)*

Santiago's *Excelencia in Education* study contradicted common economic models for college choice and provided new considerations for policy implications. Santiago additionally concluded that many Latina/o students decide on HSIs because they believe that their students' own motivation, rather than which institution they attend, determines the quality education they receive, and because HSIs are more accessible economically and culturally, located as they are within large Latina/o communities. What this means is that many Latina/o students see no difference in the quality of education between the state's flagship institutions and their local institution.

However, the broad policy strokes of Texas legislators do not consider that students from predominant ethnically diverse high schools are significantly less likely to enroll at a selective public institution, like the two top tier public universities in Texas (Tienda & Niu, 2006a). Tienda and Niu additionally concluded that for Latina/o students, the concentration of economic disadvantage rather than their segregated ethnicity is largely responsible for their lower enrollment rate at selective institutions. The implication of this creates an enormous problem as the discourse around the top 10% policy has been largely directed at the admissions of top tier universities, and not how top diverse students also attend their local public university. Differences in enrollment rates between White and Latina/o students, as well as differences in factors influencing college choice as explained above by Tienda and Niu (2006a) and Santiago (2007), highlight the importance of new considerations of diverse student college access and success. Essentially, this speaks to the different educational realities and experiences and to overall college expectations between Whites and Latina/os, especially linguistically diverse students living along the U.S.–Mexico border. Additionally, further consideration is needed about the negative impact of segregation or concentrated disadvantage on college expectations (Niu et al., 2006; Orfield & Lee, 2005). However, Frost (2007) highlighted how higher concentrations of Latina/o students at high schools with similar demographics increase college expectations, which in turn significantly improve college-going rates. Although this argument runs counter to Tienda and Niu's (2006a) idea of segregated disadvantage, these two perspectives additionally hint at the contextual differences of Latina/o students that explain varying policy results.

Method

The Data

The quantitative data were derived from the multiyear, archived, individual-level information facilitated by the Texas Higher Education Coordinating Board, which collects reports from all institutions of higher education in the state. The reports are aggregated into a large database that stores student-level information on enrollment, graduation, and admissions reports. Via permission from the Texas Higher Education Coordinating Board, I was given 2-month access to the database with enrollment, graduation, and admissions reports with student-level information spanning the 1999–2000 to 2007–2008 academic years from all public universities in Texas. For this chapter, the analyses applied are descriptive statistics in order to illustrate the access and success of top linguistically diverse students in Texas.

Analysis

The data largely used for this analysis was retrieved through Apply Texas, which is a common admissions application for all public universities in Texas. In this application, students self-reported the data used in this analysis. For language background, students were specifically asked if they spoke another language at home besides English. Students had the option not to respond, which was then reported as Unknown, or answering either (1) English Only, (2) Spanish, or (3) Other Language. Due to the few numbers of English Only respondents and the large number of Unknown respondents, I assumed a possible intent by monolingual English speakers not to respond to this question since bilingual speakers typically recognize their advantage to answer such questions. Therefore, English Only and Unknown variables were collapsed for this analysis and labeled as Monolingual/Unknown. To further justify this action, when Unknown to English Only respondents were compared, similar rates of graduation and retention were found. In fact, percentage points only varied by 1% point difference, where Unknown respondents in both cases were 1% lower in 6-year graduation rates and 1-year retention rates. Observing the linguistic breakdown in the 2007–2008 top 10% first-year enrollment that are bachelor's degree-seeking at Texas public universities, 84% of all students were Unknown, 5% were English Only, 8% were English/Spanish, and 4% were English/Other language. Lastly, in order to have an understanding of where linguistically diverse students enroll, especially in considering the literature review, comparisons were made by Borderland public universities (or local universities), top tier public universities, and other public universities in Texas.

Findings: Access and Success of Linguistically Diverse Students in Texas

When observing diverse linguistic backgrounds for the latest (2007–08) first-year college cohort that are bachelor's degree-seeking at Texas public universities, some trends highlight the importance of making distinctions among public universities and further clarify regional differences.

Differences among Language Groups

First, Monolingual/Unknown top 10% students are more likely to enroll at the top tier public universities, 55%, than Borderland public universities, 9% (Table 6.1). However, this does not necessarily translate to high concentrations of linguistically diverse students at Borderland universities since they are still vastly outnumbered by Monolingual/Unknown speakers who represent 82% of the enrollment at these universities. Nonetheless, English/Spanish Bilingual students make up 17% of the top 10% student population at Borderland universities. More importantly, it is essential to note that it is not Monolingual/Unknown speakers who have the highest proportional enrollment rate at top tier universities, it is in fact English/Other Bilingual speakers, 67% of whom choose top tier universities.

Enrollment over time across the three types of institutions indicate that

TABLE 6.1 Top 10% Enrollment Total N at TX Public Universities Type (2007–08)

Count(% Row) (% Column)	Border Univ.	Top Tier Univ.	Other TX Univ.	Grand Total
Monolingual/Unknown	1,273(9%) (82%)	7,629(55%) (89%)	5,038(36%) (90%)	13,940(100%) (89%)
English/Spanish Bilingual	268(22%) (17%)	592(48%) (7%)	364(30%) (7%)	1,224(100%) (8%)
English/Other Bilingual	18(3%) (1%)	374(67%) (4%)	169(30%) (3%)	561(100%) (4%)
Grand Total	1,559(10%) (100%)	8,595(55%) (100%)	5,571(35%) (100%)	15,725(100%) (100%)

Note. Adapted from Vazquez Heilig, J. & Rodriguez, C., & Somers, P. (2011).

English/Spanish Bilingual speakers have had an enrollment growth, whereas percentages of English Monolingual/Unknown Speakers and English/Other Bilingual speakers have had decreasing percentages over time in all available data years. In fact, from the fall of 1999 to the fall of 2007 the number of top English/Spanish students at all Texas public universities increased from 276 to 1,224, or from 2% to 8% of the total top student population. However, a surprising trend is the increase of enrollment at top tier universities of English/Spanish Bilingual students. In 2005–2006, 1.4% of all enrollment was English/Spanish Bilingual, and by 2007–2008 this enrollment increased to 6.9%. One likely explanation can be found in changes to the state's DREAM Act-like policy, whereby Texas Senate Bill 1528 (2005) allowed for a greater number of immigrant students to qualify for state residency, and thus in-state tuition, through changes of state residency requirements. To further elaborate, the Texas Comptroller of Public Accounts (2006) "estimates that there were about 135,000 undocumented children in Texas public schools during the 2004–05 school year, or about 3 percent of total public school enrollment" (p. 4). The report continued:

> according to the Texas Higher Education Coordinating Board, in fall 2001, 393 students attended institutions of higher education as Texas residents based on Section 54.052(j) of the Education Code (DREAM Act-like policy); of these, 300 attended community colleges. In fall 2004, nearly 10 times as many students received in-state rates due to Section 54.052(j) provisions—3,792, more than 75 percent of whom attended community colleges.
>
> *(p. 5)*

Also, Texas has the Texas Application for State Financial Aid (TASFA) which has been a beneficial coupling to the current state residency requirements. First with House Bill 1403 in 2001, then for greater flexibility in 2005 with Senate Bill 1528, the Texas Legislature provided Texas high school students attending a

Texas school at least three years prior to graduation to qualify for state residency (Texas Higher Education Coordinating Board, 2009). Qualifying for Texas residency also qualified students for the Texas Application for State Financial Aid. Reportedly, in the fall of 2007, from this legislation 9,062 students enrolled at a Texas public higher education institution (Texas Higher Education Coordinating Board, 2009). For further consideration of this ethnicity/linguistic or immigration link, an ethnic breakdown of top 10% English/Spanish Bilingual students for 2007–2008 demonstrates that 83% were Latina/o, 14% White, and 2% Black, based on self-reported data. In contrast, the majority of top 10% English/Other Bilingual students reported as being 66% Asian American, 23% White, 5% Black, 4% Latina/o, 1% American Indian, and 0.4% international students. Thus, the breakdown of these two groups highlights the growing ethnic and linguistic diversity in Texas. However, it is important to note that while linguistic diversity growth may be explained by growth in foreign-born populations, overall growth in ethnic diversity, especially for the U.S. Latino community, has been related to birth rates (U.S. Census, 2006).

Gender

Gender differences provide an additional perspective (see Table 6.2). Female students across the board overrepresent top 10% students; however, gender parity comes closer at the top tier universities as these universities have a higher enrollment rate of males overall (Rodriguez, 2009). Interestingly, linguistically diverse male and female students reach gender parity at these universities. There is a high percentage of female linguistically diverse students at Border-

TABLE 6.2 Top 10% Enrollment at TX Public Universities by Gender (2007–08)

	Border Univ.	Top Tier Univ.	Other TX Univ.	Grand Total
Monolingual/Unknown				
Female	64%	58%	66%	61%
Male	36%	42%	34%	39%
English/Spanish Bilingual				
Female	63%	51%	63%	57%
Male	37%	49%	37%	43%
English/Other Bilingual				
Female	78%	49%	61%	54%
Male	22%	51%	39%	46%
Grand Total	1,559	8,595	5,571	15,725
Female	1003 (64%)	4895 (57%)	3667 (66%)	9565 (61%)
Male	556 (36%)	3700 (43%)	1904 (34%)	6160 (39%)

Note. Adapted from Vazquez Heilig, J. & Rodriguez, C., & Somers, P. (2011).

TABLE 6.3 Top 10% Enrollment at TX Public Universities by College Generation Status (2007–08)

	Border Univ.	Top Tier Univ.	Other TX Univ.	Grand Total
Monolingual/Unknown				
1st Gen. College	51%	28%	44%	33%
≥2nd Gen. College	49%	72%	56%	67%
English/Spanish Bilingual				
1st Gen. College	73%	65%	72%	68%
≥2nd Gen. College	27%	35%	28%	32%
English/Other Bilingual				
1st Gen. College	43%	29%	41%	33%
≥2nd Gen. College	57%	71%	59%	67%
Grand Total	550	8209	3490	12249
1st Gen. College	319 (58%)	2503 (30%)	1647 (47%)	4469 (36%)
≥2nd Gen. College	231 (42%)	5706 (70%)	1843 (53%)	7780 (64%)

Note. Adapted from Vazquez Heilig, J. & Rodriguez, C., & Somers, P. (2011).

land universities. However, part of the case for English/Other Bilingual students at these universities might be due to population size effects.

College Generation Status

Table 6.3 shows top 10% enrollment at Texas public universities by college generation status (2007–08). Not surprising and in agreement with college success literature (Perna & Thomas, 2008), top 10% Monolingual/Unknown students are 67% second generation and beyond college students, i.e., at least one parent holds a college degree. While that same percentage (67%) is true for English/Other Bilingual students, the opposite is true of top 10% English/Spanish Bilingual students, 68% of whom are first generation college students. Additionally, where these students enroll is slightly influenced by their generation status, particularly at the top tier universities where the enrollment rates of second generation and beyond students across all linguistic backgrounds are slightly higher than at other public universities.

Economic Status

At the intersection of linguistic diversity and economic status lies an additionally important perspective in understanding the diversity within linguistic diverse groups. As with college generation literature (Perna & Thomas, 2008), it is of no surprise that in considering economic status and academic success, a majority (53%) of top 10% Monolingual/Unknown students report a family

TABLE 6.4 Top 10% Enrollment at TX Public Universities by Economic Status (2007–08)

	Border Univ.	Top Tier Univ.	Other TX Univ.	Grand Total
Monolingual/Unknown				
Less than 40K	32%	17%	22%	19%
40K–79K	35%	25%	35%	28%
≥$80K	32%	58%	43%	53%
English/Spanish Bilingual				
Less than 40K	57%	49%	51%	51%
40K–79K	33%	26%	34%	30%
≥$80K	11%	25%	15%	19%
English/Other Bilingual				
Less than 40K	47%	31%	35%	33%
40K–79K	53%	30%	37%	32%
≥$80K	0%	39%	29%	35%
Grand Total	667	7901	3252	11820
Less than 40K	280 (42%)	1553 (20%)	829 (25%)	2662 (23%)
40K–79K	231 (35%)	2013 (25%)	1139 (35%)	3383 (29%)
≥$80K	156 (23%)	4335 (55%)	1284 (39%)	5775 (49%)

income greater than $80,000; and this group has the highest enrollment at top tier universities (Table 6.4). However, such is not the case of all linguistically diverse students, where 51% of English/Spanish Bilingual students report a family income of less than $40,000; and English/Other Bilingual students are distributed less variably across all three family income levels. However, where students enroll does reflect economic status and academic success; across all linguistic backgrounds students with the highest family income have a higher rate of enrollment at the top tier universities.

College Retention

Finally, understanding college retention completes this exploration of linguistic diversity and higher education. Comparing 1-year retention rates for 8 cohort groups that first enrolled between 1999–2000 through 2006–2007 show that 92% of Monolingual English/Unknown speakers, 86% of English/Spanish Bilingual speakers, and 93% of English/Other Bilingual speakers return to school the following fall semester after their first year. Although high retention rates are to be expected for top 10% students, there is a notable difference with English/Spanish Bilingual students and a lower retention rate. This begins to highlight the ultimate reality of college success through graduation. Graduation

TABLE 6.5 Top 10% 6-Year Cohort Graduation Rate at TX Public Universities (4 Cohort Group Average Entering between 1999–2000 and 2002–2003 Academic Year)

	Border Univ.	Top Tier Univ.	Other TX Univ.	Group Average
Monolingual/Unknown	61%	85%	67%	77%
English/Spanish Bilingual	60%	72%	63%	63%
English/Other Bilingual	60%	83%	70%	79%
University Group Average	60%	80%	67%	73%

rates over 4 cohort groups that first enrolled between 1999 and 2000 and 2002 and 2003 academic years report that 77% of Monolingual English/Unknown speakers, 63% of English/Spanish Bilingual speakers, and 79% of English/Other Language Bilingual speakers graduate within 6 years (Table 6.5). Furthermore, across all three linguistic backgrounds, students had the highest graduation rates at the top tier universities, which speaks to the importance of sending linguistically diverse students to top tier universities. Interestingly enough, across all three linguistic backgrounds students had almost the same graduation rate at Borderland universities. In other words, linguistic background appears not to be a catalyst for varying success at Borderland universities.

Conclusion

Clearly, as we observe and breakdown what lies at the intersection of top linguistically diverse students and access and success at Texas public universities, there are some differences between the three linguistic backgrounds and the three types of institutions compared here. First, across linguistic backgrounds, top 10% students largely enroll at one of two top tier public universities. However, it is English/Other Bilingual students who enroll at a higher rate at top tier universities than Monolingual/Unknown students and English/Spanish Bilingual students. As the top linguistically diverse student enrollment is broken down by ethnicity, gender, college generation status, and economic status, there are further understandings that both contribute to and align with access and success literature (Bourdieu, 1977; Hurtado et al. 1997; Lareau, 1993; MacLeod, 1987; Mallette & Cabrera, 1991; McDonough, 1997; Terenzini et al., 1981; Tinto, 1993).

To further elaborate on the dynamics of linguistic diversity at Texas public universities, first, an ethnic breakdown of English/Spanish Bilingual students identifies a majority of this population as Latina/o (83%); and English/Other Bilingual students as majority identify as Asian American (66%). Considering the current gender academic gap across all ethnic groups (Rodriguez, 2009), linguistically diverse students are closer to parity at the top tier universities. However, what this means is that male linguistically diverse students have a higher enrollment rate than females at top tier universities. Rodriguez further highlights this finding for all female top 10% students by explaining that male students at a greater rate are more likely to leave home to attend either UT-Austin or Texas A&M. Observing college generation status and linguistic diversity reveal a perspective that aligns with access literature.

However, the reality that Border public universities have greater parity in graduation rates across linguistic diversity suggests that indeed there are cultural and linguistic dynamics that are either being better supported or accepted at Border public universities, or are not an issue as deficit thinking (Valencia, 2010) tends to suggest. Although my explanation of the findings align with traditional models of access and success, particularly those founded on social/cultural capital theory (Bourdieu, 1977), Yosso (2006), critically advances the concept of linguistic capital as a powerful and positive dimension in college access and success via Yosso's framework of cultural capital wealth. Yosso argues that linguistically diverse students, particularly like those attending local Border public universities, not only carry social, cultural, and linguistic capitals, but also navigational, familial, aspirational, and resistance capitals, that interact interchangeably or in unison (also known as community cultural wealth) that contribute positively to students' access to and eventual success in higher education. Although linguistically diverse students have a low 6-year graduation rate, particularly at Border public universities, and given students' community cultural wealth and living around concentrated disadvantages (Niu et al., 2006) while attending Border public universities, I interpret these findings as reflective of a high level of resiliency and eventual success beyond 6-year graduation rates; especially if high aspirational, navigational, linguistic, social, cultural, resistance, and familial capitals are acknowledged. These capitals together might be better supported in the environments at Border public universities than at top tier public universities, especially acknowledging the cultural importance that students place when enrolling at their local or Borderland university (Tienda & Niu, 2006a; Santiago, 2007). Furthermore, and most importantly, the educational opportunity afforded by local public universities, which tend to make a lesser case for admissions requirements and often have open-enrollment opportunities, in fact might be providing a greater public good and will have a greater influence on overall economic development. Therefore, linguistically diverse students attending and succeeding at local Border public universities will arguably have a far greater impact on families, communities, and our overall diverse society than what traditional models explain and what top tier public universities provide.

Implications

The implications from these findings demand that top tier universities like The University of Texas at Austin and Texas A&M University recognize that linguistically diverse students bring culturally and linguistically rich capitals, especially if Texas and the United States are to maintain global economic competitiveness. More importantly, given the vast diverse demographics concentrated in the Texas Borderlands, Borderland students' access to and success in the top tier schools needs to be both promoted and recognized with additional resources. Given that many English/Spanish bilingual students from the Borderlands are of the first generation in their families to attend college and are of lower socio-economic status, financial aid considerations to attract students to enroll at the top tier universities cannot be understated. Recognizing the rich linguistic capital of students by top tier universities will not only help further diversify these campuses but will contribute greatly to the development of diverse students, their families and communities, and our society.

At the same time, one must not undermine the vital role that Borderland and other Texas universities play in the development of linguistically diverse students regardless of lower graduation rates. Although the challenge of lower graduation rates by those students who stay close to home is a complex issue around considerations for commuter student characteristics, job and family responsibilities, economic challenges, and cultural dynamics, it is ever more important for Borderland universities, and essentially the state legislature, to provide the resources to support the success of linguistically diverse students. It is important to recognize that Borderland universities, through the success of diverse students, directly contribute to the development of families and communities of that region. This is especially the case since college graduates are more likely to stay and work in the Borderlands if they go to school in the region. Considering the challenges highlighted by Combs (2001), providing resources to Borderland universities in order to improve resources for their students is critical.

Note

1. Top tier universities refer to universities that are members to the Association of American Universities (AAU), which is a nonprofit association of 61 U.S. and two Canadian preeminent public and private research universities (Association of American Universities, 2010). Texas has three top tier universities, two public (Texas A&M University, The University of Texas at Austin) and one private (Rice University).

References

Alon, S., & Tienda, M. (2005). Assessing the "mismatch" hypothesis: Differences in college graduation rates by institutional selectivity. *Sociology of Education, 78*(4), 294–315.

Association of American Universities. (2010). *Member institutions and years of admission.* Retrieved from http://www.aau.edu/about/article.aspx?id=5476

Bourdieu, P. (1977). Cultural reproduction and social reproduction. In J. Karabel & A. H. Halsey (Eds.), *Power and ideology in education* (pp. 487–511). New York: Oxford University Press.

Combs, S. (2001). *The Border: Where we stand—January 2001 update.* Retrieved from Office of the Texas Comptroller of Public Accounts website: http://www.window.state.tx.us/border/wws/

Fisher v. Univ. of Tex. at Austin, 645 F. Supp. 2d 587, 590 (5th Cir. 2011).

Frost, M. B. (2007). Texas students' college expectations: Does high school racial composition matter? *Sociology of Education, 80*(1), 43–66.

Hopwood v. State of Texas, 78 F.3d 932 (5th Cir. 1996).

Hossler, D., Braxton, J., & Coopersmith, G. (1989). Understanding student college choice. In J. C. Smart (Ed.), *Higher education: Handbook of theory and research, Vol. 4* (pp. 231–288). New York: Agathon Press.

Hossler, D., Schmit, J., & Vesper, N. (1999). *Going to college: How social, economic, and educational factors influence decisions students make.* Baltimore: Johns Hopkins University Press.

Hurtado, S., Kurotsuchi Inkelas, K., Briggs, C., & Rhee, B. S. (1997). Differences in college access and choice among racial/ethnic groups: Identifying continuing barriers. *Research in Higher Education, 38*, 43–75.

Lareau, A. (1993). *Home advantage: Social class and parental intervention in elementary education.* Philadelphia: Falmer Press.

LULAC v. Richards, 868 S.W.2d 306 (1993).

MacLeod, J. (1987). *Ain't no makin' it: The level of aspirations of a low-income neighborhood.* Boulder, CO: Westview Press.

Mallette, B. I., & Cabrera, A. F. (1991). Determinants of withdrawal behavior: An exploratory study. *Research in Higher Education, 32*(2), 179–194.

McDonough, P. M. (1997). *Choosing colleges: How social class and schools structure opportunity.* Albany: SUNY Press.

Niu, S., Tienda, M., & Cortes, K. E. (2006). College selectivity and the Texas top 10% law. *Economics of Education Review, 25*(3), 259–272.

Orfield, G., & Lee, C. (2005). *Why segregation matters: Poverty and educational inequality.* Cambridge, MA: Harvard University, The Civil Rights Project. Retrieved from http://bsdweb.bsdvt.org/district/EquityExcellence/Research/Why_Segreg_Matters.pdf

Perna, L. W., & Thomas, S. L. (2008). Theoretical perspective on student success: Understanding the contributions of the disciplines. *ASHE Higher Education Report, 34*(1), 1–87.

Rodriguez, C. (2009). *The Texas experiment on the border: Analysis of student access and success of Borderland top 10% students at Borderland and top tier public universities.* Unpublished doctoral dissertation, The University of Texas at Austin.

Santiago, D. A. (2007). *Choosing Hispanic-serving institutions (HSIs): A closer look at Latino students' college choices.* Retrieved from Excelencia in Education website: http://www.edexcelencia.org/research/choosing-hispanic-serving-institutions-hsis-closer-look-latino-students%E2%80%99-college-choices

Sharp, J. (1998). *Bordering the future.* Retrieved from Office of the Texas Comptroller of Public Accounts website: http://www.window.state.tx.us/border/borderpdf.html

Smith, M. (2010, July 21). Affirmative action suit challenges UT admissions policy. *The Texas Tribune.* Retrieved from http://www.texastribune.org/texas-education/higher-education/affirmative-action-suit-challenges-ut-policy/

Terenzini, P. T., Lorang, W. G., & Pascarella, E. T. (1981). Predicting freshman persistence and voluntary dropout decisions: A replication. *Research in Higher Education, 15*(2), 109–127.

Texas A&M University (TAMU). (2009). *Data brochure: FY 2008–FY 2009.* Retrieved from http://www.tamu.edu/opir/reports/mis/Data_Brochure_0809.pdf

Texas Comptroller of Public Accounts. (2006). *Undocumented immigrants in Texas: A financial analysis of the impact to the state budget and economy.* Retrieved from http://www.window.state.tx.us/specialrpt/undocumented/

Texas Education Agency. (2010). *2010 state AEIS report.* Retrieved from http://ritter.tea.state.tx.us/perfreport/aeis/2010/state.html

Texas Education Agency. (2011). *Hispanics are majority in public schools.* Retrieved from http://www.tea.state.tx.us/index2.aspx?id=2147499598

Texas Higher Education Coordinating Board. (2009). *Overview: Residency and in-state tuition.* Retrieved from http://www.thecb.state.tx.us/reports/PDF/1528.PDF

Texas House Bill 588, 75th Leg., Education Code §51.801-.807 (1997).

Texas Senate Bill 175, 81st Leg. Education Code §51.801-.807 (2009).

Texas Senate Bill 1528, 79th Leg. Education Code §54.052-.056 (2005).

Tienda, M., & Niu, S. (2006a). Capitalizing on segregation, pretending neutrality: College admissions and the Texas Top 10% law. *American Law and Economics Review, 8*(2), 312–346.

Tienda, M., & Niu, S. (2006b). Flagships, feeders, and the Texas Top 10% law: A test of the "brain drain" hypothesis. *Journal of Higher Education, 77*(4), 712–729.

Tinto, V. (1993). *Leaving college: Rethinking the causes and cures of student attrition* (2nd ed.). Chicago: University of Chicago Press.

University of Texas–Austin. (2007). *Student characteristics: Fall 2006.* Retrieved from University of Texas Office of Information Management and Analysis website: http://www.utexas.edu/academic/oir/statistical_handbook/06-07/pdf/0607students.pdf

University of Texas–Austin. (2008). *Top 10% Report 11.* Retrieved from http://www.utexas.edu/student/admissions/research/topten_reports.html

U.S. Census. (2006). *2006 American community survey.* Retrieved from http://www.census.gov/population/www/socdemo/hispanic/hispanic_pop_presentation.html.

U.S. Census. (2010). U.S. Census Bureau delivers Texas' 2010 census population totals, including first look at race and Hispanic origin data for legislative redistricting. Retrieved from http://2010.census.gov/news/releases/operations/cb11-cn37.html

Valencia, R. R. (2008). *Chicano students and the courts: The Mexican American legal struggle for educational equality.* New York: New York University Press.

Valencia, R. R. (2010). *Dismantling contemporary deficit thinking: Educational thought and practice.* New York: Routledge.

Vazquez Heilig, J. & Rodriguez, C., & Somers, P. (2011). Immigrant DREAMs: The Texas 10% admissions plan, English learner college choice and academic success. *Journal of Latinos and Education, 10*(2), 106–126.

Yosso, T. (2006). *Critical race counterstories along the Chicana/o educational pipeline.* New York: Routledge.

7

WHO ARE LINGUISTIC MINORITY STUDENTS IN HIGHER EDUCATION?

An Analysis of the Beginning Postsecondary Students Study 2004

Anne-Marie Nuñez and P. Johnelle Sparks

According to the 2004 Beginning Postsecondary Students Study, 11% of college students in the United States come from Linguistic Minority (LM) backgrounds, in that they report not having spoken English as the first language in their home (U.S. Department of Education, 2007). Yet, limited research to date has explored who these students are and where they are enrolled in college (Kanno & Cromley, 2010; Rodriguez & Cruz, 2009). This chapter provides a demographic profile of LM college students, analyzes the factors associated with their enrollment in different higher education institution types, and provides a comparative perspective about LM and non–LM students in terms of their characteristics when they enter college.

Because this study's sample includes only first-year students already in college, our analysis does not address the characteristics of a critical group of less academically and linguistically proficient LM students who might never have had the academic preparation, financial support, or other opportunities to attend college in the first place (Kanno & Cromley, 2010). However, our analysis offers the advantage of including a more representative group of non-traditionally as well as traditionally-aged students who are pursuing college for the first time. This is important, since about one-fifth (19%) of students beginning college for the first time are 24 years or older (U.S. Department of Education, 2007). Using data from a national database of postsecondary students, we address the questions: Who are Linguistic Minority students in U.S. postsecondary education? How do they differ from non-Linguistic Minority students in U.S. postsecondary education? Where are they enrolled in college? What are the demographic, academic background, habitus, and college participation characteristics associated with the kinds of colleges they attend?

Literature Review and Conceptual Context

Given the increasing prevalence of LM students in the population, the current presidential administration's goal to increase U.S. postsecondary educational attainment rates will be impossible without raising LM students' postsecondary enrollment and completion rates. LM students in higher education are over-represented in community colleges and underrepresented in 4-year institutions (Rodriguez & Cruz, 2009). Although community colleges provide an impor-tant pathway into postsecondary education for LM students, students who begin in these institutions also have lower college persistence and completion rates (Arbona & Nora, 2007; Bowen, Chingos, & McPherson, 2009).

Few studies have addressed LM students' postsecondary education enroll-ment and attainment (Louie, 2005; Rodriguez & Cruz, 2009). Klein and col-leagues (2004) found that, among 18- to 24 year-old Americans, LM students were less likely than others to be enrolled in college. Kanno and Cromley (2010) found that those LM high school students not proficient in English (termed English Language Learners, or ELLs) were far less likely to have com-pleted college degrees eight years after their expected high school graduation date, compared with either their LM counterparts who were more proficient in English (termed EP students), or with monolingual English (EM) speaking students. Although these studies have addressed college-age LM students' post-secondary experiences, those of non-traditional aged LM students also merit attention.

Current educational policy concerns and research highlight the importance of better understanding the characteristics of LM students who do pursue higher education. This chapter's purpose is to examine the characteristics of LM first-year students enrolled in diverse postsecondary settings across the United States and the factors associated with where these students enroll. The assumptions guiding this exploration are that, among other factors, one's demographic char-acteristics, access to various resources (or multiple forms of *capital*), and inter-nalized perceptions and expectations of his or her educational opportunities (or *habitus*) shape where students enroll in college (Bourdieu, 1986; Bourdieu & Passeron, 1977; McDonough, 1997; Perna, 2006). Among the multiple forms of capital, *economic capital* (financial resources), *academic capital* (academic college preparation), *cultural capital* (access to information about preparing for, applying to, and selecting postsecondary options), and *social capital* (relationships with familial or non-familial agents who can offer support about going to college), have all been found to affect whether and where students enroll in college (e.g., McDonough, 1997; Perna & Thomas, 2008; Walpole, 2007), including LM students (Kanno & Cromley, 2010).

In terms of demographics, Hispanics, who have the lowest postsecondary educational attainment rates of any racial/ethnic group, also constitute the larg-est proportion of LM students (Gandara & Contreras, 2009). Factors hindering

Hispanics' college access include limited economic resources, information about preparing for and applying to college, and opportunities to complete college preparatory curricula (Gandara & Contreras, 2009). In contrast to Hispanics, Asians, who constitute most of the remainder of LM students, are often construed as a "model minority," academically high-achieving group, although much variation by ethnic subgroup exists in their educational attainment patterns (Lee, 2009).

Most LM students are either first- or second-generation immigrants, meaning that the student either came to the United States from another country or has at least one foreign-born parent (Portes & Rumbaut, 2001; Rodriguez & Cruz, 2009). Some researchers have found that being a first-generation immigrant, independent of other critical factors, is positively associated with higher K–12 educational achievement (Portes & Rumbaut, 2001) or that being an LM student is positively associated with enrollment in a 4-year versus a 2-year institution (Arbona & Nora, 2007). Explanations for these findings include that more recent immigrants have a heightened sense of optimism (Kao & Tienda, 1995) and have had less exposure to a U.S. "context of reception" (Portes & Rumbaut, 2001) that perpetuates institutionalized racism and discrimination toward marginalized groups such as immigrants (Gandara & Contreras, 2009; Portes & Rumbaut, 2001).

LM students disproportionately come from lower-income backgrounds (Rodriguez & Cruz, 2009). Moreover, undocumented immigrant students come disproportionately from LM backgrounds; undocumented immigrants are not eligible for federal financial aid, which limits their capacity to pay for college (Gandara & Contreras, 2009; Rodriguez & Cruz, 2009). Thus, limited access to economic capital can also affect where LM students enroll in postsecondary education.

LM students also disproportionately come from families with lower levels of parental education, often families in which neither parent has ever attended college (Rodriguez & Cruz, 2009). They also are less exposed to the capacity to communicate in a linguistically privileged way. These are two factors that can limit LM students' access to postsecondary cultural capital (Kanno & Cromley, 2010).

LM and immigrant students also tend to have less access to familial and nonfamilial social capital (Suarez-Orozco, Pimentel, & Martin, 2009). Social capital in schools includes support from "institutional agents" who can help students navigate the educational system (Stanton-Salazar, 1997). While such agents can benefit LM students in many ways, school personnel can also affect LM students' educational prospects in adverse ways. Experiences of exclusion in schooling, or "institutional neglect" (Gonzalez et al., 2003), can lead LM students to feel marginalized and alienated (Holmes, Fanning, Morales, and Herrera, this book). Resulting feelings of alienation can make it harder for them to seek institutional agents who could guide them in the path to college (Stanton-Salazar, 2001).

Eventually, access to social capital (or lack of it) can affect whether college students enroll in 2-year or 4-year institutions (Gonzalez et al., 2003).

High school course rigor, one important form of academic capital, or academic preparation for college (McDonough & Nuñez, 2007), can also affect whether and where LM students go to college. Taking a rigorous high school academic curriculum has been found to be the most important indicator of where students enroll in college, as well as whether students complete college (Adelman, 2006). Yet, many LM students do not have the same opportunities as their monolingual English counterparts to take rigorous and college preparatory courses, because they are tracked into lower level courses (Callahan, 2005, this book; Callahan, Wilkinson, & Muller, 2010; Mosqueda, this volume) or placed in inadequately resourced schools (Gandara & Orfield, 2010).

If LM students have relatively limited access to economic, cultural, social, and academic capital, they may not develop a habitus, or orientation, conducive to strategically considering various postsecondary options (McDonough, 1997). Moreover, once LM students enter college, they are also more likely to experience "environmental pull" (Nora, 2004) factors, such as working full-time during college, taking care of family, and being a part-time student. Environmental pull factors negatively affect the postsecondary students' college participation and persistence rates (Greene, Marti, & McClenney, 2008; Horn & Premo, 1995).

Method

Our research questions are: How do LM college students compare to their non-LM counterparts in terms of characteristics related to demographics, family capital, economic capital, cultural capital, social capital, academic capital, habitus, and college participation patterns? How are these factors associated with where LM students begin their college careers? As we address these questions, we also examine whether being LM is a significant predictor of enrolling in various sectors of higher education, as well as to what extent the factors predicting LM and non-LM students' enrollment in these sectors are similar or different.

We analyze data from the Beginning Postsecondary Students Longitudinal Study 2004 (BPS:04) conducted by the National Center for Education Statistics (U.S. Department of Education, 2007). This study involves the most recent nationally representative sample of first-time students, who were surveyed in their first year of college (the 2003–04 academic year). The survey contains information about their demographic and financial backgrounds, high school academic experiences, college application process, and reasons for choosing colleges (Cominole, Wheeless, Dudley, Franklin, & Wine, 2007). Approximately 1,700 students of the 16,500 sampled students used in this analysis report not speaking English as their primary language at home; these students comprise this study's LM student sample.

It is important to note that this study only addresses LM students and non-LM students who have already been admitted to and made the decision to go to college. An important group of LM students who might never have had the academic preparation, financial support, or other opportunities to attend college are excluded, and this group constitutes a sizable proportion of young adult LM students (Kanno & Cromley, 2010). In the BPS dataset, being an LM student was measured by the only question on the student survey that addressed language status: "Was English the primary language in your home growing up?" This is an important consideration, since there were no indicators of how proficient the student was in English, a factor which makes a significant difference in where LM students enroll in college (Kanno & Cromley, 2010). A dichotomous variable was constructed from responses to this question, indicating the student was either a LM student or non-LM student.

The dependent variable was assessed by first using two questions that indicated whether the first institution the student attended was a 4-year institution or 2-year institution, with responses of less than a 2-year institution removed from the analytic sample. Responses to a separate question of whether the 2-year institutions were not-for-profit or for-profit were used to further eliminate any 2-year for-profit institutions. Lastly, following Cunningham (2006), the selectivity of 4-year institutions was classified based on two equally-weighted criteria if they did not have an open admissions policy: (a) the centile distribution of the percentage of students who were admitted to each institution (of those who applied); and (b) the centile distribution of the midpoint between the 25th and 75th percentile SAT/ACT combined scores reported by each institution. From this information, three response options were used for the dependent variable, including whether the student was enrolled in a 4-year selective institution (defined as a 4-year institution in the most exclusive category in terms of percentage of students admitted and standardized admissions test scores), 4-year nonselective institution (defined as a 4-year institution in any of the other categories of percentage of students admitted and standardized admission test scores), or a 2-year institution (defined as 2-year academic institutions excluding 2-year for-profit institutions).

In the multivariate analysis, the first block of variables included *demographic and family capital* (including cultural and social capital) variables. These variables included the student's gender, age, race/ethnicity, immigration status (first-generation, second-generation, and third-generation), parental level of education (defined as having a high school diploma or less; some college experience, including an associate degree; and having a college degree or more, including a bachelor's degree or more) and income. Income was defined from a variable reporting income quartiles for each respondent and values were adjusted to account for whether or not the student was financially dependent or independent in their first year of enrollment.[1]

The second block of variables represented *academic capital*, or academic preparation. This set included high school GPA (3.5–4.0, 3.0–3.49, and 2.9 or below), the highest math course completed in high school (algebra I, algebra II/ trigonometry, or calculus), and whether or not the student earned AP credits in high school, excluding AP foreign language credits.[2]

The third block addressed concerns related to *habitus*. It included the extent to which the student rated as important the following reasons in choosing a college: affordability/financial reasons, location, personal/family reasons, academic programs/coursework availability, and reputation of the institution.

The fourth block included *college participation characteristics*. These included whether the student delayed enrollment, was part-time enrolled in college, and worked full-time. The latter two can be seen as environmental pull factors, and each of the three puts students at risk for not completing a college degree.

This study used bivariate and multivariate statistical techniques to address the research questions. The bivariate analysis examined whether significant differences were observed between LM college students and non-LM students on the characteristics just described. In the multivariate analysis, we used multinomial logistic regression methods to examine how key factors such as socioeconomic status and immigrant generational status were related to LM students' enrollment in 2-year, 4-year selective, or 4-year nonselective institutions. Lastly, we stratified the analysis by LM student status to create two new analytic samples and assessed how the characteristics that influence enrollment patterns in these three types of institutions compare for LM students and non-LM students.

Results

Our initial descriptive analysis indicated that among first-time and first-year students who began their postsecondary educations in the 2003–04 academic year, about 11% were LM students. In selective 4-year institutions, about 13% of students were LM, 10% of students in nonselective 4-year institutions were LM, and 13% of students in 2-year institutions were LM. About 61% of LM students, compared with 56% of non-LM students, were enrolled in 2-year institutions. More non-LM students (34%) than LM students (27%) were enrolled in nonselective 4-year institutions. Roughly equivalent proportions (12% and 10%, respectively) of LM and non-LM students were enrolled in 4-year selective institutions.

Table 7.1 compares the characteristics of LM and non-LM first-year students by institutional type. The majority of LM students were Hispanic; however, more LM Asian students (41%) were enrolled in selective 4-year institutions than Hispanic students (34%). In the other sectors, Hispanics comprised the largest ethnic group of LM students. In comparison to their non-LM counterparts, LM students tended to come from families where the parents had lower levels of postsecondary education. Among students enrolled in selective 4-year institutions, LM students were about twice as likely as non-LM students to have

TABLE 7.1 Weighted Percentages of Student Characteristics of First-Time, First-Year Beginning College Students by Linguistic Minority (LM) Status and Institutional Type, Beginning Postsecondary Students Longitudinal Study 2004 (BPS: 04), n~16.500 (Unweighted Sample Size)

Variables	Selective 4-Year Institutions (n~2,500)		Nonselective 4-Year Institutions (n~6,600)		2-Year Institutions (n~7,400)	
	LM Student	Non-LM Student	LM Student	Non-LM Student	LM Student	Non-LM Student
Gender						
Male	45.51	44.66	46.76	43.42	44.48	43.70
Female	54.49	55.34	53.24	56.58	55.52	56.30
Student's Current Age						
19 or Younger	91.05***	96.34	75.12*	82.95	50.85	55.53
20–23	7.37	2.25	11.45	7.25	18.54	15.65
24 or Older	1.58	1.41	13.43	9.80	30.61	28.82
Student's Race/Ethnicity						
White (non-Hispanic)	16.73***	72.35	19.00***	74.42	11.11***	67.72
Black (non-Hispanic)	3.38	9.54	5.53	11.76	8.59	14.37
Hispanic	33.94	5.64	45.09	6.97	52.23	11.08
Asian	41.27	7.14	22.82	1.86	21.81	1.92
Other or Multiple Races/Ethnicities	4.68	5.34	7.56	4.99	6.26	4.91
Immigration Status[a]						
First Generation	62.95	7.13	58.93***	5.70	68.23***	7.10
Second Generation	--	0.58	3.44	3.42	1.90	9.58
Third Generation	37.05	92.29	37.63	90.88	29.97	83.32

Parent's Level of Education

High School Diploma or Less	29.91***	14.48	49.19***	29.47	62.53***	46.98
Some College	14.89	11.78	11.67	20.97	11.30	24.77
College Degree or More	55.20	73.74	39.14	49.56	26.17	28.25

Income Quartiles[b]

Low Income	37.14***	13.02	44.77***	18.71	36.06***	23.09
Low-mid Income	21.00	15.64	31.06	25.03	25.62	25.65
High-mid Income	23.15	24.43	14.57	27.11	19.95	26.74
High Income	18.71	46.91	9.60	29.15	18.37	24.52

High School GPA

3.5–4.0	59.47**	67.33	22.63***	34.75	7.48**	11.42
3.0–3.49	33.26	27.02	62.44	46.15	66.87	59.12
2.9 or Below	7.27	5.65	14.93	19.10	25.65	29.46

Highest Math Course Completed in High School

Algebra	5.32*	7.66	18.70	22.58	27.14	28.48
Algebra II/Trigonometry	16.71	15.04	19.11	18.64	11.44	11.46
Calculus	73.30	73.89	41.34	42.01	13.34	13.88

Earned Advanced Placement Credit in High School

Yes	42.42	42.55	17.21	15.69	11.40**	6.35
No	57.78	57.45	82.79	84.32	88.60	93.65

Student Expects BA Degree or Better (for Students Attending 2-Year Institutions Only)

Yes					83.95*	78.63
No					16.05	21.37

(continued)

TABLE 7.1 Continued

Variables	Selective 4-Year Institutions (n~2,500)		Nonselective 4-Year Institutions (n~6,600)		2-Year Institutions (n~7,400)	
	LM Student	Non-LM Student	LM Student	Non-LM Student	LM Student	Non-LM Student
Student Expects to Transfer (for Students Attending 2-Year Institutions Only)						
Yes					69.96*	62.71
No					30.04	37.29
Reason Student Selected this Institution						
Affordable/Financial Reasons	51.82	52.46	47.20	52.16	62.84	66.38
Location	69.02**	77.20	74.13	76.19	81.61	83.77
Personal/Family Reasons	42.61	43.29	41.96	43.00	35.99	35.52
Academic Programs/Coursework	60.10	66.72	58.54	59.54	49.04	43.53
Reputation	76.29	78.18	48.54	55.74	34.60	34.67
College Participation Factors						
Delayed Enrollment	4.82	3.41	19.81	15.77	46.04	43.20
Full-Time Employment	2.00	3.19	16.21	14.28	27.53	31.20
Part-Time Student	9.70	9.32	18.41	15.57	59.90*	52.88

Weight: wta000; *p< 0.05, **p< 0.01, ***p< 0.001 for differences between Linguistic Minority students and non-Linguistic Minority students within each institutional type on the basis of chi-square tests for equal distributions.

a Adequate sample sizes were not available to test for equal distributions based on immigration status among students attending selective 4-year institutions.

b Income quartiles were provided in BPS:04 and were calculated from two variables contained in the data source, household income and dependent/independent student status. For dependent students, the quartiles correspond to the following household income groups: Low income: $0–$30,999; Low-mid income: $31,000–$56,999; High-mid income: $57,000–$88,999; and High income: incomes greater than $89,000. For independent students, the quartiles correspond to the following household income groups: Low income: $0–$7,999; Low-mid income: $8,000–$19,999; High-mid income: $20,000–$37,999; and High income: incomes greater than $38,000.

parents with a high school diploma or less (30% and 14%, respectively). Nearly two-thirds of LM students in 2-year colleges, compared with just under half of non–LM students (47%) had parents with a high school diploma or less. Moreover, all three institution types, particularly the nonselective 4-year and 2-year sectors, LM students were overrepresented in the lowest income quartiles.

Across the three sectors, a lower proportion of LM students had earned high school GPAs in the top category (3.5 or better). The proportion of LM students in the 3.0-3.49 GPA range, however, slightly exceeded that of non–LM students. In terms of the highest math course completed in high school and having earned AP credit, LM and non–LM students did not appear to differ in either 4-year sector. However, more LM than non–LM students in 2-year institutions had earned AP credit in high school.

Overall, LM students did not appear to differ significantly from non–LM students in the reasons they reported for choosing their college. LM 2-year college students, however, were more likely to indicate they expected to receive a bachelor's degree or better and had intentions to transfer. These students were also more likely to be enrolled part-time.

F-statistics, a measure of goodness-of-fit for the regression models, are presented in Tables 7.2 and 7.3. These results indicate that at least one of the coefficients in each model is significantly different than zero, and that each of these models adds predictive power to explaining the outcome over the null model that only includes the model intercept. Table 7.2 presents odds ratios for the factors related to enrollment in a selective 4-year and nonselective 4-year institution, compared with a 2-year institution. The results indicate that, holding other factors constant, LM status is not significant in determining the type of institution that LM students enroll. Factors that did have a significant effect on selective 4-year enrollment versus 2-year enrollment included race/ethnicity (Asian and multiple race), coming from a high income family, having higher high school GPAs, taking advanced high school math courses, receiving non-language AP credit, reporting on key habitus measures, and exhibiting lower levels of environmental pull. In predicting 4-year nonselective versus 2-year enrollment, most variables operated in a similar fashion as presented for the 4-year selective versus 2-year enrollment model. However, race/ethnicity, income, non-language AP credits earned in high school, and full-time employment outside of school were not statistically significant in determining whether students enrolled in a nonselective 4-year versus a 2-year college.

The analysis was then stratified by the student's LM status to create two analytic samples (Table 7.3). Of note, fewer variables were significant in determining where LM students enrolled than for their non–LM counterparts. Of the demographic and family capital characteristics, being from the lowest parental education level was the only characteristic that significantly predicted LM student enrollment in a selective 4-year versus 2-year institution; while being Asian or from a highest income background were the only demographic and

TABLE 7.2 Odds Ratios Predicting Enrollment at a Selective 4-Year Institution or Non-selective 4-Year Institution versus a 2-Year Institution, Beginning Postsecondary Students Longitudinal Study 2004 (BPS: 04), n~16,500 (Unweighted Sample Size)

Variables	Selective 4-Year	Nonselective 4-Year
Linguistic Minority Student (ref=yes)	1.22	1.12
Demographics and Family Capital		
Gender (ref=male)	1.01	0.94
Student's Current Age (ref=19 or Younger)		
20-23 Years of age	0.58**	0.76*
24 Years of Age or Older	0.89	1.08
Race/Ethnicity (ref=White, non-Hispanic)		
Hispanic	1.38	0.86
Black (non-Hispanic)	2.39	1.05
Asian	2.15**	0.69
Other/Multiple Races/Ethnicities	1.59**	1.09
Immigration Status (ref=Third Generation)		
First Generation	1.09	0.94
Second Generation	0.75	0.85
Parent's Level of Education (ref= College Degree or More)		
High School Diploma or Less	0.41**	0.65***
Some College	0.38***	0.65***
Income Quartiles (ref=Low Income)		
Low-mid Income	0.90	1.17
High-mid Income	1.28	1.17
High Income	2.02***	1.29
Academic Capital		
High School GPA (ref=2.9 or below)		
3.5-4.0	9.76***	2.72***
3.0-3.49	3.17***	1.76***
Highest Math Course Completed in HS		
Algebra (ref=yes)	1.40	1.64***
Algebra II/ Trigonometry (ref=yes)	4.34***	2.65***
Calculus (ref=yes)	8.96***	3.90***
Earned Advanced Placement Credit in HS (ref=yes)	2.80***	1.21

Variables	Selective 4-Year	Nonselective 4-Year
Habitus		
Reason Student Selected this Institution		
Affordable/Financial Reasons (ref=yes)	0.33★★★	0.37★★★
Location (ref=yes)	0.63★★★	0.68★★★
Personal/Family Reasons (ref=yes)	1.13	1.20★★
Academic Programs/Coursework (ref=yes)	1.57★★★	1.68★★★
Reputation (ref=yes)	4.10★★★	1.76★★★
College Participation Factors		
Delayed Enrollment (ref=yes)	0.27★★★	0.56★★★
Full-time Employment (ref=yes)	0.37★★★	0.89
Part-time Student (ref=yes)	0.25★★★	0.25★★★

Weight: wta000; F = 30.81, prob> F = 0.0000 *p < 0.05, **p < 0.01, ***p < 0.001

family capital factors that held significance in predicting LM students' nonselective 4-year versus 2-year enrollment. Meanwhile, for non-LM students, the demographic and family capital factors of age, race/ethnicity, parent's level of education, and income were all significant in determining whether non-LM students enrolled in a selective 4-year institution versus a 2-year institution. With the exception of race/ethnicity and age (which became non-significant), these findings held in predicting non-LM students' 4-year nonselective versus 2-year enrollment.

Academic capital, habitus, and college participation factors were significant in determining enrollment patterns for both the LM and non-LM student samples. Given that demographic and family capital variables were generally not significant in determining enrollment patterns for LM students, academic preparation factors were particularly significant for them. In most cases, for both LM and non-LM students, high school preparation, habitus, and environmental pull factors were significantly related to enrolling in a selective 4-year institution versus a 2-year institution.

Discussion

This analysis of a nationally representative sample of first-time, first-year beginning postsecondary students across different institutional sectors indicates that LM students are a significant presence in higher education. The finding that LM students are evenly distributed across the sectors probably reflects the differentiation between EP students and ELL students in their pathways from high school to college (Kanno & Cromley, 2010). Although variables for EP

TABLE 7.3 Odds Ratios Predicting Type of Institution Attended By Linguistic Minority Status, Beginning Postsecondary Students Longitudinal Study 2004

Variables	Linguistic Minority Students (n~1,700) (F=60.79, prob>F=0.0000)		Non-Linguistic Minority Students (n~14,800) (F=28.37, prob>F=0.0000)	
	Selective 4-Year vs. 2-Year	Nonselective 4-Year vs. 2-Year	Selective 4-Year vs. 2-Year	Nonselective 4-Year vs. 2-Year
Demographics and Family Capital				
Gender (ref=male)	1.32	1.27	0.98	0.91
Student's Current Age (ref=19 or Younger)				
20-23 Years of age	0.92	0.68	0.51★★	0.77
24 Years of Age or Older	1.31	1.57	0.84	1.03
Race/Ethnicity (ref=White, non-Hispanic)				
Hispanic	0.84	0.61	1.29	0.87
Black (non-Hispanic)	1.00	0.52	2.49★	1.10
Asian	0.87	0.46★	2.82★★★	0.73
Other/Multiple Races/ Ethnicities	1.35	0.90	1.46★	1.03
Immigration Status (ref=Third Generation)				
First Generation	0.87	0.72	1.28	0.97
Second Generation	--	4.01★	0.78	0.80
Parent's Level of Education (ref=College Degree or More)				
High School Diploma or Less	0.46★★★	0.72	0.41★★★	0.63★★★
Some College	0.67	0.67	0.36★★★	0.64★★★
Income Quartiles (ref=Low Income)				
Low-mid Income	0.89	1.12	0.93	1.21★
High-mid Income	1.25	0.65	1.34★	1.27★★
High Income	0.92	0.49★★	2.23★★★	1.45★★★
Academic Capital				
High School GPA (ref=2.9 or below)				
3.5-4.0	12.31★★★	3.37★★★	9.65★★★	2.67★★★
3.0-3.49	3.70★★★	2.76★★★	3.19★★★	1.68★★★
Highest Math Course Completed in HS				
Algebra (ref=yes)	0.80	1.54	1.52	1.66★★★
Algebra II/ Trigonometry (ref=yes)	4.66★★	3.57★★★	4.30★★★	2.58★★★
Calculus (ref=yes)	11.46★★★	6.84★★★	8.80★★★	3.67★★★
Earned Advanced Placement Credit in HS (ref=yes)	1.75	0.94	3.09★★★	1.28★

Variables	Linguistic Minority Students (n~1,700) (F=60.79, prob>F=0.0000)		Non-Linguistic Minority Students (n~14,800) (F=28.37, prob>F=0.0000)	
	Selective 4-Year vs. 2-Year	Nonselective 4-Year vs. 2-Year	Selective 4-Year vs. 2-Year	Nonselective 4-Year vs. 2-Year
Habitus				
Reason Student Selected this Institution				
Affordable/Financial Reasons (ref=yes)	0.32***	0.36***	0.32***	0.37***
Location (ref=yes)	0.36***	0.65*	0.68***	0.70***
Personal/Family Reasons (ref=yes)	1.23	1.26	1.13	1.20**
Academic Programs/ Coursework (ref=yes)	0.83	1.21	1.72***	1.75***
Reputation (ref=yes)	6.65***	1.86***	3.95***	1.79***
College Participation Factors				
Delayed Enrollment (ref=yes)	0.15***	0.42***	0.31***	0.58***
Full-time Employment (ref=yes)	0.17***	1.01	0.40***	0.88
Part-time Student (ref=yes)	0.15***	0.19***	0.26***	0.26***

Weight: wta000; *p< 0.05, **p< 0.01, ***p< 0.001

and ELL students were not available in the study, the EP students are probably more likely to be in selective and 4-year institutions, while ELL students are more likely to be in 2-year institutions.

This study suggests that it is not being of LM background per se that determines where one begins college, but that several factors associated with being LM do affect where postsecondary students begin their college careers. This is important, because where LM students begin their college educations will have an influence on whether or not they persist (Bowen et al., 2009). LM students in 4-year colleges are slightly older than others, and so may have similar needs to other nontraditionally aged students. Across all sectors, LM students are more likely to be of Hispanic or Asian backgrounds. Thus, many of the challenges that Hispanics and Asians face in pursuing and completing higher education overlap with the challenges that LM students face. For example, Hispanics beginning college often face additional familial or financial responsibilities that may pull them away from being able to focus on their studies (Gandara & Contreras, 2009; Nora, 2004), while Asian students could find that they do not receive the services they need because there are assumptions that these students are successful and do not need extra support in college (Lee, 2009).

LM students across sectors are most likely to be first-generation immigrants, and they may have higher optimism (Kao & Tienda, 1995) about pursuing college. It is possible that they are less vulnerable to racial/ethnic stereotypes about their groups because they have spent less time in the United States (Portes & Rumbaut, 2001); this condition may also contribute to higher levels of optimism or motivation (Arbona & Nora, 2007; Gandara & Contreras, 2009). Despite these potential strengths, first-generation immigrant students have less access to cultural capital in terms of information about college and social networks that could offer support for pursuing college (Louie, 2005). It is important to build on LM students' potential assets, but also to target the areas where they need more support.

LM students are also quite likely to be the first-generation college-goers. Again, this could mean that their access to cultural capital about postsecondary education is limited (McDonough, 1997). Moreover, these students' and their families' limited knowledge of English could compromise their capacity to acquire such information (Kanno & Grosik, this volume). Promoting LM students' access to familial and nonfamilial cultural and social capital about higher education appears critical in enhancing their longer-term degree attainment (McDonough, 1997; Walpole, 2007).

Our results suggest that two central areas where LM college students need the most support are in accessing economic and academic capital necessary to pursue college successfully. Strikingly, over one-third of LM students in either selective 4-year institutions or community colleges, and half in nonselective 4-year institutions, come from the lowest income quartile among all college students. Meanwhile, their non-LM counterparts are far more likely to come from the *highest* income quartile; half of non-LM students in 4-year selective institutions come from the highest income quartile.

Although the tracking of LM students into lower level high school courses has been well documented (Callahan, 2005; Callahan, Wilkinson, & Muller, 2010), this study indicates that, among students who have already begun college, there are few significant differences between LM and non-LM students in the level of math they have taken or whether they have ever earned non-language AP credit. This reflects the fact that the sample only included students who had already made it to college, so many underprepared LM students would have been filtered out prior to the study. Across all sectors, LM students beginning college were less likely to have achieved high school GPAs in the "A" range—3.5 and above. This suggests that even those LM students who made it to college were academically underprepared in comparison to their non-LM peers.

Although LM community college students are more likely to have the "environmental pull" (Nora, 2004) factor of being enrolled part-time, they are also more likely than non-LM students to indicate that they expect to earn bachelor's degrees and to transfer institutions. LM community college students also have lower incomes and levels of parental education, but are more likely to have earned AP credit than their non-LM counterparts. While LM students are overrepresented in community colleges, they are underrepresented in non-selective 4-year institutions. It is possible that some academically qualified LM students choose community colleges over nonselective 4-year institutions as an alternative and lower-cost route to the bachelor's degree—in other words, they could be academically "undermatching" where they enroll, according to their qualifications (Bowen et al., 2009). This is one important place where having access to economic capital for LM students is critical in terms of finding a college in which they are most likely to succeed.

This study suggests that while habitus and environmental pull factors tend to similarly influence both LM and non-LM students' college enrollment patterns, key family capital and economic capital factors do not have the same explanatory power for LM students that they do for non-LM students. One explanation for the lack of effects of key family capital and economic capital factors is that other motivational or cultural characteristics that were unmeasured in this study influence LM students' college enrollment patterns. Our study shows that, regardless of institutional sector, the majority of LM college students are first-generation immigrants. These students could have increased immigrant optimism (Kao & Tienda, 1995) about the potential for education to advance their socioeconomic mobility and less exposure to negative stereotypes about their ethnic groups (Portes & Rumbaut, 2001). Therefore, they may have higher levels of motivation and lower levels of alienation from the K–12 schooling system (Arbona & Nora, 2007; Gandara & Contreras, 2009; Portes & Rumbaut, 2001). These levels of immigrant optimism, motivation, and alienation from schooling may all have a more important influence on where LM students go to college than where non-LM students go to college.

One habitus characteristic that is influential for non-LM students, but does not have a significant effect for LM students in predicting enrollment in either of the 4-year sectors, is ranking academic programs or coursework as important in college choice. Having less access to cultural and social capital about college, LM students could be less cognizant than non-LM students of the diversity of academic programs in different colleges and institution types. Therefore, they may be less attuned to this factor in choosing colleges. On the other hand, an institution's reputation appears far more important for LM students than non-LM students in choosing selective 4-year institutions. Perhaps when choosing 4-year selective institutions, LM students are more cognizant of how college degrees from institutions with more prestigious reputations will afford them valuable symbolic capital for educational and career advancement (Bourdieu & Passeron, 1977; McDonough & Nuñez, 2007), which is particularly important for these students, given that so many of them are starting out from lower socioeconomic backgrounds. This perspective could also reflect increased immigrant optimism (Kao & Tienda, 1995) about the power of selective institutions to garner more economic and social benefits in the longer term.

Implications for Research

This study suggests several directions for further research. First, to highlight traditionally and nontraditionally aged LM college students' experiences, more federal, state, and institutional data must be collected on their experiences (Rodriguez & Cruz, 2009) that accounts for factors like proficiency level and high school background (Kanno & Cromley, 2010). Second, our research suggests that limited financial resources hinder LM students' college access to 4-year and more selective institutions, as some relatively academically prepared LM students could be enrolled in 2-year instead of 4-year institutions, which could hinder their longer-term educational attainment prospects (Arbona & Nora, 2007; Bowen et al., 2009). Moreover, typical family capital indicators appear to have far less influence on where LM students enroll in comparison to non–LM students. More research is needed about how socioeconomic and financial factors uniquely affect LM students' college access.

In addition, far fewer variables in our model were significantly related to where LM students enrolled than where non–LM students enrolled. This raises more questions about what variables and conditions actually do affect where LM students enroll in college, and how their college choice and access dynamics could be different from those of other students. For example, how does the variation among LM students by race/ethnicity, income, and immigration status, affect where these students enroll? What additional elements of academic capital affect where LM students enroll? What are other variables or conditions that could explain where LM students enroll in college?

Implications for Policy and Practice

Because LM students disproportionately come from low-income backgrounds, ensuring that LM students apply for and receive appropriate financial aid is a key step in enhancing their postsecondary options. Given these students' possibly limited cultural capital and language skills, having professionals assist these students and their families in the financial aid application process could help them access federal aid (Bettinger, Long, Oreopoulos, & Sanbonmatsu, 2009). For students coming out of high school, programs like Indiana's 21st Century Scholars Program and the Gates Millennium Program could provide academically high-achieving LM students with scholarships to pursue college (Hurtado, Laird, & Pierorazio, 2003; St. John, Musoba, & Simmons, 2003).

For students transitioning from K–12 into college, outreach programs can offer another strategy for facilitating access to academic, cultural, and social capital. Programs such as Puente (Gandara, 2002; Rendon, 2002) and BESITOS (Holmes, Fanning, Morales, Espinoza, & Herrata, this volume) emphasize the strengths of students from LM backgrounds and incorporating culturally responsive curricula to effect positive change in their college access and success. P-20 partnerships linking K–12 schools and higher education institutions could also smooth the high school to college transition for LM students (Nuñez & Oliva, 2009). Beyond educational initiatives, broader approaches that involve stakeholders like community and health agencies, can also broaden pathways to higher education for LM students, particularly those of nontraditional age (Gandara & Orfield, 2010). Involving families as well as students in these efforts is critical to enhancing college access (Louie, 2005).

In light of increasing segregation in American communities, schools, and neighborhoods (Orfield, 2009), higher education can offer unique opportunities for students of diverse backgrounds to interact with and learn from one another (Gurin, Dey, Hurtado, & Gurin, 2002). LM students have much to contribute to postsecondary settings, particularly if their skills of navigating different cultures and their multilingual competence are valued as a form of "intercultural capital" (Nuñez, 2009) and as a critical asset in an increasingly globally connected world (Gandara & Orfield, 2010). Serving these students in postsecondary education poses great challenges, but also great opportunities.

Notes

1. For financially dependent students, adjusted incomes corresponded to the following income quartiles: low income (between $0 and $30,999, reference); low-mid income (between $31,000 and $56,999); high-mid income (between $57,000 and $88,999); and high income (equal to or greater than $89,000). For financially independent students, adjusted incomes corresponded to the following income quartiles: low income (between $0 and $7,999, reference); low-mid income (between $8,000 and $19,999); high-mid income (between $20,000 and $37,999); and high income (equal to or greater than $38,000).
2. We excluded AP language credits in the analysis because LM students might have the opportunity to take an AP test in their native language.

References

Adelman, C. (2006). *The toolbox revisited: Paths to degree completion from high school through college.* Washington, DC: U.S. Department of Education.

Arbona, C., & Nora, A. (2007). The influence of academic and environmental factors on Hispanic college degree attainment. *The Review of Higher Education, 30*(3), 247–270.

Bettinger, E. P., Long, B. T., Oreopoulos, P., & Sanbonmatus, L. (2009). *The role of simplification and information in college decisions: Results from the H&R Block FAFSA experiment.* Retrieved from Harvard University website: http://gseacademic.harvard.edu/~longbr/Bettinger_Long_Oreopoulos_Sanbonmatsu_-_FAFSA_experiment_9-09.pdf

Bourdieu, P. (1986). The forms of capital. In J. G. Richardson (Ed.), *Handbook of theory and research for the sociology of education* (pp. 241–258). New York: Greenwood.

Bourdieu, P., & Passeron, J. (1977). Cultural reproduction and social reproduction. In J. Karabel & A. H. Halsey (Eds.), *Power and ideology in education* (pp. 487–511). New York: Oxford University Press.

Bowen, W., Chingos, M., & McPherson, M. (2009). *Crossing the finish line.* Princeton, NJ: Princeton University Press.

Callahan, R. M. (2005). Tracking and high school English learners: Limiting opportunity to learn. *American Educational Research Journal, 42*(2), 305–328.

Callahan, R. M., Wilkinson, L., & Muller, C. (2010). Academic achievement and course taking among language minority youth in U.S. schools: Effects of ESL placement. *Educational Evaluation and Policy Analysis, 32*, 84–117.

Cominole, M., Wheeless, S., Dudley, K., Franklin, J., & Wine, J. (2007). *2004/06 Beginning Postsecondary Students Longitudinal Study (BPS:04/06) methodology report* (NCES 2008-184). Retrieved from National Center for Education Statistics website: http://nces.ed.gov/pub-search/pubsinfo.asp?pubid=2008184

Cunningham, A. F. (2006). *Changes in patterns of prices and financial aid* (NCES 2006-153). Retrieved from National Center for Education Statistics website: http://nces.ed.gov/pubs2006/2006153.pdf

Gandara, P. (2002). A study of high school Puente: What we have learned about preparing Latino youth for postsecondary education. *Educational Policy, 16*, 474–495.

Gandara, P., & Contreras, F. (2009). *The Latino education crisis: The consequences of failed social policies.* Cambridge, MA: Harvard University Press.

Gandara, P., & Orfield, G. (2010). Moving from failure to a new view of language policy. In P. Gandara & M. Hopkins (Eds.), *Forbidden language* (pp. 216–226). New York: Teachers College Press.

Garcia, E., Lawton, K., & Diniz de Figueirido, E. H. (2010). *The education of English Language Learners in Arizona: A legacy of persisting achievement gaps in a restrictive language policy climate.* Retrieved from UCLA Civil Rights Project website: http://civilrightsproject.ucla.edu/research/k-12-education/language-minority-students/the-education-of-english-language-learners-in-arizona-a-legacy-of-persisting-achievement-gaps-in-a-restrictive-language-policy-climate/garcia-az-ell-gaps-2010.pdf

Greene, T. G., Marti, C. N., & McClenney, K. (2008). The effort-outcome gap: differences for African American and Hispanic community college students in student engagement and academic achievement. *Journal of Higher Education, 79*(5), 513–539.

Gurin, P., Dey, E., Hurtado, S., & Gurin, G. (2002). Diversity and higher education: Theory and impact on educational outcomes. *Harvard Educational Review, 72*(3), 330–366.

Horn, L., & Premo, M. (1995). *Profile of undergraduates in U.S. postsecondary education institutions: 1992–1993.* Retrieved from National Center for Education Statistics website: http://nces.ed.gov/pubsearch/pubsinfo.asp?pubid=96237

Hurtado, S., Laird, T. N., & Pierorazio, T. (2003). *The transition to college for low-income students: The impact of the Gates Millennium Scholars Program.* Retrieved from Melinda Gates Foundation website: http://www.gatesfoundation.org/learning/Documents/Final-Transitionto-College-Hurtado.pdf

Kanno, Y., & Cromley, J. (2010). *English Language Learners' access to and attainment in postsecondary education.* A paper presented at the annual meeting of the Association for Institutional Research, Chicago, IL.

Kao, G., & Tienda, M. (1995). Optimism and achievement: The educational performance of immigrant youth. *Social Science Quarterly, 76*(1), 1–18.

Klein, S., Bugarin, R., Beltranena, R., & McArthur, E. (2004). *Language minorities and their educational and labor market indicators: Recent trends. NCES 2004-009.* Retrieved from National Center for Educational Statistics website: http://nces.ed.gov/pubsearch/pubsinfo.asp?pubid=2004009

Lee, S. (2009). *Unraveling the "model minority" stereotype: listening to Asian American youth.* New York: Teachers College Press.

Louie, V. (2005). Immigrant newcomer populations, ESEA, and the pipeline to college: Current considerations and future lines of inquiry. *Review of Research in Education, 29*, 69–105.

McDonough, P. (1997). Choosing colleges: *How schools and social class structure opportunity.* Albany: State University of New York Press.

McDonough, P., & Nuñez, A.-M. (2007). Bourdieu's sociology of education: Identifying persistent inequality, unmasking domination, and fighting social reproduction. In C. A. Torres & A. Teodoro (Eds.), *Critique and utopia: New developments in the sociology of education* (pp. 139–154). Lanham, MD: Rowman & Littlefield.

Nora, A. (2004). Access to higher education for Hispanic students: Real or illusory. In J. Castellanos & L. Jones (Eds.), *The majority in the minority* (pp. 47–70). Sterling, VA: Stylus.

Nuñez, A.-M. (2009). Latino students' college transitions: A social and intercultural capital perspective. *Harvard Educational Review, 79*(1), 22–48.

Nuñez, A.-M., & Oliva, M. (2009). Organizational collaboration to promote college access: A P-20 framework. *Journal of Hispanic Higher Education, 8*(4), 322–339.

O'Connor, N., Hammack, F. M., & Scott, M. A. (2010). Social capital, financial knowledge, and Hispanic student college choices. *Research in Higher Education, 51*(1), 195–219.

Orfield, G. (2009). *Reviving the goal of the integrated society: A 21st century challenge.* Retrieved from UCLA Civil Rights Project website: http://www.civilrightsproject.ucla.edu/research/deseg/reviving_the_goal_mlk_2009.pdf

Perna, L. W. (2006). Studying college access and choice: a proposed conceptual model. In J. Smart (Ed.), *Higher education: Handbook of theory and research* (Vol. XXI, pp. 99–157). Cambridge, MA: Springer.

Perna, L. W., & Thomas, S. L. (2008). *Theoretical perspectives on student success: Understanding the contributions of the disciplines.* San Francisco: Jossey-Bass.

Portes, A., & Rumbaut, R. G. (2001). *Legacies.* Berkeley: University of California Press.

Rendon, L. I. (2002). Community college Puente: A validating model of education. *Educational Policy, 16*, 642–667.

Rodriguez, G. M., & Cruz, L. (2009). The transition to college of English Learner and undocumented immigrant students: Resource and policy. *Teachers College Record, 111*(10), 2385–2418.

Stanton-Salazar, R. (1997). A social capital framework for understanding the socialization of racial minority children and youth. *Harvard Educational Review, 67*, 139.

Stanton-Salazar, R. (2001). *Manufacturing hope and despair.* New York: Teachers College Press.

St. John, E. P., Musoba, G. D., & Simmons, A. B. (2003). Keeping the promise: The impact of Indiana's Twenty-First Century Scholars Program. *The Review of Higher Education, 27*(1), 103–123.

Suarez-Orozco, C., Pimentel, A., & Martin, M. (2009). The significance of relationships: Academic engagement and achievement among newcomer immigrant youth. *Teachers College Record, 111*(3), 712–749.

U.S. Department of Education. (2007). *2004/06 Beginning Postsecondary Students Longitudinal Study restricted data set* (NCES 2007185). Washington, DC: National Center for Education Statistics.

Walpole, M. B. (2007). Economically and educationally challenged students in higher education: Access to outcomes. *ASHE-Higher Education Report Series, 33*(3), 1–113.

8

IMMIGRANT ENGLISH LEARNERS' TRANSITIONS TO UNIVERSITY

Student Challenges and Institutional Policies

Yasuko Kanno and Sarah Arva Grosik

There are compelling reasons to encourage more English learners (ELs), linguistic minority students who have been classified as in need of ESL services by their respective academic institution, to consider going to four-year colleges. At the individual level, a bachelor's degree makes a tremendous difference in one's earning power and employability. Over a worker's lifetime, a bachelor's degree is worth about $1.1 million more than an associate degree, which in turn is worth about $487,000 more than a high school diploma (Carnevale, Smith, & Strohl, 2010). It has also been predicted that two thirds of the 18.9 million new jobs created between 2004 and 2014 will be filled by workers with at least some level of postsecondary education; of these positions, 63% of the particularly high-growth, high-paying jobs will require a bachelor's degree or higher (U.S. Department of Labor, 2006). Further, college education is associated not only with better economic outcomes but also with better health and more active civic participation (Baum & Ma, 2007).

At the macro level, the United States needs more college graduates than it is currently producing in order to maintain its competitive edge over other developed nations. Carnevale et al. (2010) warn that by 2018 the U.S. labor market is likely to have a shortage of 3 million college-educated workers. Several organizations and private foundations have recently called for concerted efforts to increase the number of college graduates (Bowen, Chingos, & McPherson, 2009; College Board, 2010; Lumina Foundation, 2010; Southern Regional Education Board, 2010), including President Obama's initiative to increase community college graduates by 5 million by 2020 (Office of Social Innovation and Civic Participation, 2009). However, none of these initiatives would succeed if they did not consider how to address the specific needs of ELs who wish to advance to postsecondary education as ELs are currently the fastest growing segment of the K–12 student population (Wolf, Herman, Bachman, Bailey, & Griffin, 2008). By 2025, the proportion of ELs in U.S. public schools will jump from 10.8 % to 25% (National Clearinghouse for English Language Acquisition, 2011; Spellings, 2005).

Nonetheless, when it comes to the education of ELs, researchers' and educators' focus has been on their high school graduation, rather than their college access and graduation (Callahan & Gándara, 2004; Harklau, 1999). Although for other traditionally underrepresented students, such as ethnic minorities, low-income, and first-generation college students, research has long shifted its emphasis to exploring college access, and more recently, college completion (e.g., Bowen et al., 2009), research on ELs seems "stuck" at the K–12 level. Very little information is available on the experiences of ELs making a transition to postsecondary education, especially to four-year institutions.

This study, then, examines the factors that inhibit immigrant ELs from gaining access to four-year institutions. We address the following research questions:

1. What are the unique and additional challenges that ELs face because of their EL status when they try to access four-year college education?
2. To what extent do the receiving universities' language policies and institutional climates affect ELs' transition experiences?

Literature on ELs' College Access and Success

Compared with research on the college access and success of other diversity groups, we lack both quantitative and qualitative data on ELs' participation and experiences in college. Nonetheless, the small but growing body of research clearly shows that only the most accomplished ELs manage to reach four-year colleges and universities and that there are considerable barriers—not only linguistic but nonlinguistic and institutional barriers—that inhibit ELs' college participation.

First of all, we know that ELs access and graduate from four-year institutions at much lower rates than their more English proficient peers. Kanno and Cromley's (2011) recent analysis of the National Education Longitudinal Study of 1988 found that only 18% of ELs advance to four-year colleges right after high school graduation compared with 43% of monolingual English-speaking students and 38% of English-proficient linguistic minority students. With regard to graduation, only 12% of ELs attain a bachelor's degree, compared with 32% of monolingual English speakers and 25% of English-proficient linguistic minority students within eight years of high school graduation.

Other studies have found that it is not simply ELs' English proficiency per se, but other risk factors often associated with ELs, that cause these disparities in educational outcomes. A series of studies conducted by Callahan and colleagues (Callahan, 2005; Callahan, Wilkinson, & Muller, 2010; Callahan, Wilkinson,

Muller, & Frisco, 2009), for instance, have found that ELs are disproportionately more likely to be placed in low-level courses, which in turn leads to low
academic achievement (see also Callahan & Shifrer, this volume). Particularly
alarming is their finding that students' placement in ESL classes itself, even
when controlling for their English proficiency, contributes to lower academic
achievement and reduced opportunity to take college preparatory courses, in a
direct contradiction to the intent of the Lau Remedies (Callahan et al., 2009).
Also, Harklau's (2000) well-known study on ELs' transition from high school
to a community college found that the same ELs were perceived and treated
quite differently in high school and in college. Harklau's EL participants were
considered model students in high school, and yet when they moved onto a
community college, they were perceived as troublemakers. Likewise, Kanno
and Varghese's (2010) recent interview study of ELs who had been admitted
to a major public university identified both linguistic and nonlinguistic barriers to ELs' pursuit of four-year college education. They found that although
the ELs reported significant linguistic challenges, such as academic reading
and writing, they found such challenges to be manageable. What they found
much harder to overcome were nonlinguistic barriers; more specifically, institutional barriers that applied only to ELs (such as remedial ESL requirements)
and financial stresses. They also reported that many ELs eliminate themselves
from applying to four-year institutions, assuming that four-year colleges are
beyond their reach.

This study expands on Kanno and Varghese's study (2010). Although that
study began to identify important and varied difficulties that ELs face in making the transition to a four-year institution, it was based on data from one
university. We wondered whether students at another four-year institution,
especially one that differs on important dimensions such as selectivity, diversity, and ESL requirements, would have similar experiences. This study, then,
compares and contrasts the data from Kanno and Varghese's study with the data
collected at another major public university.

Theoretical Framework

For the theoretical framework of this study, we draw on George Kuh's theory
of student engagement (Kuh, Kinzie, Buckley, Bridges, & Hayek, 2007; Kuh,
Kinzie, Schuh, Whitt, & Associates, 2005). The central tenet of this theory is
that the more students engage in their studies and other educational activities
on campus, the more likely they will persist and graduate from college. What is
unique and important about Kuh's theory is that it invokes institutional commitment to promoting student engagement rather than focusing solely on students' attitudes. Thus, Kuh's conceptualization of student engagement consists
of two parts: (a) the student's investment of time and energy into curricular and
extracurricular activities on campus, and (b) the institution's role in enhancing

student engagement. In other words, it is not just the students' sole responsibility to engage fully in collegiate educational activities; the institutions' climate, policies, and practices have a strong bearing on the quality and quantity of student engagement.

Kuh's theory is useful as we examine how institutional differences between the two universities we studied, Northern Green University (NGU) and Speakman University, affected ELs' experiences. Although the two universities shared many commonalities—both were large, public research universities located in urban areas—there were several key differences. Speakman was less selective than NGU and was also more diverse. With regards to language policy, NGU adopted a remedial approach to EL education while Speakman provided for-credit ESL academic writing training in the context of the first-year writing program. A major focus of our analysis is to explore how these institutional characteristics impacted our participants' engagement.

The Study

This chapter draws on two sets of data. The first set of data was collected in the 2006–07 academic year at a major public university on the West Coast called Northern Green University (Kanno & Varghese, 2010).[1] NGU is a research-intensive state flagship university. It is routinely rated as one of the top 50 U.S. universities in *U.S. News and World Report*. In 2010, 86% of the first-year students were in top 10th percentile of the graduating class in their high school and 55% had a high school GPA of 3.75 or higher. The racial composition of the school consisted of 47% White, 31% Asian/Pacific Islander, 6% Hispanic, and 2% Black, and 1% American Indian/Alaskan Native.

At NGU, 33 ELs who were matriculated undergraduate students of the university were interviewed to examine the challenges they had experienced as they tried to gain access to university. These students were recruited, on a voluntary basis, from noncredit remedial ESL classes. Only immigrant and refugee students were included in the data; international students on F-1 visas were excluded (see Table 8.1 for a summary of participant characteristics).

The second set of data was collected during the 2009–10 academic year at another major public university, this time on the East Coast, called Speakman University. Speakman is also a research university; however, it is less selective than NGU. In 2010, 21% of the first year students were in the top 10th percentile of the graduating high school class; 22% had a high school GPA of 3.75 or higher. The racial composition of the university consisted of 60% White, 14% Black, 11%, Asian/Pacific Islander, 3% Hispanic, and less than 1% American Indian/Alaskan Native.

At Speakman, 21 matriculated ELs were interviewed. In this university, there are no remedial ESL classes; the students were thus recruited through the ESL sections of the first-year writing program.

TABLE 8.1 Summary of Participant Characteristics

	NGU (33)	Speakman (21)
National Origin	Taiwan (7), Vietnam (4), Iran (3), China (2), Ethiopia (2), Peru (2), Somalia (2), Ukraine (2), Laos (1), Indonesia (1), Korea (1), Sudan (1), India (1), Mexico (1), UAE (1), Fiji (1), Russia (1)	Vietnam (5), Dominican Republic (2), India (2), Russia (2), Korea (1), Japan (1), Thailand (1), Guatemala (1), Colombia (1), Liberia (1), Nigeria (1), Ethiopia (1), Romania (1), Albania (1)
Gender (Female)	21 (64%)	12 (57%)
Age (Mean)	20	21
Community College Transfer	14 (42%)	1 (5%)
Low Income Student	21 (64%)	16 (76%)
First-Generation College Student	10 (30%)	13 (62%)
At Least 1 AP Course in High School	13 (39%)	9 (43%)
Currently Working	19 (58%)	14 (67%)

Interviews at both universities were semi-structured and guided by comparable interview protocols. In order to ensure comprehensiveness and uniformity across all participant interviews, a common set of questions was asked of every participant, but the interviewers also asked follow-up questions to explore each student's unique narrative. Both sets of data were analyzed using ATLAS.ti. The NGU dataset had been analyzed to identify the types of challenges that the 33 ELs faced in reaching the university (Kanno & Varghese, 2010). However, once the Speakman dataset was collected, we read both sets of data several times and devised a new set of analytic codes that could be applied to both datasets. These codes were meant to identify both the common challenges shared by NGU and Speakman ELs and the unique challenges experienced by ELs at one institution but not at the other, as well as factors contributing to the differences. Once all the data were analyzed by the first-level codes, we then clustered these codes into several larger categories of challenges (Strauss & Corbin, 1990).

In what follows, we first discuss the common challenges that both NGU and Speakman ELs experienced. We then discuss differences in the experiences of NGU and Speakman ELs and analyze what instructional factors can account for these differences.

Common Challenges

Four challenges emerged as commonly experienced by both NGU and Speakman ELs as they made their transitions to universities: (a) academic English, (b) lack of information, (c) financial hardship, and (d) difficulty accessing high-level courses in high school. We discuss each of these themes in turn.

Academic English

The first type of challenges that were identified by students at both NGU and Speakman were problems with college-level academic English, with the majority of these problems involving reading and writing. One linguistic hurdle that was directly associated with college application was the writing of college essays. Most students were aware that the college essay was a critical component of the college application, but they also worried that the unsophisticated vocabulary and awkward grammar in their essays may compromise their image in the eyes of the admissions officers. Shammy, a Vietnamese student at NGU, noted,

> I think essay, essay is the more challenging. 'Cause you know, we still lack of grammar, vocabulary. I was like really scared what if I just use you know all the easy words, they might not accept me because my vocabulary level, not really good. So, I try to look in the dictionary for you know, more big word and then when I use it I don't really know where should I put it in my sentence.

Several students in this study also indicated that their limited English proficiency negatively affected their performance on college entrance exams such as the SAT and hence, their acceptance to selective institutions. This disadvantage was more relevant to EL students at NGU than students at Speakman, since several of our NGU participants applied to Ivy League and other highly selective schools whereas none of the ELs at Speakman did. For example, Andrew, an academic high achiever from Taiwan, had intended to apply to Stanford and UC Berkeley but ultimately "settled on" NGU. The reason was that even with multiple attempts, he simply could not score higher than 360 on the SAT Critical Reading although he always scored higher than 700 on the mathematics portion of the exam. "It's always 360, I don't know. [Pause] I gave up," he said.

Even after students overcame the linguistic barriers to gain acceptance to college, they continued to encounter difficulties with academic reading and writing throughout their coursework. Writing, in particular, seemed to be the linguistic challenge that plagued our participants the most. Many students discussed a lack of confidence in their writing abilities and often seemed to focus on the mechanical errors that they made in their essays as a result of their nonnative proficiency level. Many students described their writing-intensive courses as their least preferred classes, favoring instead the courses in which writing was not a major component (e.g., math and science courses). Another ongoing problem many participants identified was the extra time that it took to complete academic tasks in their L2. Arina, a Russian student from Speakman, illustrated the difficulty she faced when encountering new academic vocabulary in her course readings: "Cuz a lot of words, you would never know all of them. Have to translate, if it's take for American one hour, for me I'm gonna take like five hours." Our participants reported having to spend three or four times as long to complete the same task as their native-speaking peers, and these extra academic demands allowed little time for them to engage in extracurricular activities.

Lack of Information

Another major theme that emerged from the data was a lack of information about college. Many ELs are placed in familial and institutional settings where college information is not readily available because many of them are the first people in their family to go to college (*Education Week*, 2009) and/or attending urban schools with limited resources (Fry, 2008). As a result, we found that even among our participants, all of whom eventually reached universities, some students initially lacked the most basic knowledge of the college-going process. The basic rules of the college-going process such as "You need to take college entrance exams such as the SAT and the ACT if you want to apply to a four-year college," "the personal statement is a critical part of your application and should be carefully crafted," and "it is a good idea to visit colleges that you are seriously considering," were not necessarily obvious to some of our students. Roderick, Nagaoka, and Coca (2009) call such procedural knowledge "college knowledge," arguing that it is a vital part of college readiness.

Interviews with several students revealed that they had been in many ways "clueless" about essential aspects of the college application process. Ali, a Romanian student from Speakman, was one such student who was unfamiliar with many aspects of the application process and as a result did not realize the importance of the college essay. Thus, instead of taking the time to draft and revise her college essay, Ali simply wrote her application essay directly into the online application in one sitting. Another example of how this lack of information can impair students' chances of college acceptance was illustrated by Sanskruti, an Indian student from Speakman, who explained how her EL status caused her to be oblivious to the logistics of the college application process:

> No, I had no clue that you even had to take SAT to go to college really because you know I told you I was in ESL, where we learn English and kind of being connected or something, so we had no knowledge.

In this case, Sanskruti attributed her lack of information about college entrance exams to the fact that she was an EL student in her high school and was thus not prepared by high school personnel to take the steps necessary to apply to four-year institutions.

Lack of information can seriously derail or complicate ELs' college transition. Dania, an Ethiopian student who transferred to NGU from a community college, had initially planned to become a pharmacist and was pursuing a major in pharmacy at community college. However, when she started seriously considering transferring to a four-year institution, she discovered that all pharmacy programs in area universities required a personal interview as part of the admissions process. Intimidated by the prospect of a formal interview, she abruptly shifted her major to nursing even though it involved an adjustment in her coursework and prolonged her stay at the community college. Dania commented, "When I switched my major from pharmacy to nursing, it's not because [of] the biology or chemistry; it's just because of the English." Had she been better informed of the transfer process to pharmacy schools, she might have been able to avoid such a drastic and costly change of plan.

Lack of information can also prevent students from receiving the financial aid for which they are eligible. There were several low-income students who, as far as we could tell, were clearly eligible for Pell Grants and other needs-based financial aid and yet were not receiving them. For example, Ali was living with her sister and receiving no financial assistance from her parents back in Romania. She was working 46 hours a week as a sales clerk in a clothing store. And yet, she was not receiving any financial aid because she did not know how to file her FAFSA application despite her effort to seek the help of an advisor at Speakman. Ali said, "Not a lot of people can explain or can tell me what should I do in order to get that [i.e., financial aid]." Thus, in addition to the college application process, getting financial aid is another area where lack of information can cause severe negative consequences.

Financial Hardship

Many EL students at both NGU and Speakman also experienced considerable financial stresses, which limited their initial college choice and restricted the amount of time and energy they were able to invest in engagement in college life. ELs in the United States on average come from families that are more socioeconomically disadvantaged than their non-EL peers (*Education Week*, 2009). This general economic disadvantage of ELs is also reflected in our sample. Thirty-seven of the 54 students in our study (68.5%) were low-income students.[2] Many of the students in this study originally came from a middle-class background in their countries of origin; however, when they immigrated to the United States, many families experienced downward economic mobility because the parents did not speak English fluently and lacked relevant qualifications in the United States.

Students' lack of economic capital affected their choice of colleges and college participation on many fronts. First of all, when discussing why they chose to apply to and ultimately enrolled in either Speakman or NGU, a number of students attributed their decision to the fact that these universities were more affordable than private universities. Proximity to their home was stated as another reason they enrolled in these universities because they could not afford to live on campus. Steven, a Mexican student at NGU, explained that financially speaking, his choice of colleges was limited to public institutions that were close enough to his home: "I made sure that by my junior year I was going to get into college for sure. Specifically, NGU. I wanted to because there was no other option. Either it was NGU or community college. But I didn't want to go to community college." Such a matter-of-fact acceptance of where these students could and could not afford to attend was common throughout our interviews.

Once in college, a large number of these students had to cope with the difficult task of balancing a job and their studies. Fourteen of the 21 students at Speakman and 19 of the 33 students at NGU were working while attending university. Sometimes students were not only paying for their own expenses but were also contributing to the family finances or even sending remittances back to extended family members in their native countries. Luniyinla, a Liberian student at Speakman, described the pressure that he felt from his family in Liberia:

> They know that I am going to university but uh sometime they—they might call [from Liberia] and leave me a message uh you know help me with this, help me with that. Average college student over here most—most of the time like what you do is like work to help yourself out but uh the extra pressure from back there sometime you can't just tell everybody I can't—I can't afford it. Sometime you going to pinch the little one you have to help one or two person out.

Thus, ELs' financial constraints forced them to work long hours and commute from home (sometimes involving more than two hours of commuting time). These constraints, compounded by the long hours they needed to devote to their studies because of linguistic challenges, left little time for them to socialize on campus and engage in extracurricular activities. When asked about their engagement in campus life, 16 of the 22 Speakman students and 20 of the 33 NGU students reported that they were not involved in any student associations or clubs on campus. Because of the many demands on their time, most commuting students only came to the campus when they had classes and strategically bundled their courses in a way that allowed them to come to the campus only a few days a week. While such a strategy allowed working ELs to spend the minimal amount of time on campus, from the perspective of student engagement (Kuh et al., 2007; Kuh et al., 2005), it also meant that they were foregoing many opportunities for personal and professional growth that colleges offered outside of the structured class time.

Difficulty Accessing High-Level Courses in High School

Another limitation that ELs faced concerned high school course-taking. Students in this study reported encountering hurdles in taking a required set of college preparatory courses in high school for admission to four-year institutions (Callahan, 2005; Callahan et al., 2010) or honors and advanced placement (AP) courses that would make them competitive for selective institutions (Geiser & Santelices, 2006). Given that our participants were those who had been admitted to public research universities, it is not surprising that 22 of the 54 students (40%) took at least one AP course in high school. What is disturbing, however, is that several students reported that ELs were actively discouraged from taking AP courses or had dramatically limited access to them because of their EL status. Celia, a Dominican student from Speakman, described the limited course-taking opportunities for EL students in her high school:

> I didn't get into many of the other AP classes because I was in—an ESOL student. Many of the opportunities in the high school were given to those English speakers like native English speakers, if you were in those—in the ESOL program you won't be able to do the—uh there were they had cooking classes and baby-sitting classes and beauty salon classes ... but no ESOL students [in the AP classes] and they didn't put—put it in our roster and we didn't have the chance to take it.

Celia's and other ELs' experiences suggest that the institutional personnel in high school may have limited course-taking expectations for EL students, which is difficult for ELs to overcome.

Differences between the Two Institutions

A comparison of ELs from two institutions also sheds some light on how particular institutional climates and policies directly affect ELs' engagement (Kuh et al., 2007; Kuh et al., 2005). The ways in which NGU and Speakman supported their ELs' linguistic development especially had a tremendous impact on the students' framing of their EL identity and their status on campus.

ESL Requirements

One major difference between the two institutions was their approaches to ESL education. NGU took a remedial approach: Any incoming students who were non-U.S. citizens *and* nonnative speakers of English were required to either demonstrate their English proficiency with test scores or enroll in the university's Academic ESL Program (AEP). A student was considered English proficient if he or she scored at least 490 on the SAT Critical Reading, 70 on the TOEFL iBT, or passed the NGU-made placement test. Students who were not able to demonstrate their English proficiency were required to take up to five remedial AEP courses, depending on their performance on the placement test. AEP courses were noncredit courses, and each course cost approximately $1,000, which was significantly more expensive than the tuition for regular undergraduate courses.[3]

Three aspects of NGU's ESL policy struck our participants as particularly unfair: (a) that they were noncredit courses, (b) that the tuition was disproportionately high, and (c) that only noncitizen students had to demonstrate their English proficiency. A few students acknowledged that the course content itself was useful, but an overwhelming majority of the students resented being placed in the AEP program and focused on trying to test out of the program as fast as possible or passing the required courses with minimal effort. For example, Roger, a Peruvian student, expressed his sentiment for having to pay $1,000 for learning so little:

> They made me, they practically made me take the class for [learning the present perfect] "have been" because it was pretty much really basic. And you have to pay a thousand dollars. I have been here, what, six years. I got out of high school with honor and they made me take ESL. What kind of—I don't wanna say the word.

In our interview transcripts, we have a number of equally strongly worded complaints about the ESL requirement. In other words, the policy that was designed to facilitate ELs' academic success was ironically perceived by the majority of ELs as a major barrier to their success on campus. It added an extra financial burden on their already tight budget and prolonged the time for a degree completion by imposing noncredit courses.

In contrast to NGU's remediation model, Speakman took the first-year writing program approach to ESL instruction.[4] Upon arriving at Speakman University, all undergraduate students were required to take an English language placement test to determine their writing proficiency. However, if students had previously stated in the freshman survey that they spoke another language in their home, this placement test was utilized to determine whether those students should be classified as ELs. If such students received a score that was below a certain threshold on this placement test, they were required to take the ESL sections of the two mandatory first-year writing courses: Introduction to Academic Reading and Writing (English 113) and Advanced Reading and Writing (English 213). These were taken instead of the general sections of these courses (English 103 and English 203) and were specifically designed to address the needs of students with limited English proficiency. Thus, students at Speakman were not required to take any additional courses as a result of their

ESL placement. The ESL classes were smaller than the general sections and the instructors, who were trained in second language writing, spent extended time with the students in tutorial conferences.

When we examined NGU ELs' attitudes towards their ESL requirement, we were not at all surprised by their resentment, given that problems associated with a remedial approach to college ESL have long been documented (e.g., Benesch, 1988; CCCC Committee on Second Language Writing, 2001; Williams, 1995). However, we were surprised by Speakman ELs positive attitudes towards their ESL requirement. We had predicted that the Speakman ELs were likely to be less hostile towards their ESL requirement since it did not involve any extra tuition or courses. However, we had thought that the ELs would still be unhappy about being singled out and placed in separate sections from their native-speaking peers, since Holten (2009) had reported ELs' grudge against a similar arrangement at UCLA. However, the ELs at Speakman were overwhelmingly positive about their ESL courses. Twenty of the 21 ELs reported that they found these courses useful and most sang high praise for the ESL instruction that they received. Joy, a Guatemalan student, expressed her enthusiasm towards her ESL course: "I love it [laughs]. I'm not leaving. [Interviewer: Really? Why?] I think I've learned so much more in ESL class than I've ever learned in AP classes."

There seem to be two key factors in Speakman ELs' positive perception of ESL placement. The first factor, of course, is that their ESL courses were for credit and considered full equivalents of non-ESL first-year writing courses. They did not have to take any extra courses or pay extra tuition because of their EL status. However, we believe an equally critical second factor is that through their advisors and first-year writing instructors, ELs at Speakman heard on repeated occasions that the ESL sections offered a smaller class size, more individualized attention, and instruction that was designed to meet their specific needs as EL writers. Nowhere in this message was any hint that they were placed in ESL because their English—and by extension, they—were inferior. ELs seemed to "buy into" this message, and being value-conscious consumers of education that they were, seemed to believe that they were receiving a better deal for the same tuition. Consequently, many ELs at Speakman, even when they were given a choice to choose a "regular" section of the writing program, opted for an ESL section.

Campus Climate

In addition to the differences in ESL requirements, NGU and Speakman also differed in terms of overall campus climate. To begin with, NGU was more selective than Speakman in terms of admissions requirements. The admission rates at the two institutions appear comparable at first glance: Speakman had an admission rate of 61%, whereas NGU had an admission rate of 58%. In spite of these similar admissions rates, it is clearly the case that students of a higher caliber applied to, and were subsequently accepted to, NGU as opposed to Speakman as judged by the applicants' high school class standings and GPAs. The increased selectivity of NGU might have made ELs feel less adequate as compared to their high achieving native-speaking peers on campus. Indeed, many of our NGU participants spoke of the high academic standards at the university and the competitive atmosphere among students. Jason, who transferred to NGU from a community college, noted that while she had felt no qualms about asking English language questions at the community college, she refrained from asking such questions at NGU. When asked why she felt that way, she said,

> I think a lot of people who go to [community] college [are] just average people. You know. Maybe like people here are more smart. And if you go ask something like, they think it's so basic, maybe you not really intelligent, you know.

Jason's comments illustrate the ways in which ELs interpret the institutional climate of their university and how they adjust their behaviors according to their interpretation. In Jason's case, the presence of academic achievers around her intimidated her and prevented her from asking for the linguistic support which would have enhanced her engagement.

Beyond the difference in academic standards at the two institutions, Speakman was also a much more diverse environment than NGU. Speakman prided itself on being diverse and was home to a large number of nontraditional college students. Speakman had a higher percentage of African American and Hispanic students combined (17%) than NGU (8%). Moreover, 35% of Speakman undergraduate students were part-time students compared to 14% at NGU. Eighty-five percent of Speakman students received some kind of financial aid while only 57% of NGU students did. In sum, academically, ethnically, and socioeconomically, Speakman represented a more diverse student community than did NGU. Given that ELs are not simply linguistically diverse but often come from a racial minority and lower socioeconomic background (*Education Week*, 2009), Speakman's diverse environment likely offered a climate that was easier for ELs to fit into than the more selective, and therefore more homogeneous, environment at NGU. Joy, whose mother was Jewish Guatemalan and whose father was African American, had always been an academic achiever (she graduated from high school with a 3.9 GPA), one consequence of which was that she was taking most of her honors and AP courses with her White peers. She expressed the pleasure of being "part of the majority" for the first time:

> I struggled with identity issues trying to relate to more—like more than one group of people … because I went to a majority White school my whole life. I kind of like—people kind of, oh, you are this and you're this and people try to put you in a box. And here everyone's in the same box

because everyone is different. So you're no longer stratified. [Interviewer: Stratified.] Yeah, I am part of the majority.

Conclusion and Implications

Expanding on Kanno and Varghese (2010), this study compared and contrasted the specific factors—both linguistic and nonlinguistic—that inhibited ELs from gaining access to two different research universities. Several common obstacles were identified. Unfamiliarity with writing college essays, low scores on the verbal sections of the college entrance exams, and the burden of managing college-level reading and writing demands emerged as major linguistic challenges. Lack of information about college was also a prevalent problem, one that sometimes further complicated ELs' already difficult college transition processes. Many ELs experienced financial hardship, which limited their choice of colleges and negatively affected their engagement in campus life. Finally, ELs sometimes encountered discouragements from their high school teachers and administrators to take honors and AP courses because of their EL status.

On the other hand, we found a few critical differences in the experiences of ELs at the two institutions. The majority of ELs at NGU resented being institutionally labeled as "English learner" while ELs at Speakman were much more positive about their position as ELs. We attributed this difference to two reasons. First, NGU adopted a remedial approach to ESL education while Speakman incorporated ESL education into the regular first-year writing program. Second, Speakman offered a more diverse environment—not only linguistically but academically, ethnically, and socioeconomically—into which it was easier for linguistically diverse students to fit.

The findings of this study offer a number of pedagogical and policy implications for a better college transition process for ELs. First, the results make it clear that access to relevant and reliable information is a key to college access and success. In this regard, we see a larger role for ESL teachers in high school to play. The ELs in this study expressed lacking the information essential to successfully navigate the college-going process. In most high schools, college guidance is the responsibility of the guidance counselor, and not part of the job assignments of ESL teachers. However, given the extraordinarily high student-to-counselor ratio, ELs may not receive adequate guidance. Also, ELs may not feel confident enough in their communication skills (Baum & Ma, 2007) to assert themselves and vie for their counselors' attention. Even when they do manage to meet with their counselors, the counselors may assume too much background knowledge of the U.S. education system on the part of the ELs, and may not explain the college-going process in language that the ELs can understand. ESL teachers, on the other hand, already have an existing relationship with ELs. Because of their knowledge of the students, their daily contact, and their expertise, ESL teachers are much more likely to be able to break down the process of college-going in terms that ELs can understand and follow-up on their progress.

We are not suggesting that ESL teachers should take over the entire task of college guidance for ELs. Rather, we are suggesting that ESL teachers be the first point of contact for ELs to develop their relationship with other institutional agents and acquire cultural capital in school. In our interviews, we found that ELs who had received the support of a caring teacher who took the time to introduce them personally to another institutional agent (e.g., a counselor, a university admissions officer, an outreach program officer) had a much smoother college transition than those who received no such support. For most ELs, ESL teachers are the institutional agents they have daily contact with and therefore are most likely to succeed as long-term, stable mentors for these students.

Second, we need to do more to ensure that ELs receive all the financial aid for which they are eligible. Lack of economic capital limits college choice, and once in college, inhibits student engagement in educational activities. There were several students in our study who we believe were eligible to receive Pell Grants. Yet, they failed to file their FAFSA application and consequently had to work long hours to make ends meet. Once again, lack of information was the biggest barrier. Financial aid application is often a confusing process even for native-English-speaking, U.S.-born students (Roderick, Nagaoka, Coca, & Moeller, 2008). Some of the ELs in this study tried to file their FAFSA but gave up after struggling for hours to decode what was asked of them. For most ELs, it is not enough to be directed to the FAFSA website; they need someone sitting down with them as they apply online, or at the very least need a hands-on workshop, specifically designed for ELs, that explains what information they need to gather and walks them through the application process step by step. ELs' parents should also be invited to attend such workshops, with translators made available when necessary.

Third, the experiences of ELs at NGU strongly indicate that the remedial approach to ESL is seen by the students as punitive and costly. The findings of this study indicate that ELs tend to interpret such a requirement as an institutional stamp of their "deficiency," rather than an offer of additional help. They resent having to take noncredit courses that incur extra tuition. Clearly, if students resent their ESL placement so much that they start sabotaging classes, the institutional goal of providing linguistic support is not being accomplished.

Much more promising is Speakman's approach to place ELs in ESL sections of the first-year writing program and scaffold the development of their academic literacy in that context. In this way, ELs are not required to take additional courses and their ESL courses are counted as full equivalents of the "regular" writing classes. However, our study suggests that this arrangement by itself is not sufficient: After all, some ELs may still resent being singled out, labeled ELs, and placed in a separate class from native-English-speaking students. Thorough communication of the rationale for this policy and its benefits for ELs is critical. Speakman ELs appreciated their ESL classes because this arrangement made sense to them. They understood that (a) they were not penalized for being ELs, and (b) they might in fact be getting a better deal for the same tuition, with a smaller class size and more individualized attention from their writing teachers. They did not perceive their ESL placement as an imposition the way NGU ELs did. In all, the contrast between the experiences of NGU and Speakman ELs speaks to the pivotal role of the institution in promoting or inhibiting student engagement.

Notes

1. We would like to thank Manka Varghese for allowing us to reanalyze and use the NGU data for this chapter.
2. We first identified low-income students on the basis of whether or not they were receiving Pell Grants; however, it quickly became evident that some did not apply for a Pell Grant (because of the lack of knowledge about the FAFSA) or were not eligible for one (because of their immigration status) even when it was clear from our interviews that they were low-income students. Therefore, whenever there were obvious signs of financial hardship in their narratives, we identified those students as low-income even when they were not receiving Pell Grants.
3. In 2006–07, full-time, resident undergraduate students paid a little over $2,000 in tuition each quarter. Full-time study at NGU typically consisted of taking three courses for 15 credits. Thus, $1,000 for a noncredit AEP course struck many students—and many AEP instructors—as unreasonably high tuition. Several ELs complained that it represented the university's exploitation of students who were the least able to pay.
4. This was purely a difference in institutional policy and was not indicative of the superior English proficiency on the part of Speakman ELs. In fact, the average SAT Critical Reading score for admission to Speakman (550) was lower than the average score of students at NGU (585). Also, NGU had a minimum SAT Critical Reading score for admission (430) whereas Speakman had no cutoff score. Therefore, in all likelihood, the English proficiency of Speakman ELs on average was likely to be lower than that of NGU ELs.

References

Baum, S., & Ma, J. (2007). *Education pays 2007: The benefits of higher education for individuals and society* Retrieved from College Board website: http://www.collegeboard.com/prod_down loads/about/news_info/trends/ed_pays_2007.pdf

Benesch, S. (1988). Introduction. In S. Benesch (Ed.), *Ending remediation: Linking ESL and content in higher education* (pp. 1–5). Washington, DC Teachers of English to Speakers of Other Languages.

Bowen, W. G., Chingos, M. M., & McPherson, M. S. (2009). *Crossing the finish line: Completing college at America's public universities.* Princeton, NJ: Princeton University Press.

Callahan, R. M. (2005). Tracking and high school English learners: Limiting opportunity to learn. *American Educational Research Journal, 42*(2), 305–328.

Callahan, R. M., & Gándara, P. (2004). On nobody's agenda: Improving English-language learners' access to higher education. In S. Michael (Ed.), *Teaching immigrant and second-language students: Strategies for success* (pp. 107–127). Cambridge, MA: Harvard Education Press.

Callahan, R. M., Wilkinson, L., & Muller, C. (2010). Academic achievement and course taking among language minority youth in U.S. schools: Effects of ESL placement. *Educational Evaluation and Policy Analysis, 32*(1), 84–117.

Callahan, R. M., Wilkinson, L., Muller, C., & Frisco, M. (2009). ESL placement and schools: Effects on immigrant achievement. *Educational Policy, 23*(2), 355–384.

Carnevale, A. P., Smith, N., & Strohl, J. (2010). *Help wanted: Projections of jobs and education requirements through 2018*. Retrieved from Center on Education and the Workforce, Georgetown University website: http://www9.georgetown.edu/grad/gppi/hpi/cew/pdfs/FullReport.pdf

CCCC Committee on Second Language Writing. (2001). *CCCC statement on second language writing and writers*. Retrieved from http://www.ncte.org/cccc/resources/positions/secondlangwriting

College Board. (2010). *The college completion agenda*. Retrieved from http://www.CompletionAgenda.CollegeBoard.org

Education Week. (2009, January). A distinctive population. *Quality counts 2009: Portraits of a population, how English language-learners are putting schools to the test*, 15.

Fry, R. (2008). *The role of schools in the English language learner achievement gap*. Retrieved from Pew Hispanic Center website: http://pewhispanic.org/files/reports/89.pdf

Geiser, S., & Santelices, V. (2006). The role of Advanced Placement and honors courses in college admissions. In P. C. Gandara, G. Orfield, & C. Horn (Eds.), *Expanding opportunity in higher education: Leveraging promise* (pp. 75–114). Albany: State University of New York Press.

Harklau, L. (1999). Representations of immigrant language minorities in US higher education. *Race Ethnicity and Education, 2*(2), 257–279.

Harklau, L. (2000). From the "good kids" to the "worst": Representations of English language learners across educational settings. *TESOL Quarterly, 34*(1), 35–67.

Holten, C. (2009). Creating an inter-departmental course for generation 1.5 ESL writers: Challenges faced and lessons learned. In M. Roberge, M. Siegal, & L. Harklau (Eds.), *Generational 1.5 in college composition: Teaching academic writing to U.S. educated learners of ESL* (pp. 170–184). New York: Routledge.

Kanno, Y., & Cromley, J. (2011). *English language learners' college access and attainment: A national level analysis*. Paper presented at the American Association for Applied Linguistics, Chicago, IL.

Kanno, Y., & Varghese, M. (2010). Immigrant English language learners' challenges to accessing four-year college education: From language policy to educational policy. *Journal of Language, Identity, and Education, 9*(5), 1–19.

Kuh, G. D., Kinzie, J., Buckley, J. A., Bridges, B. K., & Hayek, J. C. (2007). *Piecing together the student success puzzle: Research, propositions, and recommendations, ASHE Higher Education Report, 32*(5). San Francisco: Jossey-Bass.

Kuh, G. D., Kinzie, J., Schuh, J. H., Whitt, E. J., & Associates. (2005). *Student success in college: Creating conditions that matter*. San Francisco: Jossey-Bass.

Lumina Foundation. (2010). *Lumina's big goal: To increase the proportion of Americans with high-quality degrees and credentials to 60 percent by the year 2025*. Retrieved from http://www.luminafoundation.org/goal_2025

National Clearinghouse for English Language Acquisition. (2011). *NCELA FAQ: How many school-aged Limited English Proficient (LEP) students are there in the U.S.?* Retrieved from http://www.ncela.gwu.edu/faqs/view/4

Office of Social Innovation and Civic Participation. (2009). *Investing in education: The American Graduation Initiative*. Retrieved from White House website: http://www.whitehouse.gov/blog/Investing-in-Education-The-American-Graduation-Initiative/

Roderick, M., Nagaoka, J., Coca, B., & Moeller, E. (2008). *From high school to the future: Potholes on the road to college*. Retrieved from Consortium on Chicago School Research at the University of Chicago website: http://ccsr.uchicago.edu/downloads/1835ccsr_potholes_summary.pdf

Roderick, M., Nagaoka, J., & Coca, V. (2009). College readiness for all: The challenges for urban high schools. *The Future of Children, 19*(1), 185–210.

Southern Regional Education Board. (2010). *No time to waste: Policy recommendations for increasing college completion*. Retrieved from http://publications.sreb.org/2010/10E10_No_Time_to_Waste.pdf

Spellings, M. (2005). *Academic gains of English language learners prove high standards, accountability paying off*. Retrieved from U.S. Department of Education website: http://www.ed.gov/news/speeches/2005/12/12012005.html

Strauss, A. C., & Corbin, J. M. (1990). *Basics of qualitative research: Grounded theory procedures and techniques*. Newbury Park, CA: Sage.

U.S. Department of Labor. (2006). *America's dynamic workforce: 2006*. Retrieved from Cornell Universeity ILR School website: http://digitalcommons.ilr.cornell.edu/key_workplace/288/

Williams, J. (1995). ESL composition program administration in the United States. *Journal of Second Language Writing, 4*(2), 157–179.

Wolf, M. K., Herman, J. L., Bachman, L. F., Bailey, A. L., & Griffin, N. (2008). *Recommendations for assessing English language learners: English language proficiency measures and accommodation uses* (CRESST Report 737). Retrieved from National Center for Research on Evaluation, Standards, and Student Testing website: http://www.cse.ucla.edu/products/reports/R737.pdf

9

A LINGUISTIC MINORITY STUDENT'S DISCURSIVE FRAMING OF AGENCY AND STRUCTURE

Manka M. Varghese

Studies that have looked at students' postsecondary transitions and experiences have leaned significantly towards structural reasons to explain their success or lack of success, such as various institutional resources or barriers (Bowen, Kurzwell, & Tobin, 2005; McDonough, 1997). This chapter shifts the focus from these structural explanations to linguistic minority students' sense of agency. This conceptual framework that highlights the agency of the students was used to frame and analyze findings from a study that I along with others (Kanno & Varghese, 2010; Kanno, Varghese, & Fuentes, 2011; Oropeza, Varghese, & Kanno, 2010) conducted using interviews of linguistic minority students at the undergraduate level. In a recent article (Kanno et al., 2011) based on this same study and using follow-up case studies of five students, we show how these students framed and used their agency (often in relation to their history and environment) to navigate the institutions of high school and college as well as how their agency was relationally and symbiotically created with their environment.

This chapter builds upon these previous analyses but adds a new perspective on the role of agency in linguistic minority students' academic careers. While previous work looked at agency as the intent or completion of actualized events, here I seek to show that the discursive construction of agency and how a student sees himself or herself as an agent are equally important. I trace the saliency and construction of agency in one linguistic minority student's narrative, showing how she viewed herself, her actions, and her relationship with institutional resources and challenges. I attempt to understand the discourses that the student draws upon to explain her actions in relation to the environment. In doing so, this chapter sheds significant light on the discourses that college-going linguistic minority students see as being available to them, and how and why they draw on these discourses as they construct narratives of college-going and college persistence. I suggest that how students talk about themselves, the ways in which they create narratives of self, and the discourses they draw on to create them are key to understanding their agency. Such an analysis underscores that what is important is how students actually discursively create agentive narratives.

Literature Review

Increasing the number of underrepresented students in higher education has been a critical area of research and policy at both the federal (Bowen et al., 2005; Venezia, Kirst, & Antonio, 2004) and state levels (Contreras et al., 2008; Vasquez-Heilig & Darling-Hammond, 2008). A substantial slice of research on college access for underrepresented students has focused on immigrant students in particular (Gray, Rolph, & Melamid, 1996; Louie, 2008; Vernez & Abrahamse, 1996). Within this immigrant population, linguistic minority students have received increasing attention but remain significantly under-researched. Although their academic underachievement in K–12 schools has become widely recognized (Contreras et al., 2008; Thomas & Collier, 1997; Wright, 2006), their transition from secondary to tertiary levels of education has received scarce regional and national attention.

In their recent statistical analysis of the postsecondary attainment of linguistic minority students from the National Education Longitudinal Study of 1988 dataset (NELS: 88), Kanno and Cromley (2010) conclude that one in five English learner (EL) students drops out of high school. One in two EL students does not attend any form of postsecondary education and within 8 years of high school graduation, while one in three native speakers of English receives a bachelor's degree, only one in eight ELs does. Through quantitative analyses, Callahan (2005) and her colleagues (Callahan, Wilkinson, & Muller, 2010) have attempted to understand the underachievement of linguistic minorities in high school. Her study of a California high school (2005) suggests that tracking and course enrollment rather than language proficiency were better predictors of these students' academic achievement. More recently, by examining linguistic minority students and their performance in the Education Longitudinal Study (ELS) of 2002 dataset, Callahan et al. (2010) conclude that designation as ELs actually can hinder these students' pursuit of postsecondary education, either because ESOL course scheduling does not allow for these students to take higher-level college requirements or because they are viewed by gatekeepers as incapable of taking such classes. Callahan et al. further found that these students were significantly less likely than their native English speaker counterparts to take advanced classes in math and science, which are critical to applying to a four-year college. Mosqueda's (2007) dissertation analysis of Latino ELs in the same ELS dataset of 2002 concludes that Latino ELs underachieve in math compared to their non-EL counterparts mainly due to lack of prior access to high level math courses and to teachers certified in math (see also Mosqueda, this volume).

These studies have provided useful statistical information and indicators of structural barriers impeding linguistic minority students' access to and retention in college. However, they have not been able to provide as much information about how students negotiate such barriers as they make life decisions. Louie's (2007) overview of college transitions argues that what is missing is an understanding of "specifically how (an) individual negotiates and is received by the educational system, to become prepared for, to get access to, (and) obtain financing for college (or not)" (p. 2224). A limited number of qualitative studies on this topic, such as Harklau (2000a, 2000b, 2001, 2009) and the study we conducted (Kanno et al., 2011; Kanno & Varghese, 2010; Oropeza, et al., 2010) provide more of a window into the process of this type of negotiation. Only a limited number of scholars have examined minority students' agency in their efforts to acquire a postsecondary education (Knight, 2003; Morales, Herrera, & Murry, 2009; Stanton-Salazar, 2001) and none have done so from linguistic minority students' perspectives. Focusing on understanding the agency of linguistic minority students as we have done in our work and in this chapter contributes to our understanding of how linguistic minority students do or do not exert individual will to overcome limited linguistic, material, and cultural resources, as well as how they negotiate these resources.

Oropeza et al. (2010), Kanno and Varghese (2010), and Kanno et al. (2011) have provided initial information about the challenges and the individual agency of linguistic minority students who had been successfully admitted into college, specifically a four-year college, and how this agency developed and was used to negotiate institutional resources and challenges. However, as of yet we lack studies regarding how the agency of these students is also created by them through their narratives and discourse. In this chapter I draw on one specific linguistic minority student's narrative to show that college-bound linguistic minority student agency can be indicated most powerfully not necessarily by what actions students take but by students' discursive constructions of themselves as powerful agents. I show that agency can be seen in the ways that students construct themselves discursively as agents who can overcome barriers. Therefore, I show that the way individual students are able or unable to access and articulate particular discourses needs to be taken into account when analyzing their potential success in accessing and navigating college. I also argue that this sort of analysis makes the relationship between agency and structure salient, by showing that the availability of these discourses and students' ability to avail themselves of such discourses are often connected to particular forms of capital.

Theoretical Framework: Constraint Agency and Discursive Construction

The theoretical framework I use here is based on the work of Bourdieu (1977, 1986) as articulated by Mills and Gale (2007) and the work of Bakhtin (1981, 1986). The relationship between agency and structure has been one of the most enduring problems in anthropology and sociology (e.g., Archer, 2003; Ortner, 1984; Sewell, 1992) and a significant aspect of the work done by Bourdieu. Fundamentally, the debate concerns how social structures condition human conduct and to what extent agency can be enacted: i.e., how individuals can exercise their will to determine their own fate. Bakhtin's work (1981,1986), on the other hand, is used in this chapter to understanding the discursive nature of this agency—viewing the student narratives and the narratives of their agency as "resolutely grounded in language" (Johnston, 1997, p. 687).

The framework, therefore, draws on Bourdieu's (1977; Bourdieu & Passeron, 1990) conceptualization of the relationship between *agency* and *capital*, which Mills and Gale (2007) articulate as *constraint agency*. Although Bourdieu's work has been criticized significantly in that it has been viewed as being overly deterministic (Caillé, 1992; Jenkins, 1982), scholars such as Mills and Gale (2007) have recently revisited it to counter this accusation. The notion of *constraint agency,* as referred to by Mills and Gale and present in Bourdieu's work, suggests that individuals can make choices although such choices are constrained by their habitus and the resources to which they have access:

> All activity and knowledge [are] always informed by a relationship between where the agent has been and how their history has been incorporated, on the one hand, and their context or circumstances (both in a general sense and "of the moment"), on the other.
>
> *(Mills & Gale, 2007, p. 437)*

Mills and Gale argue that what is significant about Bourdieu's interpretation of social action is that it is not constituted by norms and people following internalized rules; rather, individuals take certain actions based on who and what they are, and who and what they are is constrained by the varying forms and amounts of capital to which they have access.

In this chapter, I therefore argue that linguistic minority students are able to talk about making decisions by accessing resources beyond the networks to which they belong, the classes in which they are placed, and the economic resources they have at hand. Their talk and the decisions they are able to make are nevertheless influenced by the different forms of capital initially available to them.

This approach of focusing on "constraint agency" specifically—that is, looking at the different forms of capital these students bring, create, and are provided with both in and outside school—along with the characteristics of individual students, supports an in-depth and broad look at the process by which student and institutional dynamics come into play in shaping how students make decisions about their postsecondary pursuits and experiences.

In this chapter, the focus is more specifically on how students actually construct their narratives about these decisions: what discourses they view as compelling, what discourses are present, and what they draw upon in constructing their agentive selves. The work of Bakhtin (1981, 1986) and his theory of language have been used by a number of scholars in various fields for this purpose. What is significant about using his work is that it enables me to look at students' narrative of how they got into college and how they stayed as discursively constructed but amidst competing and sometimes contradictory discourses which are ideologically saturated (Blackledge, 2002; Johnston, 1997). A Bakhtinian framework allows me not only to consider how agency plays out in this narrative but also to look at how it is related to available and compelling discourses in the particular social context of college access and the lives of linguistic minority students. Here I do not apply detailed linguistic analysis but I draw on Johnston's (1997) use of Bakhtin to analyze the discursive construction of life history narratives. In a study of EFL teachers' life stories as discursive constructions, Johnston explains his approach, arguing that

> rather than simply describing a preexisting reality—the life story—each telling of a life is created for the specific occasion of that telling, partly using "available forms of discourse" (Weiler, p. 41) but also in that are sensitive to the various interests at stake.
>
> (p. 683)

I draw on some of the same Bakhtinian methodology for looking at narratives in interviews as used by Johnston in analyzing one linguistic minority student's agentive construction of herself.

Method

This chapter is based on a study that I, along with colleagues (Kanno et al., 2011; Kanno & Varghese, 2010; Oropeza et al., 2010), conducted regarding linguistic minority students' experiences accessing and experiencing college. We conducted 1.5- to 2-hour in-depth qualitative interviews with 33 first-generation immigrant and refugee freshman students during their first year of college at "Northern Green University," a major public university. We also interviewed seven institutional personnel (e.g., the past and present directors of the campus ESL programs). Student participants were selected based on initial surveys distributed in ESL classes. Relevant documents were also collected such as curriculum guidelines for ESL classes, statistics on number of ESL students, university policy guidelines on English language requirements and state policies. During the interviews, questions focused on the challenges the students faced in applying to college as well as their initial experiences in college. Students responded in interviews about their academic and social college experiences and college application process in high school. While an interview protocol based on the literature was used, we also modified questions in each interview to explore the unique circumstances of each participant. All the student interviews were audio-recorded and transcribed.

In this chapter, I focus on the interview with one particular student, Mickey, to show how student agency and navigation within a postsecondary institution is discursively constructed. I read through the interview multiple times, making notes about when and how she talked about barriers that presented themselves and when and how she overcame them. As Johnston (1997) makes clear, a Bakhtinian approach requires not a content analysis of the narrative but more of a holistic examination of the text. I therefore examine in particular how Mickey narrates the story of how she accessed college and her experiences in college, the discursive moves she makes in doing so as well as the discourses that are available and that she draws on in the narration itself. Some specific Bakhtinian discursive strategies that Johnston (1997) uses in his analysis and that I looked for included: (a) "primary and secondary discourses," when one discourse was prominent or the most important but another less prominent one was still present; (b) "double voicing," when competing discourses existed together; (c) "authoritative," discourses that were personally salient and compelling for the student; and (d) use of "quotatives," discourses that Mickey had drawn from elsewhere but that she repeated as her own.

Mickey was a Somali who was raised in Kenya and came to the United States with her mother and siblings at age 14. They joined Mickey's father, who had immigrated to the United States 2 years earlier. Mickey's parents completed high school and had strong English skills prior to immigrating. Mickey's father worked in information technology and her mother worked as a teacher with refugees. Mickey completed seventh grade in Kenya and had 8 years of English language instruction before coming to the United States. Mickey also attended summer school in the United States the summer before entering eighth grade, which she said helped her transition. Mickey did not participate in ESL instruction in school in the United States. She learned about resources for college from her school counselor and through a university minority outreach program. Mickey was also required to take remedial ESL courses at Northern Green. I focus on Mickey and her narrative for this chapter for several reasons. First, she was institutionally defined as disadvantaged. She was part of the Educational Opportunity Program (EOP) at Northern Green because she was a racial minority and also a low-income student. As part of the EOP, she had access to tutoring services, a counselor, and a general advising center. However, in spite of these numerous structural barriers, her narrative contained a strong element of how she saw herself as having agency as well as particular discourses she was drawing from to overcome any barriers. In addition, out of all the students we interviewed, Mickey's responses were the lengthiest and she had a remarkable ability to express why she took certain actions and made certain decisions. Therefore, her interview and narrative made the most sense to select in terms of a discursive approach and analysis.

In this chapter, I explore several major insights gained through this analysis. First, I show how Mickey developed a discursive presentation of herself as capable of overcoming significant challenges. While this was a discourse that one would assume would come mainly from mainstream U.S. ideologies of immigrants and success, she actually talked about it as coming from her father. Second, I argue that although Mickey's primary discourse is of her ability to overcome challenges, she also demonstrates a secondary discourse of the importance of familial capital to help her in terms of emotional support. Third, I show how in her narrative, Mickey shows competing discourses of the superiority of both the Somalian/Kenyan educational system and that of the United States but draws on the latter to describe her agency and her ability to gain access to college. Finally, I illustrate the presence in Mickey's narrative of the awareness of structural challenges that exist for linguistic minorities like herself and her ability to present them as having "constraint agency"—that is, agency within structural confines. In all, I suggest that it is important to consider not only the material actions and effects of student agency, but also how students construct and narrate themselves as agentive through the discourses they avail themselves of and articulate. By putting forth this definition of agency, I show that in understanding the path towards accessing college, we need to examine how students talk about themselves and their view of themselves as agentive in this path. This type of analysis, I show, can also reveal the different discourses as well as forms of capital and resources that students access as they articulate themselves as agentive.

Findings

"You Can Do It": Mickey's Discursive Presentation of Agency in Accessing and Staying in College

The main discursive version that Mickey presents of herself in her narrative of how she got into college and her persistence in college is that she made an effort and made it happen whatever the obstacles were. This could be viewed as mainly an American ideological discourse of individualism that Mickey has strongly endorsed as a first generation immigrant. However, her constant references to her father's belief in getting ahead, especially through quotatives, allows us to see that it is a discourse that has been made available to her repeatedly from her home.

Mickey describes three key incidents; taken together, these make a coherent narrative of how she views her path to college. The first incident is her establishment of a relationship with her high school counselor. When asked about the barriers for EL students, Mickey responds that a major barrier for them is to learn a new system and provides the following as an example:

> So even in high school some of things I didn't know they had a scholar-ship, what is it called? A counselor. I knew they had—I knew what a counselor was, someone who can helps you. I didn't know it was someone you could go and say, "I don't know what I am doing actually should I take this class? Or da-da-da." I didn't know that stuff until I was in my junior year of high school that's when I realized that all this information was available to me and that's when I started making use of it. I went to my counselor and said, "Hi, my name is Mickey. I don't believe you met me before, but you have been my counselor for two years. But anyway, we are going to be friends now."

The second incident relates how Mickey befriended a staff person in her high school who was part of the scholarship committee and who provided her information about various scholarships to apply to. Once again, Mickey casts herself as the agent responsible for making this happen: "I just made that con-nection and then she eased up slowly and slowly and slowly and this time I tell her my stories."

The third incident narrates Mickey's persistence when she was initially denied Equal Opportunity Program (EOP) counseling and services at North-ern Green. In institutes of higher education, students receive services based on their categories. By receiving EOP services, Mickey would be getting academic and personal counseling, advocacy, and support with financial aid and hous-ing, placement testing, academic tutoring, and special instruction—services she would not be getting as an ESL student. When Mickey went to see an advisor in the EOP office to ask some questions, the advisor asked whether she was an ESL student. Mickey did not know how to answer because she had never taken an ESL course in high school. The counselor then checked her SAT verbal score and told her that she probably had ESL requirements, and that if she was an ESL student, her office could not advise her. But Mickey por-trayed herself in this narrative as not budging. She "just kept asking her—'why, why, why?'" As a result of her persistence, Mickey reported that she persuaded the advisor to check her records again and on a second perusal, the counselor noticed that Mickey was in fact a recipient of the Diversity Scholars Award, a Northern Green scholarship given to high-achieving underrepresented minor-ity freshman students. When Mickey confirmed that she was indeed a Diversity Scholar, the advisor told her that, in that case, the EOP office was able to help her after all. What is clear about Mickey's discursive representation of how she got into college is the primacy of agency. The incidents she chooses to describe highlight what she sees herself as being able to accomplish.

Throughout the interview, Mickey refers to her father's words when talking about the importance of striving for things. Early in the interview, when asked how much her family knew about the educational system in the United States, she talks about her father's interest in Americans who had become successful:

> We basically watched movies and we saw the lifestyle and thought that is a better lifestyle probably. But my dad was the one who actually inspired us all. He actually read this book that was called um—what was it? *"Think Big,"* um, um what is it? *"Think Big* something" *"Become Rich"* or something like that and then it has all of the most famous success-ful people. Like George, like the guy who invented peanut butter and Fredrick Douglas and all these people that found that education actually something much more successful than just doing general labor work. He was really inspired by that book and he wanted more for his kids and he's like "The only way to do that is come here and give my kids that oppor-tunity." And I am glad that he did that because once I came here a lot opened up for me and I realized a lot of things. Yeah.

Mickey's narrative is peppered with these quotatives, where in her discourse she has internalized her father's voice of trying hard and working hard to achieve success. In all, then, the primary discourse Mickey draws on and presents is that of her individual strength to overcome the number of challenges that have arisen. This primary discourse is one that her father has provided for her family although one can argue that the societal norms of the United States have played a critical part in amplifying their importance.

Selective Acculturation: Drawing on a Secondary Discourse of Familial Capital

Although Mickey's primary discourse of being agentive was that of individual-ism and her own ability to overcome challenges, as I showed above, she also constructed herself as agentive by drawing upon a secondary discourse of her familial support. In this secondary discourse that Mickey draws upon in her narrative, she portrays her family as providing her stability and strength, as well as connections to the Somali community and the Muslim religion. Throughout the interview, Mickey talks voluminously about her family and how her family has helped her in supporting her decisions and also providing her with stability. When asked about her friends on campus, for example, Mickey explains that she is not accustomed to the idea of hanging out. She relates a story about when she was in high school and one of her good friends asked her over for a slumber party, and she could not go because her priority was her family. When explain-ing why she could not accept her friend's invitation, she observes:

> I have a different system of living. I can't go out and say "oh mom you know what, I have a different life from you. I am going to live my own

life." My life revolves around my family ... it's like even if they didn't say stay home, I am just so accustomed to it that it's too odd for me to go out and hang out and stuff, you know ... the idea of coming together and that's one that most American people miss out.

In the Mickey's discursive construction of agency, what is important is not as much whether Mickey directly drew on her family's strength (which she undoubtedly did), but rather how salient the discursive strategy of familial capital was in her narrative of accessing and staying in college as a means of providing her stability and reassurance.

Mickey's discursive construction of her family as contributing to her agency resonates with recent theories of how immigrants integrate into U.S. society. In particular, work has focused on the notion of selective acculturation where immigrant groups who have become upwardly mobile have also maintained strong ties to their families and ethnic community. In a review of the literature, Gibson (2010) confirms the importance of such a category and group:

> A major finding to emerge from the international cases cited here, as well as recent studies is that minority students do better in school when they feel strongly anchored in the identities of their families, communities and peers and when they feel supported in pursuing a strategy of selective or additive acculturation.... Conversely, those at greater risk of failure are those who feel disenfranchised from their culture.
>
> *(p. 19)*

Somalia/Kenya and the United States: Double-Voicing in Mickey's Dual Frames of Reference

Mickey's dual frames of reference were constructed with two different voices: one that positioned the United States' educational system as superior, and the other that favored the Kenyan/Somalian educational system over that of the United States. These discourses existed together. However, it is also important to note that it is the U.S. educational system that has primacy in her narrative and is the most compelling for how she got into college. She describes the Kenyan/Somali system of education mainly as one that is restrictive—both in terms of opportunities as well as creativity:

> Most of the people they just go to eight grade and try to start a general business ... and so coming here was actually much more beneficial; one this is you get aid from the government, another thing is they have wonderful facilities.
>
> Here I have noticed that most of the teachers in elementary they get the kids, they get the kids to think and to reason about things and explore while back there it's just like ok, "2 plus 2 = 4, got it? Got it."

But interestingly, she also speaks of the Kenyan/Somali system as being superior in the sense that it is based on a deeper understanding of content:

> So one thing I realized was most of the American student was doing things based on "Get it done." Get it done, you are finished, you are free, you can go. That's it. For us it's completely different. We have been taught that when you learn something it is valuable to you and it sticks to you.

Mickey's comparisons of the American and Somali educational systems seem to draw upon "dual frames of reference." These have been theorized to be a significant aspect of immigrants' attitudes towards schooling and the host society (Ogbu, 1991; Suarez-Orozco, 1989). The dual frames of reference refer to the frame of reference towards their country of origin and their host society. In the case of voluntary immigrants and first generation immigrants, the observation has been that they have more positive attitudes towards their host society and this makes them achieve better than in school than immigrants who feel more negatively towards the host society. Even though this concept is a psychological or psychosocial one, it also useful to view it discursively: i.e. as a way that someone talks about their perspective of their home country and the country that has taken them in.

Bakhtin's idea of double voicing provides us with the ability to view Mickey's dual frames of reference as discursively constructed in a more complex way than dual frames of reference are usually portrayed. Two discourses are able to co-exist together for Mickey, each that claims the superiority of one educational system over the other; however, it is the U.S.-based one that she draws on primarily in her narrative and seems most compelling to her in discussing her ability to navigate high school and get into college.

The Discursive Context of Agency and Structure

Although, as I show repeatedly in this chapter, Mickey's discursive presentation of gaining access to college focuses on her agency and ability to overcome barriers, there is nevertheless a sense of awareness of constraint agency in the discursive context that Mickey narrates in her story. It is interesting and relevant to note that when asked about the challenges ELs face in this process, she repeatedly states that they (although she does not include herself) are not given enough information about how to successfully navigate this pathway. Structural aspects are highly salient in the discursive context of trying to get into college. Even when she narrates her agentive moves, she simultaneously provides a detailed accounting of potential structural constraints for ELs unfamiliar with the American educational system such as knowledge of the different classes needed to apply to college, the establishment of a strong relationship with the school counselor, working on and writing the college application, and becoming aware and applying for scholarships. Such structural constraints—meeting the pre-requisites for college, having a roadmap for college, having strong relationships with counselors, being able to successfully fill out a college application—have been discussed in the literature as major factors that can act as barriers for minority students to access college (Bowen et al., 2005; McDonough, 1997; McLanahan & Sandefur, 1994; Schneider & Stevenson, 1999).

Constraint agency is also indicated in Mickey's talk about ELs having "not enough exposure to information and not knowing that they can get help" as well as not having "tactics on how to deal with their problems." Therefore, the discursive context that Mickey operates in is one where she is aware of these kinds of barriers—more for other ELs than for herself. In fact, when asked what she thought was the biggest barrier for ELs, she responds that it is "self-esteem," underscoring the primacy of the discourse of agency and the importance of something from within that would help in overcoming such barriers. Therefore, these discourses of agency and structure are not contradictory for Mickey but exist together in creating a discursive context where both have to be viewed as acting together and providing a backdrop for Mickey's narrative.

Conclusions

The study presented in this chapter adds to a few others that have underscored the primacy of agency and how agency is related to structural challenges in minority students'—in this case, linguistic minority students'—access to college. However, this study also shows that when we highlight agentive selves as being crucial to how linguistic minority students see themselves successfully, the discourses they draw on and the discursive construction of these agentive selves are critical to examine. This analysis emphasizes that the concept of agency is not necessarily one of intention or completed action alone but equally that of a discursive strategy or set of strategies that students deploy to narrate themselves and their pathways to college. Such a discursive approach and analysis provides multiple insights. First, it shows that even if interviews and narratives (of actions) cannot be viewed as "the truth" or something that the individual has actually done, they should be viewed as critical tools that can reveal how students articulate themselves, their sense of agency, and what resources, ideas, and ways of talking/being are compelling to them. By using a Bakhtinian framework, we can see that what we may assume as the single root of a belief or an idea may have other beliefs connected to it. For instance, I show how in Mickey's case, her father's discourse of agency and making an effort has also permeated and reinforced her narrative of individualism and meritocracy.

A discursive approach also shows that discourses that may seem contradictory on the face of it might nevertheless co-exist together. Examining this interview as a word-world correspondence would have forced us into a psychological or cognitive analysis that would have made us interpret these ideas as purely contradictory. In this chapter, I show that Mickey's sense of agency is connected to discursive strategies that incorporate a positive dual frame of reference and familial capital. However, I propose that such discourses can also exist alongside others, such as aspects of a negative dual frame of reference, which are part and parcel of competing discourses that exist for all individuals.

I also show that the discursive context that Mickey's narrative exists within is that where structure and agency are interrelated—both negatively and positively. She both implicitly and explicitly describes the structural challenges faced by linguistic minority students. But she is also aware of her familial capital: Albeit from a family of a lower socioeconomic status, she talks about having other forms of capital at her disposal, such as her parents' and her ability to speak English, her parents' employment and especially that of her mother as well as her family and community network. Her sense of agency must therefore be considered in relationship to both the challenges she describes as well as the advantages she talks about herself as having.

Finally, what Johnston (1997) writes about EFL teachers' careers in Poland can also be said of the narratives of linguistic minority students' access to and persistence in college: "These lives are lived in complex contexts in which personal, educational, political, and socioeconomic discourses all influence the way the life is told" (p. 708). Examining these narratives through a lens and analytical framework of discursive construction can shed some light on what such discourses are as well as how agency is articulated discursively for linguistic minority students in the way they narrate their own stories.

References

Archer, M. S. (2003). *Structure, agency and the internal conversation.* Cambridge, England: Cambridge University Press.

Bakhtin, M. M. (1981). *The dialogic imagination* (C. Emerson & M. Holquist, Trans.). Austin: University of Texas Press.

Bakhtin, M. M. (1986). *Speech genres and other late essays* (V. W. McGhee, Trans.). Austin: University of Texas Press.

Blackledge, A. (2002). The discursive construction of national identity in multilingual Britain. *Journal of Language, Identity and Education 1*(1), 67–87.

Bourdieu, P. (1977). Cultural reproduction and social reproduction. In J. Karabel & A. H. Halsey (Eds.), *Power and ideology in education* (pp. 487–511). New York: Oxford University Press.

Bourdieu, P. (1986). The forms of capital. In J. G. Richardson (Ed.), *Handbook of theory and research for the sociology of education.* (pp. 241–258). Westport, CT: Greenwood Press.

Bourdieu, P., & Passeron, J.-C. (1990). *Reproduction in education, society and culture* (R. Nice, Trans., 2nd ed.). London: Sage.

Bowen, W. G., Kurzwell, M. A., & Tobin, E. M. (2005). *Equity and excellence in American higher education.* Charlottesville: University of Virginia Press.

Caillé, A. (1992). Esquisse d'une critique de l'économie générale de la pratique [A critique of the general economy of an outline of a theory of practice]. *Cahiers du LASA, 12/13,* 109–219.

Callahan, R. M. (2005). Tracking and high school English learners: Limiting opportunity to learn. *American Educational Research Journal, 42*(2), 305–328.

Callahan, R. M., Wilkinson, L., & Muller, C. (2010). Academic achievement and course taking among language minority youth in U.S. schools: Effects of ESL placement. *Educational Evaluation and Policy Analysis, 32*(1), 84–117.

Contreras, F., Stritikus, T., O'Reilly-Diaz, K., Torres, K., Sanchez, I., Esqueda, M. Ortega, L., Sepulveda, A., & Guzman, B. (2008). *Understanding opportunities to learn for Latino students in Washington.* Report prepared for the Washington State Commission on Hispanic Affairs and the Washington State Legislature. Retrieved from http://www.kcts9.org/files/WA%20 Latino%20Achievement%20Gap%20Executive%20Summary.pdf

Gibson, M. A. (2010, October). *Exploring and explaining the variability: The school performance of today's immigrant students.* Paper presented at the Conference on the Second Generation, Jerome Levy Economic Institute, Bard College, Annandale-on-Hudson, NY.

Gray, M. J., Rolph, E., & Melamid, E. (1996). *Immigration and higher education: Institutional responses to changing demographics.* Santa Monica, CA: RAND.

Harklau, L. (2000a). From the "good kids" to the "worst": Representations of English language learners across educational settings. *TESOL Quarterly, 34*(1), 35–67.

Harklau, L. (2000b). Representations of immigrant language minorities in U.S. higher education. *Race Ethnicity and Education, 2*(2) 257–276.

Harklau, L. (2001). From high school to college: Student perspectives on literacy practices. *Journal of Literacy Research, 33*(1), 33–70.

Harklau, L. (2009, April). *Why Izzie didn't go to college: Choosing work over college as emergent Latina feminism.* Paper presented at the American Educational Research Association Annual Meeting, San Diego, CA.

Jenkins, R. (1982). Pierre Bourdieu and the reproduction of determinism. *Sociology, 16*(2), 270–281.

Johnston, B. (1997). Do EFL teachers have careers? *TESOL Quarterly, 31*, 681–712.

Kanno, Y., & Cromley, J. (2010, March). *How many ELLs go to college?* Paper presented at the TESOL Convention, Boston, MA.

Kanno, Y., & Varghese, M. (2010). Immigrant English language learners' challenges to accessing four-year college education: From language policy to educational policy. *Journal of Language, Identity and Education, 9*(5), 310–328.

Kanno, Y. Varghese, M., & Fuentes, R. (2011). *Agency and structure in immigrant English language learners' access to four-year college education.* Manuscript submitted for publication.

Knight, M. G. (2003). Through urban youth's eyes: Negotiating K-16 policies, practices, and their futures. *Educational Policy, 17*(5), 531–557.

Louie, V. (2007). Who makes the transition to college? Why should we care, what we know and what we need to do. *Teachers College Record, 109*(10), 2222–2251.

Louie. V. (2008). Second generation pessimism and optimism: How Chinese and Dominicans understand education and mobility through ethnic and transnational orientations. *International Migration Review, 40*(3), 537–572.

McDonough, P. M. (1997). *Choosing colleges: How social class and schools structure opportunity.* Albany: State University of New York Press.

McLanahan, S., & Sandefur, G. (1994). *Growing up with a single parent.* Cambridge, MA: Harvard University Press.

Mills, C., & Gale, T. (2007). Researching social inequalities in education: Towards a Bourdieuian methodology. *International Journal of Qualitative Studies in Education, 20*, 433–477.

Morales, A., Herrera, S., & Murry, K. (2009). Navigating the waves of social and political capriciousness: Inspiring perspectives from DREAM-eligible immigrant students. *Journal of Hispanic Higher Education, 8*, 1–18.

Mosqueda, E. (2007). *English proficiency, tracking, and the mathematics achievement of Latino English learners.* Unpublished doctoral dissertation, Harvard University, Cambridge, MA.

Ogbu, J. (1991). Immigrant and involuntary minorities in comparative perspective. In M. Gibson & J. Ogbu (Eds.), *Minority status and schooling: A comparative study of immigrant and involuntary minorities* (pp. 249–285). New York: Garland Press.

Oropeza, M., Varghese, M., & Kanno, Y. (2010). Linguistic minority students in higher education: Using, resisting, and negotiating multiple labels. *Equity and Excellence in Education, 43*(2), 216–231.

Ortner, S. B. (1984). Theory in Anthropology since the Sixties. *Comparative Studies in Society and History, 26*(1), 126–166.

Schneider, B., & Stevenson, D. (1999). *The ambitious generation: America's teenagers, motivated but directionless.* New Haven, CT: Yale University Press.

Sewell, W. H. (1992). A theory of structure: Duality, agency, and transformation. *American Journal of Sociology, 98*(1), 1–29.

Stanton-Salazar, R. D. (2001). *Manufacturing hope and despair: The school and kin support networks of U.S.-Mexican youth.* New York: Teachers College Press.

Suarez-Orozco, M. (1989). *Central American Refugees and U.S. High Schools: A pyschosocial study of motivation and achievement.* Stanford, CA: Stanford University Press.

Thomas, W. P., & Collier, V. (1997). School Effectiveness for Language Minority Students. *NCBE Resource Collection Series, No. 9.* Washington, DC: National Clearinghouse for Bilingual Education.

Vasquez Heilig, J., & Darling-Hammond, L. (2008). Accountability Texas-style: The progress and learning of urban minority students in a high-stakes testing context. *Educational Evaluation and Policy Analysis. 30*(2), 75–110.

Venezia, K., Kirst, M., & Antonio, A. (2004). *Betraying the college dream: How disconnected K-12 and post-secondary systems undermine student aspirations.* San Francisco: Jossey-Bass.

Vernez, G., & Abrahamse, A. (1996). *How immigrants fare in U.S. education.* Santa Monica, CA: RAND Center for Research on Immigration Policy.

Wright, W. (2006). A catch-22 for language learners. *Educational Leadership, 64*(3), 22–27.

PART III

College Experiences and Persistence

10

NAVIGATING "OPEN ACCESS" COMMUNITY COLLEGES

Matriculation Policies and Practices for U.S.-Educated Linguistic Minority Students

George C. Bunch and Ann K. Endris

Increasing attention has been paid by researchers and educators to the fact that U.S.-educated linguistic minority (US-LM) students, sometimes called "Generation 1.5,"[1] do not fit the typical profiles of native-born English speakers or other groups of students learning English, such as adult immigrants with lower levels of English proficiency or students on international visas who often arrive in the United States with high levels of academic preparation (e.g., Harklau, Losey, & Siegal, 1999; Roberge, Siegal, & Harklau, 2009; Valdés, 1992, 2004). While this work has shed light on issues relevant to the instruction of US-LM students in college writing and English as a Second Language (ESL) courses, less research has focused on institutional policies and practices these students must navigate in order to pursue their academic goals (Gray, Rolph, & Melamid, 1996; Kanno & Varghese, 2010), especially at the community college level (Bunch, 2008, 2009; Bunch, Endris, Panayotova, Romero, & Llosa, 2011; Bunch & Panayotova, 2008).

Nationwide, two-thirds of all Latino students beginning postsecondary education do so in community colleges (Katsinas & Tollefson, 2009, cited in Goldrick-Rab, 2010; Solórzano, Rivas, & Velez, 2005), and almost half of all Asian and Pacific Islander students in higher education attend community colleges (Lew, Chang, & Wang, 2005; U.S. Government Accountability Office, 2007). Although the number of these racial and ethnic minority students who can be considered *linguistic* minority is unknown, there is evidence that students from immigrant backgrounds are more likely to attend community colleges than are their U.S.-born counterparts (Vernez & Abrahamse, 1996). Regardless of the precise numbers, immigrant and linguistic minority students are part of a "New Mainstream" that challenges educators and researchers to rethink the traditional normalization of "white, middle-class, [monolingual] English speaking experiences" as "mainstream" (Enright, 2011, p. 111).

Open Access to *What?*

Community colleges are often known as "open-access" institutions because admission is open to almost all students. However, access to courses that bear credit toward degrees, professional certificates, or transfer to four-year institutions is often regulated through placement tests, prerequisites, remedial course sequences, and other gatekeeping measures. Despite the fact that placement results are sometimes characterized as "recommendations" by community colleges, results of the placement process can be used to determine whether students have met prerequisites for college-level courses in English, mathematics, and other disciplines, and what levels of ESL or remedial courses they must take in order to gain access to these courses.

Research on the general student population has shown that students often do not understand the stakes involved in testing and placement, do not prepare for placement tests, and receive little guidance, either in high school or upon entering community college, about the academic expectations of community college or how to navigate the matriculation process (Bueschel, 2004; Grubb, 2006; Rosenbaum, Deil-Amen, & Person, 2006; Venezia, Bracco, & Nodine, 2010). Rosenbaum et al. (2006), studying Midwestern community colleges, documented a wide range of "information problems" stemming from "meager, vague, and even inconsistent information" provided to students as they attempted to make the transition from high school to higher education (p. 98). Students, many of them first-generation college students from working-class backgrounds, often misunderstood the implications of remedial placements, attending courses for months or even an entire year before realizing they were not earning credits toward a degree or transfer to a four-year institution. Students also faced bureaucratic barriers, limited availability of counselors, contradictory or ill-advised guidance from staff, delays in detecting costly mistakes, and a system that placed the responsibility on students to initiate requests for information they did not know they needed (Rosenbaum et al., 2006, pp. 114–126). In California, Venezia et al. (2010) found that students at sample community colleges had encountered little information about community college while in high school, developing "incorrect or misguided" (p. 7) perceptions about higher education at this level. Upon transitioning to community colleges, students were uninformed about the stakes of the placement testing process, rarely took steps to prepare for the assessments, had to wait in long lines for counseling or make appointments weeks in advance, and experienced "post-assessment confusion and frustration" (p. 13).

US-LM students, many of whom are the first in their families to pursue higher education, are likely to encounter the range of problems documented in research on the general student population. But immigrant and linguistic minority students encounter additional hurdles as well (Gray et al., 1996). First, students from immigrant backgrounds are even less likely than other first generation college students to be familiar with the culture and bureaucracy of American institutions of higher education, including the need to seek information proactively and advocate for themselves in negotiating institutional policies. Second, the low amount and quality of information available to students about college-going expectations and procedures may disproportionately impact students from linguistic minority backgrounds. Harklau (2008) observed that much information in high schools about college is available only orally, through morning announcements and class visits from guidance counselors. Written information, when it is available, often has a "generic, abstract quality" (p. 183) that is not helpful to immigrant students in need of detailed information. On the opposite end of the spectrum, Biber, Conrad, Reppen, Byrd, and Helt (2002) have documented the linguistic demands inherent in the "gatekeeping" (p. 12) language of course catalogs, college websites, and interactions with college officials. Frequently, the written and oral language encountered in these "service encounters" (p. 12) is actually more "structurally complex" (p. 33) than the language used in course textbooks and lectures.

In addition to negotiating matriculation policies that apply to all students, US-LM students may also encounter perceptions of their English language abilities and academic potential that reproduce inequalities they faced in their primary and secondary schooling (Enright, 2011; Oropeza, Varghese, & Kanno, 2010; Valdés, 2001). On one hand, US-LM students may encounter deficit orientations that are similar to those ascribed to monolingual English-speaking students assigned to remedial courses (Hull, Rose, Fraser, & Castellano, 1991). In addition, US-LM students face the prospects of being urged, or even required, to "re-become ESL" (Marshall, 2010), an assignment that they often resist due to their experiences in K–12 schools, the stigma associated with the label in higher education (Kanno & Varghese, 2010), and their perception of the amount of time it will take to progress through multiple levels of ESL. Neither ESL nor remedial English course sequences have typically been designed with the strengths and needs of US-LM students in mind, and few mechanisms exist to provide faculty in either program with fundamental knowledge about the nature of bilingualism (e.g., Grosjean, 1982; Valdés, 1992) important for informing the teaching of US-LM students (Bunch et al., 2011).

Chapter Overview and Description of the Study

This chapter explores the testing and placement process that US-LM students in California encounter upon transitioning from high schools to community colleges and how information about this process is, or is not, made available to students. We focus on California because it has the nation's largest linguistic minority population and a community college system that plays a particularly important role in the higher education aspirations of the state's population. Because California's Master Plan for Higher Education reserves initial entry into its public four-year institutions (University of California and California State University) to the top one-third of high-school graduates, the overwhelming majority of the state's population must access higher education through one of the state's 112 community colleges (Woodlief, Thomas, & Orozco, 2003).

We reviewed state policy documents; analyzed information available on 25 California community colleges' websites; interviewed over 50 faculty members, counselors, matriculation staff, and administrators at 10 colleges; and conducted site visits at 5 of these colleges.[2] Our analysis and interpretation of the findings is based on three assumptions (Bunch et al., 2011). First, US-LM students are circumstantial bilinguals who exhibit linguistic strengths in more than one language (Valdés, 1992), have experienced inadequate and inequitable education in U.S. schools (Gándara, Rumberger, Maxwell-Jolly, & Callahan, 2003), and are in need of expanding their linguistic repertoire to include a wider range of academic language and literacy skills in English. Second, interventions for US-LM students should integrate a focus on language development and academic content, provide access to and support in settings that feature authentic uses of academic language and literacy, and accelerate students' progress through credit-bearing academic sequences toward terminal goals (degrees, certificates, transfer). Finally, US-LM students are in need of high-quality, transparent information about placement tests, matriculation procedures, and instructional options so that they can make informed decisions about their own education.

As we discuss in the remainder of the chapter, at most colleges we found a disturbing lack of information provided to US-LM students to help them understand and prepare for the high-stakes testing, placement, and course selection process. We also found little institutional focus on or understanding of the backgrounds, characteristics, strengths, and needs of US-LM students. When this population was targeted, it was often to find ways to refer students to ESL courses, most of which had not been designed with this population in mind. In contrast, at several colleges, personnel articulated the importance of providing high-quality information to US-LM students so that they can make informed decisions about their own education, and explicit efforts were made to provide useful and transparent information to students about the placement process and its relevance for students' pursuit of their academic goals.

Navigating the Matriculation Process

As US-LM students transition from California high schools to community colleges, they encounter a matriculation process designed to include a number of different steps: application to the college; orientation (on-line or in-person);

placement testing in mathematics and either English or ESL (administered either at students' high schools or at the college itself); counseling; the use of multiple measures for placement decisions; and course enrollment. Due in part to a lawsuit settled between the community college system and the Mexican American Legal Defense Fund in 1991, a number of regulations govern how colleges manage the matriculation process, including the selection and validation of testing instruments, the use of multiple measures in the assessment process, and the rights of students to challenge the imposition of course prerequisites (California Community College Assessment Association [CCCAA], 2005; Chancellor's Office, 1998; Grubb, 1999; Perry, Bahr, Rosin, & Woodward, 2010; Shulock & Moore, 2007).

However, the enactment of matriculation steps and enforcement of regulations are complicated by decentralized authority in California's community college system, a strong history and culture of local college autonomy, and the state's perennial budgetary crises (Venezia et al., 2010). As we completed our research, funding for California community colleges continued to deteriorate, with direct impact on matriculation policies and services. Due to funding cuts, soon after the completion of our data collection, the state legislature excused community colleges and districts from adhering to state matriculation regulations. However, even before the suspension of enforcement of these regulations, we found that colleges varied widely in the ways in which the regulations were enacted. At the same time, severe underfunding of counseling services has left students virtually on their own in attempting to navigate the testing and placement processes (Consultation Council Task Force on Assessment, 2008; Gándara, Alvarado, Driscoll, & Orfield, in press; Grubb, 2006; Venezia et al., 2010; Woodlief et al., 2003). Student to counselor ratios in California community colleges have been reported to be over 1,000 to 1, and counselors at some colleges describe how it is virtually impossible for many students to get even short appointments in time for them to act on the advice (Bunch et al., 2011).

ESL or English?

Because US-LM students are neither recent immigrants nor native English speakers, one of the first decisions they face upon entering community college is whether to take an ESL placement test or regular English placement test. This is a high stakes decision, because students who take the ESL test, regardless of their score, are typically placed into an ESL course, and students taking the English test are usually placed into an English course. A full discussion of the relative merits of placement of US-LM students into ESL or developmental English courses is beyond the scope of this chapter, as is a discussion of the appropriateness (or lack thereof) of community college ESL and English placement tests for this population (see Bunch, 2008, 2009; Bunch et al., 2011; Bunch & Panayotova, 2008; Llosa & Bunch, 2011; Valdés & Figueroa, 1994).

Although neither ESL nor remedial English courses are typically designed for US-LM students, it is possible to envision curricula and instructional practices in either program that could promote US-LM students' academic language and literacy development and progress toward academic goals (Kibler, Bunch, & Endris, 2011). Here, our primary focus is on the extent to which students have information on, or even choices regarding, their potential placement in either ESL or remedial English course sequences.

According to guidance the state Chancellor's office provides to colleges on matriculation regulations, students cannot be required to take an ESL test, nor can they be obligated to enroll in ESL courses (CCCAA, 2005, p. 14). However, at many colleges we examined, students were not informed of their right to choose which sequence to enroll in, and little information was provided to guide their choices. Although slightly over half the college websites we reviewed (14 of 25) included some information regarding how students from linguistic minority backgrounds should decide between taking an ESL or a regular English placement test, many used "self-evident" language, such as "the ESL test is for students whose native language is not English and who wish to enroll in ESL classes." Such descriptions provide limited guidance for students who may not identify with either the ESL or native English speaker label (Harklau et al., 1999; Oropeza et al., 2010). Other websites attempted to guide students to either the ESL or English test based on whether students believed English or another language was their strongest, by asking students to consider questions about their linguistic practices (such as whether they use English to speak with friends and coworkers), or what the language of instruction was in their elementary and secondary education. While such questions were undoubtedly designed to assist students in making informed decisions, the requested information oversimplifies the complex linguistic backgrounds of many US-LM students and is not always relevant to whether an ESL or English instructional setting might be best for them (see Bunch & Panayotova, 2008; Matsuda, Canagarajah, Harklau, Hyland, & Warschauer, 2003; Valdés & Figueroa, 1994).

Both our review of websites and interviews with college faculty and staff indicated that many colleges attempt to steer US-LM students toward ESL placement tests and courses. One college website directed students to choose ESL if they were undecided between ESL and English: "If you are not sure, take the ESL test." Other colleges included information on websites or handouts that were clearly designed to attract students to ESL programs, highlighting the "advantages" of ESL while excluding mention of any potential downsides. At one college, the assessment director referred to the ESL test as the "bilingual test" and the English test as the "native speaker test," terminology that suggests that bilingual students, regardless of their proficiency in English, should take the ESL test. An ESL instructor at this college explained that when students take the community college placement tests in high schools (a program coordinated by counselors from the college), if students' home language is not English, they are given the ESL test. As a result, according to the instructor, "half of your [Advanced Placement] English kids … take the ESL test." If this is true, then even those students proficient enough in English to be enrolled in Advanced Placement courses are steered into ESL courses by virtue of being raised in a household where English was the nondominant language.

Instructors and staff at several colleges expressed concern that US-LM students are referred to ESL at times simply because of a "foreign" accent. One interviewee pointed out that when students speak with assessment center receiving staff, which often includes student assistants, they are referred to the ESL test if students "obviously [have] trouble expressing themselves." At a different college, considering it "unfortunate" that US-LM students were often referred to regular English tests, an English instructor reported that efforts were underway to educate counseling and assessment staff to identify "Generation 1.5" students and steer them toward ESL.

Finally, students at some colleges had no choice between taking an ESL or English test, because both tests were embedded into a single placement test session using the ACCUPLACER. The computer-adaptive nature of the ACCUPLACER allows colleges to set up mechanisms whereby students can be branched from ESL to English tests and back again based on background questions asked of students or on students' performance on test items. As they take the ACCUPLACER the way it is set up in some colleges, students are unaware that they have branched into an ESL test or an English test. Some college officials praise this branching capability as an effective response to dilemmas regarding whether ESL or English tests are more appropriate for US-LM students. However, the practice raises ethical questions about the transparency of information provided to students and the extent to which it is consistent with the Chancellor's guidelines stating that students cannot be forced to take an ESL test. In addition, matriculation staff at one college pointed out that native English speakers frequently get automatically branched into the ESL portion due to poor performance on either the regular English or ESL components of the test. As a result, these students receive recommendations to enroll in ESL courses. Although these monolingual English speakers do not actually enroll in ESL courses, it is likely that a number of US-LM students are referred in a similar way, without the option native English speakers have to question their placement into ESL.

What to Expect on Placement Tests

College website information on testing and placement was dominated by discussions of logistics, such as how students should sign up for a testing session and test times and locations. Most websites (21 of 25) also included at least minimal information about the areas tested on ESL and English placement tests (e.g., writing, sentence structure, and reading) and the format of the test (e.g. the number of questions on the test or whether the test was timed or untimed). However, only 14 of the 25 colleges provided the names of the actual placement tests used for both English and ESL, meaning students at almost half of the colleges had no way to seek information or resources outside of the college that might help them prepare for the exams, even if they knew that test preparation was important. Less than half of the websites (11) provided information on where students could find sample questions for ESL tests, 18 did so for regular English, and only 10 colleges referred students to test-taking tips, study guides, or full-length sample tests for either test.

All 25 websites included at least some information about stakes associated with the assessment process, although the websites differed widely in how they described those stakes. Just over one-quarter (7 out of 25) emphasized the stakes of the assessment process, such as one colleges that stated, "Taking math/English assessments is one of the most important steps you will complete in your college life." In contrast, other websites explicitly de-emphasized the stakes involved:

> Please do not worry that your scores on the math and English assessment tests might prevent you from attending college. Test results are used by the college's staff only to help you select the English and/or math classes that best correspond to your skills so you can be a successful student.

Although such language was undoubtedly crafted in part to reduce students' anxiety going into the testing and placement process, the message is also somewhat disingenuous given the high stakes involved, and it could have the unintended consequence of reducing students' chances of preparing themselves to do their best on the exam.

Multiple Measures

One of the fundamental principles of testing in educational settings is that no single test should be used for high stakes decisions (American Educational Research Association, American Psychological Association, & National Council on Measurement in Education, 1999). Particularly for US-LM students, who may perform poorly on placement tests that focus primarily on grammar skills but may be able to fulfill many language functions in English (Llosa & Bunch, 2011; Valdés & Figueroa, 1994), additional measures are particularly important. Based on state regulations, California community college policy requires that colleges use multiple measures to create "a holistic profile of student strengths and weaknesses based on a variety of informational sources" (CCCAA, 2005, p. 3) in order to recommend placements and judge whether students have satisfied prerequisite requirements. According to information provided to the colleges by the Chancellor's office, "typical" measures include standardized placement tests, writing samples, performance-based assessments such as listening comprehension tests and oral interviews, self-evaluation, and surveys and questionnaires eliciting information about college plans (intended major and number of units), hours worked, and "motivation" (CCCAA, 2005). Choice of which specific multiple measures used is left to individual colleges. While a placement test score plus one additional measure (such as an interview with a counselor) constitutes an appropriate use of multiple measures, colleges are directed to err on the side of eliciting and using more rather than less information (CCCAA, 2005, p. 4).

Little publically available information exists regarding what multiple measures colleges use in practice and how these measures are used to inform student placement. At several colleges, according to faculty and staff members, no information other than the placement test score is used for placement unless students question the results of the test. This means that for the vast majority of students at some colleges, there is no use of multiple measures for placement purposes. At one college, in order for a counselor to use multiple measures to assess students' placement and potentially re-place them, students must question their placement recommendations during a group orientation session with between 40 and 150 students.

At a number of colleges, websites emphasized that it was students' responsibility to supply any information beyond placement test scores that they wished to be used for placement purposes. Yet little or no information was made available to students regarding the multiple measure process. Slightly over half of the CC websites (14 out of 25) made some reference to multiple measures or "additional information" used to place students, but these websites rarely stated which measures could be used, how students' might provide additional information, and how colleges use multiple measures in the placement process. In fact, only 1 of the 25 colleges we examined both defined the term and specified the measurement tools on its website.

Meanwhile, although students may not be aware of the practice, several colleges embed multiple measures into the placement test itself, through a set of questions delivered as part of computer-based placement tests. Computer-delivered tests such as ACCUPLACER give local colleges the option of developing their own set of questions that appear as part of the placement test, either before, during, or after the actual test questions. At some colleges, students' responses to questions, such as when they last took an English course, grades received in high school, and what language skills they typically use in their job, are quantified and integrated into students' overall placement test score.

From Placement Test to Course Selection

College websites provided contrasting messages regarding the role students play in using assessment information to make their own course-taking decisions, both across colleges and sometimes within each college's website. Over half of the websites (14) included references to students themselves using the information garnered from the assessment process; 12 described the use of assessment information as a joint one between students and counselors; and 9 presented the information provided to students as "recommendations," "suggestions," or "guidance." On the other hand, over half of the websites (16), including some of the same websites that elsewhere suggested that students could use information from assessments to make their own decisions (with or without consulting with a counselor), also included references that de-emphasized student or counselor agency, describing assessment results as "determining" (the word most frequently used) student placement. Students at many colleges, therefore, were presented with mixed messages regarding their own role in using placement information to make educational decisions. On one website, students were informed that placement test results give students and counselors "an indication of which classes are right for you," and that the matriculation process helps "students make better, more informed educational choices." On the other hand, the same website stated that "it is important to follow your placements because they include prerequisites," which are "strictly enforced."

Such ambiguity represents a fundamental tension in California's testing and placement system. Technically, neither testing nor following placement recommendations is mandatory. Yet in practice, as one interviewee explained it, students are "basically obligated" to take courses they have tested into "because of the prerequisites and the way they're written." An administrator at a different college concurred, stating, "We can't require students to enter these [pre-collegiate] courses … but we have a fairly robust set of prerequisites" for college-level, credit-bearing courses. Thus, students must comply with the testing and placement process in order to progress toward their academic goals.

Meanwhile, some of the most important aspects concerning the stakes of the assessment and placement process were often missing on college websites: how test scores are translated into placement "recommendations," how students should go about selecting courses, and whether those courses carry credit for degrees, certificates, or transfer to four-year institutions. Most websites were silent on these issues, and those that did provide information tended to steer students towards the classes that the placement test recommended, rather than outlining the relative merits of different course-taking decisions. As a result, US-LM students attempting to learn about, and perhaps compare, sequences of both ESL and English courses could do so on less than half of the colleges' websites (11 out of 25). Slightly over half of the colleges (17) provided any website information about ESL or English course sequences. Regarding the crucial issue of which courses include credit that can be used toward either a terminal degree or transfer, only 6 colleges addressed this topic for ESL and only 9 colleges did so for English. Meanwhile, only 3 of the 25 colleges presented information for *both* ESL and English on which courses carry degree credit *and* which courses carry transfer credit.

Challenging Placement Results

Instructors indicated that students are often surprised, and sometimes upset, by unexpectedly low test scores and placements, and state policy requires that colleges have a process in place whereby students can challenge course prerequisites. Nonetheless, interviewees reported that students usually accept their placement recommendations without challenging them. Several college personnel commented that marginalized students, including nonnative English speakers, are the least likely to challenge their placements, due to lack of information about the process as well as having been socialized to respect institutional authority. According to this instructor, "There tends to be more of a sense among our Latino students that the college is the expert," and that the tests "must be good measures if that's what the college is using."

Website information provided to US-LM students about the challenge process is often incomplete or difficult to comprehend. Over one-quarter of the websites we analyzed (7 out of 25) included *no* information about the challenge process. Among colleges that did discuss challenges, only 6 included information about how students can challenge their *placement* recommendation, as opposed to challenging the existence of the prerequisite in the first place. The two types of challenges are related, in that placement exams and multiple measures serve as the fulfillment of a prerequisite. However, this distinction might not always be clear to students, especially when reading college websites that describe the prerequisite challenge process without explaining that the placement exams and multiple measures serve as prerequisites. College websites varied as to the extent to which they clarified the difference between the two types of challenges.

Colleges also differed in whether their presentation of information about the challenge process seemed designed to encourage or discourage students from using this option. Some websites provided information that would likely be inaccessible or intimidating to LM students. For example, one website used bureaucratic and legalistic language to describe its college's challenge process:

> In keeping with the requirements and provisions of Section 55201(f) of Title 5 and Section I.B 1-3 of the XX Community College District Model Policy, XX College has established a procedure by which any student who does not meet a prerequisite or corequisite, or who is not permitted to enroll due to a campus limitation on enrollment, but who provides satisfactory evidence, may seek entry into the class according to the college's challenge process.

A different college's website explained that in order to challenge placements, students must challenge the prerequisite for the course. The website provided detailed information about the grounds for challenging prerequisites but did so using language that would likely be intimidating and discouraging to any student actually considering such a challenge. Students considering mounting a challenge were told that they would have to do one or more of the following, depending on the grounds on which they were challenging the prerequisite:

> Cite the State regulation or District-approved process the prerequisite has violated. Indicate the chapter and section of the law, if known. If available, attach a copy of the regulation or District-approved process to the Challenge Form ... Explain how the prerequisite, corequisite or limitation on enrollment is discriminatory. Does it discriminate against a person on the basis of age, ethnicity, religion, gender or sexual preference? What is it, specifically, about the enrollment limitation that results in discrimination against a person from one or more of these groups?

This same college's description of the challenge process concluded by stating, "It is the responsibility of the student to provide compelling evidence and documentation to support the challenge," and "If there is no documentation provided, then the challenge will automatically be denied." Whether or not such language was intended to be intimidating, discouraging, or difficult to understand, it is unlikely that US-LM students, or others inexperienced with higher education bureaucracies, would find these descriptions encouraging, even if they felt they had strong grounds to mount a challenge.

Promoting Informed Decision Making

As discussed above, the websites we reviewed provided little information for US-LM students about important aspects of their transitions into community college. The information presented on some websites was clearly not designed to be easily accessible or "student-friendly," especially for students from immigrant and linguistic minority backgrounds. Although lack of staff time to maintain websites due to budgetary constraints undoubtedly played a role in the quality of information available on college websites, there were also indications at some colleges of a belief that students should have limited access to information and fewer choices in the matriculation process. For example, some college personnel questioned whether students should be provided information that would encourage them to prepare for placement tests, or even if they should be allowed to prepare. In the words of one testing coordinator, "I don't feel that [they] should [prepare]. It should be based on where they are now." Similarly, a matriculation staff member at a different college stated that students who retake placement tests are "cheating the system."

Even at some colleges that had developed hardcopy material to guide students in various aspects of the matriculation process, the information was withheld from most students. An official at one college reported that staff members at the matriculation office window were not displaying a sheet that matriculation officials had designed to help US-LM students choose between ESL and English placement tests because there was not room on the counter for it. During a site visit to the testing center at another college, a staff member told us that the flyer providing information about the college's placement tests was kept behind the desk and not provided to students unless they asked for it. Yet there was no notice posted or any other way for students to know about the existence of the flyer or that they should ask for it.

Countering policies and practices at some colleges that, intentionally or not, seemed to limit the ability of US-LM students to make informed decisions, personnel and websites at other colleges attempted to provide explicit, comprehensive, and comprehensible information. One ESL instructor, who was also involved in broader efforts to improve developmental education for linguistic minority students, described how oftentimes college personnel misunderstood the challenges US-LM students face in navigating the matriculation and course-selection process:

> It seems as if it's a really straightforward way to people who are inside the system, but it isn't really that clear, you know, what it takes and how you can take certain classes and how you can choose to take classes, especially when you come from cultures where there is more of a hierarchy of information and authority figures and so on where you don't have that many choices. Being aware of those choices and knowing how to negotiate them is important.

A counselor at a different college, frustrated with the fact that students often do not have information about the challenge process, pointed out that students do not know what they can ask for and that they should question policies they see as counter to their interests. Reflecting on his own experiences as attending college as a US-LM student, the counselor said, "I wish I would have questioned this all along, during my [own] education."

Another counselor advocated for orientation sessions to occur before the assessment process, to provide opportunities to discuss with students the importance of placement tests and encourage them to prepare for the tests. She argued that this was particularly important for US-LM students, in order to ensure their best performance on placement tests which would in turn create more accurate placements into courses that would challenge students and enable them to move more quickly through course sequences. At a different college, in response to concerns about testing conditions, the testing director attempted to ensure that students were not overtaxed when they take placement tests by not administering the math test and the ESL or English test to the same students on the same day. A counselor at another college, describing her approach to students interested in enrolling in a course that is slightly higher than the placement test recommends, discussed how she neither encourages nor discourages students to take the higher-level course, but rather attempts to make clear the expectations of the higher-level class in a way that is "realistic" and contains no "sugar-coating."

One college website attempted to communicate clearly with students about how multiple measures can be used to inform placement, describing the practice as follows:

> Multiple measures refers to the use of additional information or assessment tools that may be used for course placement. Counselors are prepared to discuss with you and review additional measures that may impact your success in a course.

The college then listed "examples of other measures that may be used to determine appropriate course placement," including high school transcripts, college transcripts indicating work completed at other institutions, SAT or ACT test scores, educational goals, "skills and knowledge that have been gained through working," and the number of hours students spend working each week.

Several colleges also demonstrated explicit attempts to provide clear and comprehensive information for students to understand what kind of credit is granted for each ESL and English course. One college, for example, organized its list of the entire English course sequence into three categories, making it clear what kind of credit was involved for every English course: "READINESS for college-level reading"; "COLLEGE LEVEL (AA/AS degree-applicable)"; and "TRANSFER LEVEL (satisfies reading competency for AA/AS degree and transfer to [California State University])."

A different college, in its website's explanation of how students should use placement results to select courses, guided students through the placement results, suggested students might want to retake certain sections if they scored close to the next highest level, and provided explicit guidelines for how students could do so. The same website provided guidance for students to make informed decisions regarding what course to take if they scored on the "borderline" between two levels:

> If your score falls in a "Decision Zone," this will be noted under the course listed on the computer printout. Your skills appear to be on the borderline in terms of your readiness for the higher course.... You will need to decide which course will be best for you to enroll in. You may find you must apply good study skills and probably more time than other students to be successful if you choose to enroll in the higher course. You may wish to discuss your options with a counselor before you make your decision.

Finally, one college promoted informed decision making through its use of directed self-placement for ESL. Students who had already either self-selected or been referred to ESL were provided target materials representing reading and writing levels associated with each ESL course. After reviewing examples of written materials from various ESL course levels, considering the topics and skills covered in each course, attending a 45-minute general orientation to college, and consulting with assessment staff, students chose the ESL level they felt was most appropriate and received assistance with enrollment. College administrators reported that results of the self-placement process demonstrated validity on par or greater than the college's previous use of a standardized ESL placement test.[3]

Conclusion

As we have argued throughout this chapter, community college assessment and placement represent high stakes for the education of US-LM students. Yet our analysis found that many colleges, at least in California, provide little or no information regarding the mechanisms of assessment and placement, or the stakes involved. Some colleges provide relevant information, but the information is either difficult to comprehend, presented using a tone that likely discourages students from using it, or is nearly impossible for students to find. As argued earlier, although all students face obstacles because of the unavailability or inaccessibility of information, linguistic minority students are likely to face particular challenges given their still-developing English language proficiency, unfamiliarity with norms and institutional procedures of U.S. higher education, and misperceptions regarding their linguistic strengths and needs as circumstantial bilinguals.

Our study revealed that US-LM students are often provided little information about ESL or English course sequences, the nature of the instruction provided in either, or which courses bear credit toward certificates, degrees, or transfer. At some colleges, US-LM students are encouraged to take ESL courses, often with little actual information provided. At other colleges, students have no choice, either because all linguistic minority students are referred to ESL placement tests, or because a single placement test is used that branches students into ESL or English courses without their knowledge or consent. Meanwhile, colleges underutilize aspects of the matriculation system that could potentially assist them in learning more about US-LM students' strengths and needs, soliciting little information from students to use as multiple measures, and providing students with either minimal or inaccessible language about their rights to challenge their placements and prerequisites.

It is indisputable that California's budget crises and severe underfunding of the community college system hinders efforts to communicate effectively with students, to provide the array of counseling and other matriculation services necessary, to adequately support students' navigation of the testing and placement process, and to promote greater knowledge among faculty, staff, and administrators about how to support US-LM students' language and academic development. However, it is also clear that at some colleges, operating in the same statewide budgetary climate, efforts are underway to provide clear and useful information. Such information addressed the stakes of the matriculation process, the tests used, multiple measures that can be employed, what credit ESL and English courses carry for what purposes, and how students can interpret placement results, choose courses, retake assessments, and challenge placement results. At these colleges, to use the words of interviewees excerpted earlier, the emphasis is not on preventing students from "cheating the system," but rather on helping students to become "aware of [their] choices and [know] how to negotiate them."

Research is clearly necessary to document the impact of different amounts and types of student information on the academic progress of US-LM students in community colleges, an endeavor that was beyond the scope of this study. In the meantime, unless efforts are made to provide US-LM students with high quality, transparent information to assist them in making decisions about their own education, it is likely that traditional patterns of inequity that have placed them in a marginalized position in the first place will be replicated. Fortunately, as demonstrated by the examples presented in the final section of this chapter, both researchers and practitioners can turn to community colleges themselves for ideas on how to provide such information, even in the toughest of financial climates.

Acknowledgments

This research was supported by the William and Flora Hewlett Foundation and the Academic Senate Committee on Research at UC Santa Cruz. Dora Panayotova and Michelle Romero made significant contributions to the data collection and analysis, and we received valuable research assistance from Brian Vickers and Alexandra Pucci. We also benefitted from ongoing conversations with Lorena Llosa during the completion of the project.

Notes

1. Due to the tendency of the term *Generation 1.5* to be used to highlight students' linguistic deficits instead of resources and potential (see Benesch, 2008; Matsuda et al., 2003), we prefer to use *US-educated linguistic minority (US-LM) students* to describe students who were raised in homes where English was not the dominant language, who have attended U.S. high schools, and whose English at the community college level is still considered "suspect" by faculty, staff, or assessment measures.
2. We developed a systematic procedure for website data collection and analysis, capturing every instance of matriculation-related information on each website. We coded and analyzed interviews using a grounded approach that identified predominant themes within and across colleges. More details on the colleges selected, and the research methodology, can be found in Bunch et al. (2011).
3. Despite these results, the practice generated considerable opposition from ESL faculty

members, and the college has recently abandoned self-placement and moved back to the use of a standardized ESL test.

References

American Educational Research Association, American Psychological Association, & National Council on Measurement in Education (1999). *Standards for educational and psychological testing.* Washington DC: American Psychological Association.

Benesch, S. (2008). "Generation 1.5" and its discourses of partiality: A critical analysis. *Journal of Language, Identity, and Education, 7,* 294–311.

Biber, D., Conrad, S., Reppen, R., Byrd, P., & Helt, M. (2002). Speaking and writing in the university: A multidimensional comparison. *TESOL Quarterly, 36*(1), 9–48.

Bunch, G. C. (2008). Language minority students and California community colleges: Current issues and future directions. *Community College Policy Research, 1,* 1–17. Retrieved from http://escholarship.org/uc/item/6x39n5kd#page-1

Bunch, G. C. (2009). Immigrant students, English language proficiency, and transitions from high school to community college. In T. G. Wiley, J. S. Lee, & R. Rumberger (Eds.), *The education of language minority immigrants in the United States* (pp. 263–294). Clevedon, England: Multilingual Matters.

Bunch, G. C., Endris, A., Panayotova, D., Romero, M., & Llosa, L., (2011). *Language testing and placement in California's community colleges: Mapping the terrain.* Report prepared for the William and Flora Hewlett Foundation. Retrieved from http://escholarship.org/uc/item/31m3q6tb

Bunch, G. C., & Panayotova, D. (2008). Latinos, language minority students, and the construction of ESL: Language testing and placement from high school to community college. *Journal of Hispanic Higher Education, 7*(1), 6–30.

California Community College Assessment Association [CCCAA]. (2005). *Assessment Q&A: Questions and answers on assessment for use in the California Community Colleges.* Author.

Chancellor's Office. (1998). Matriculation Regulations: Rev. March, 1998. Student Services and Special Programs Division, California Community Colleges. Retrieved from http://www.cccco.edu/LinkClick.aspx?fileticket=Wn%2fUsAsDJyY%3d&tabid=628&mid=1718

Consultation Council Task Force on Assessment. (2008). *Report of the Consultation Council Task Force on Assessment to the Board of Governors of the California Community Colleges.* Retrieved from http://www.cccco.edu/Portals/4/Executive/Board/2008_agendas/january/3-5_Assessment%20TF%20Report%2001-08.pdf

Enright, K. A. (2011). Language and literacy for a new mainstream. *American Educational Research Journal, 48*(1), 80–118.

Gándara, P., Alvarado, E., Driscoll, A., & Orfield, G. (in press). *Building pathways to transfer: Community colleges that break the chain of failure for students of color.* University of California, Los Angeles.

Gándara, P., Rumberger, R., Maxwell-Jolly, J., & Callahan, R. (2003). English learners in California schools: Unequal resources, unequal outcomes. *Education Policy Analysis Archives 11*(36). Retrieved 12/12/2006, from http://epaa.asu.edu/epaa/v2011n2036/

Goldrick-Rab, S. (2010). Challenges and opportunities for improving community college student success. *Review of Educational Research, 80*(3), 437–469.

Gray, M. J., Rolph, E., & Melamid, E. (1996). *Immigration and higher education: Institutional responses to changing demographic.* Santa Monica, CA: Rand Center for Research on Immigration Policy.

Grosjean, F. (1982). *Life with two languages.* Cambridge, MA: Harvard.

Grubb, W. N. (1999). *Honored but invisible: An inside look at teaching in community colleges.* New York: Routledge.

Grubb, W. N. (2006). "Like, what do I do now?": The dilemmas of guidance counseling. In T. Bailey & V. Smith Morest (Eds.), *Defending the community college equity agenda* (pp. 195–221). Baltimore, MD: Johns Hopkins University Press.

Harklau, L. (2008). Through and beyond high school: Academic challenges and opportunities for college-bound immigrant youth. In L. S. Verplaetse & N. Migliacci (Eds.), *Inclusive pedagogy for English language learners: A handbook of research-informed practices* (pp. 181–194). New York: Taylor & Francis.

Harklau, L., Losey, K. M., & Siegal, M. (Eds.). (1999). *Generation 1.5 meets college composition: Issues in the teaching of writing to U.S.-educated learners of ESL.* Mahwah, NJ: Erlbaum.

Hull, G., Rose, M., Fraser, K. L., & Castellano, M. (1991). Remediation as social construct: Perspectives from an analysis of classroom discourse. *College Composition and Communication, 42*(3), 299–329.

Kanno, Y., & Varghese, M. M. (2010). Immigrant and refugee ESL students' challenges to accessing four-year college education: From language policy to education policy. *Journal of Language, Identity, and Education, 9*(5), 310–328.

Katsinas, S. G., & Tollefson, T. A. (2009). Funding and access issues in public higher education: A community college perspective: Education Policy Center, University of Alabama. Retrieved from http://www.insidehighered.com/content/download/317858/4098893/version/1/file/report.pdf

Kibler, A. K., Bunch, G. C., & Endris, A. K. (2011). Community college practices for U.S.-educated language-minority students: A resource-oriented framework. *Bilingual Research Journal, 34*(2), 201–222.

Lew, J. W., Chang, J. C., & Wang, W. (2005). The overlooked minority: Asian Pacific American students at the community colleges. *Community College Review, 33*, 64–84.

Llosa & Bunch, 2011. *What's in a test? Constructs and characteristics of California's community college ESL and English placement tests and implications for language minority students.* Report prepared for the William and Flora Hewlett Foundation. Retrieved from http://escholarship.org/uc/item/10g691cw

Marshall, S. (2010). Re-becoming ESL: Multilingual university students and a deficit identity. *Language and Education, 24*(1), 41–56.

Matsuda, P. K., Canagarajah, A. S., Harklau, L., Hyland, K., & Warschauer, M. (2003). Changing currents in second language writing research: A colloquium. *Journal of Second Language Writing, 12*, 151–179.

Oropeza, M., Varghese, M., & Kanno, Y. (2010). Linguistic minority students in higher education: Using, resisting, and negotiating multiple labels. *Equity & Excellence in Education, 43*(2), 216–231.

Perry, M., Bahr, P. R., Rosin, M., & Woodward, K. M. (2010). *Course-taking patterns, policies, and practices in developmental education in the California Community College* (A report to the California Community College Chancellor's Office). Retrieved from EdSource: Clarifying Complex Education Issues website: http://www.edsource.org/assets/files/ccstudy/FULL-CC-DevelopmentalCoursetaking.pdf

Roberge, M., Siegal, M., & Harklau, L. (Eds.). (2009). *Generation 1.5 in college composition: Teaching academic writing to U.S.-educated learners of ESL.* Mahwah, NJ: Erlbaum.

Rosenbaum, J. E., Deil-Amen, R., & Person, A. E. (2006). *After admission: From college access to college success.* New York: Russell Sage Foundation.

Shulock, N., & Moore, C. (2007). *Beyond the open door: Increasing student success in California community colleges.* Sacramento, CA: Institute for Higher Education Leadership & Policy.

Solórzano, D. G., Rivas, M., & Velez, V. (2005). *Community college as a pathway to Chicana/o doctorate production.* Los Angeles: UCLA Chicano Studies Research Center.

U.S. Government Accountability Office (GAO). (2007). *Information sharing could help institutions identify and address challenges some Asian Americans and Pacific Islander students face* (GAO-07-925): Author.

Valdés, G. (1992). Bilingual minorities and language issues in writing: Toward a professionwide response to a new challenge. *Written Communication, 9*(1), 85–136.

Valdés, G. (2001). *Learning and not learning English: Latino students in American schools.* New York: Teachers College Press.

Valdés, G. (2004). Between support and marginalization: The development of academic language in linguistic minority children. *International Journal of Bilingual Education and Bilingualism,* 7(2&3), 102–132.

Valdés, G., & Figueroa, R. A. (1994). *Bilingualism and testing: A special case of bias.* Norwood, NJ: Ablex.

Venezia, A., Bracco, K., & Nodine, T. (2010). *A one shot deal? Students' perceptions of assessment and course placement at the California Community Colleges.* San Francisco: WestEd.

Vernez, G., & Abrahamse, A. (1996). *How immigrants fare in U.S. education.* Santa Monica, CA: Rand.

Woodlief, B., Thomas, C., & Orozco, G. (2003). *California's gold: Claiming the promise of diversity in our community colleges.* Oakland, CA: California Tomorrow.

11

RETENTION OF ENGLISH LEARNER STUDENTS AT A COMMUNITY COLLEGE

Cate Almon

With their open admissions policies and comparably affordable tuitions, community colleges in the United Students enroll more than half of the nation's first-time freshmen (FF) (Miller, Pope, & Steinmann, 2005) and more of the nation's English learners (EL) than four-year institutions (Kuo, 1999). Whereas these two facts alone should make community colleges an important site for research, there is in fact a dearth of studies on community colleges (Townsend, Donaldson, & Wilson, 2005) and even fewer on the ELs who attend them. Perhaps the gap in research is not surprising, as community colleges generally do not require research from faculty and tend to lack funding for institutional research and record keeping (Sylvia, Song, & Waters, 2010). The gap in research is problematic nonetheless, as it allows for a deficit in knowledge about the effectiveness of the colleges' ability to retain and graduate so many of the nation's students. The empirical study presented here begins to address the performance of ELs at one community college in the hope that it will generate more inquiry into this area.

Perhaps the first extensive study on ELs at a community college was conducted by Belcher (1988). Belcher's institutional report, conducted in response to tremendous growth at Miami-Dade Community College, found dismal success rates where only 16% of ELs completed the English as a second language (ESL) program, and just 7% of ELs who indicated a major graduated. The graduation rate of all ELs was 3%, much lower than the graduation rate at the college (20%). However, ELs seemed to perform better than the rest of the college in terms of grade point average (GPA). Belcher also found that students who began college in lower levels of ESL had lower rates of completing the program, passing the college English placement test, and graduating. While Belcher noted that the EL sample included more nontraditionally-aged students than the rest of the college population, she did not compare performance among ELs by age or other demographic categories to determine whether success rates varied.

Since Belcher's report (1988), a few additional studies have investigated EL success in academic ESL and content courses (Curry, 2001; Song, 2006a, 2006b). Some recent initiatives have looked more comprehensively at community colleges, particularly in California. For example, Patthey-Chavez, Dillon, and Thomas-Spiegel (2005) tracked students who attended ESL and developmental courses at nine community colleges and two universities to determine their percentage rates of completing college. Patthey-Chavez et al. observed that students starting in remedial courses experienced the most difficulty accomplishing their goals, and students who indicated transfer as their goal performed best. ELs who began in high levels of ESL also performed well while those who began in low levels did not.

Spurling, Seymour, and Chisman (2008) reported on a large longitudinal study that tracked ELs who began in noncredit literacy courses at the City College of San Francisco, and made comparisons to those who began college in for-credit ESL courses. They observed that students who began in lower levels of the for-credit courses actually persisted more semesters than those starting in higher levels, converse to what was found in Belcher (1988) and Patthey-Chavez et al. (2005). Spurling et al. (2008) also found that students at the high and low ends of the age distributions (ages 16–19 and ages 35 and over) performed best. They observed that Asian/Pacific Islander students had higher than average persistence whereas Hispanic/Latino students had poorer than average persistence. The EL graduation rate was 26%, similar to the overall graduation rate at the college. Of those who did not graduate, 38% transferred to a university in the state, also close to the overall transfer rate at the college. The authors noted that they were uncertain whether the students had previous college experience, which would have likely made them more successful than FF as has been found in Belcher (1988) and Patthey-Chavez et al. (2005). Although the strength of the study lies in its comprehensiveness, data analyses were limited to descriptive statistics, similar to the studies above, leaving little room for broad interpretations.

There have been retention studies at community colleges on populations other than ELs. For example, Kolajo (2004) used transcript analysis to follow the progress of students who began college in developmental courses. Results suggested that while students performed as well as the rest of the college, the courses added to length of time in college, creating an obstacle to graduation. Sorey and Duggan (2008) concluded that age is related to obstacles to retention where lack of finances was a predictor of withdrawal for nontraditionally-aged students (age 25 and older), and low GPA was a predictor of withdrawal by traditionally-aged students (18–24 years). Race and ethnicity have also been examined in community college retention studies. Lewis and Middleton (2003), for example, synthesized research on African Americans, Lujan, Gallegos, and

Harbour (2003) focused on Latino experience, and Lew, Chang, and Wang (2006) studied Asian Pacific American students. Socioeconomic status has also been linked to dropping out (e.g., Dowd & Melguizo, 2008). In addition, part-time enrollment has been discussed as a predictor for persisting and graduating at the community college (Schmid & Abell, 2003).

The present study aims to include ELs in this line of inquiry since so little is known about ELs' trajectories through community colleges, a context that figures prominently in their education. It contributes to the fields of retention and ELs by using inferential statistics to analyze college-going among ELs as a group as well as among demographic groups within the EL population, and by making comparisons between patterns for ELs and patterns for the rest of the college. It addresses the following research questions:

1. What are the retention patterns of students at one community college who begin college by taking ESL courses, in terms of persistence, ESL program completion, graduation, and GPA?
2. How do persistence, program completion, graduation and GPA vary among students who start college with varying language proficiency levels and demographic characteristics?
3. Are there any significant differences in persistence, degree completion, and GPA between EL and non-EL students at a community college? If so, what are they?

Method

Context

Data for the study were drawn from the FF student records database of the East Penn Community College (EPCC, a pseudonym). The ESL program at EPCC was a four-level for-credit program which aimed to prepare ELs for academic programs of study that were either career-oriented or transferrable to four-year institutions. The majority of ELs immigrated to the United States while others came with student visas. Students generally self-selected into the ESL program and were given a placement test to establish their course level. From the beginning level, the program could be completed in four semesters. Students placed into the beginning two levels were encouraged to take only ESL courses whereas students in the higher two levels could take content courses simultaneously. ELs in the ESL program comprised only 2% of EPCC's students.

Participants

Participants were drawn from the population of 7,129 FF in EPCC's database of students who attended fall semesters 2001–2004. Analysis took place in 2008 in order to allow enough time for students to have graduated given the often part-time and intermittent attendance of community college students. ELs were selected from this group if they began college by taking at least one ESL course. They totaled 161, leaving 6,968 non–ELs (Table 11.1). These 161 ELs are the main focus of this study.

Research Design

The method of transcript analysis is widely regarded as the most accurate and comprehensive way to investigate retention at institutions of higher education (Hagedorn, Chi, Cepeda, & McLain, 2007; Kolajo, 2004; Maxwell et al., 2003).

Variables. Student transcripts in the EPCC database were examined for persistence, GPA, graduation, and demographic information. Dependant variables included GPA, number of falls completed, ESL program completion, and graduation. GPA ranged from 0.00 ("F") to 4.00 ("A"). Graduation included earning an associate degree (60 credits), a certificate (30 credits), or a specialized diploma (6 credits). Age was classified as traditional (18–24 years)

TABLE 11.1 All EL and Non-EL FF at EPCC and Their Characteristics, Falls 2001-2004

Characteristic	Complete samples		Matched samples	
	ELs (n = 161)	Non-ELs (n = 6,968)	ELs (n = 139)	Non-ELs (n = 139)
Age 18-24	72 (45%)	5667 (81%)	58 (42%)	58 (42%)
Age 25+	89 (55%)	1301 (19%)	81 (58%)	81 (58%)
Part-time	130 (81%)	2538 (36%)	109 (78%)	109 (78%)
Full-time	31 (19%)	4430 (64%)	30 (22%)	30 (22%)
Not U.S. resident	43 (27%)	25 (0.4%)	4 (17%)	24 (17%)
U.S. resident	118 (73%)	6943 (99.6%)	115 (83%)	115 (83%)
Hispanic	50 (31%)	575 (8%)	50 (36%)	50 (36%)
White	42 (26%)	5582 (80%)	42 (30%)	42 (30%)
Asian American	16 (10%)	77 (1%)	13 (9%)	13 (9%)
African American	1 (1%)	407 (6%)	1 (1%)	1 (1%)
Unknown/not coded	9 (6%)	283 (4.4%)	9 (7%)	9 (7%)
Native American	0	19 (0.3%)	0	0
Men	57 (35%)	3018 (43%)	48 (35%)	39 (28%)
Women	104 (65%)	3950 (57%)	91 (66%)	100 (72%)
Pell	34 (21%)	1622 (23%)	34 (25%)	29 (21%)
No Pell	127 (79%)	5346 (77%)	105 (76%)	110 (79%)

(see, e.g., Sorey & Duggan, 2008), or nontraditional (25 plus years).[1] Race/ethnicity categories were based on the college database categories. Pell grant receipt was used as a proxy for SES, but it is important to note that Pell receipt is not an exact measure to identify all low-income students. Students who began college with 12 or more credits were categorized as full-time and those with 11 or fewer credits as part-time. The category of number of fall semesters enrolled was also created. Since information on spring enrollments was not available, I had to rely on the total number of falls students enrolled to gauge student persistence. Further, ELs' completion of the ESL program (with C or higher in the final course of the ESL sequence) and the ESL levels in which they began were also analyzed. ELs and non-ELs were matched on race/ethnicity, age, and enrollment status as these were the most disproportionate in number and the most relevant categories based on previous research (Table 11.1).[2]

Data Analysis. The alpha level for *t* tests was set at $a < .05$ with a two-tailed decision since the directionality of the outcomes was uncertain (Brown, 2001).[3] Linear regression was used for GPAs and persistence and logistic regression for program completion and graduation. Due to the low number of ELs, not all demographic variables could be included in every regression, as a minimum sample size of 50 per predictor is recommended for logistic regression (Wright, 1995) and 15 per predictor for linear regression (Licht, 1995). Aside from these practicality constraints, I referred to the retention literature as another method of determining the most relevant predictors (Wright, 1995). I also ran exploratory *t* tests on the GPAs and number of falls enrolled between each variable so that any significant differences could assist in determining relevant factors (Licht, 1995). I used age (traditional and nontraditional), ethnicity (Hispanic and non-Hispanic) and ESL level upon entry into college (high and low) for each regression. Age was included since there were enough numbers, the literature indicated age as a predictor for retention (Sorey & Duggan, 2008), and there were significant differences in the preliminary *t* test where students aged 25 and older had significantly lower first GPA, $t (154.56) = 2.84$, $p = .01$, lower final fall GPA, $t (155.87) = 2.08$, $p = .04$, and fewer falls enrolled, $t (147.54) = 2.51$, $p = .01$.[4] ESL course level was included as it yielded enough numbers when collapsed into a high and a low level. Although no significant differences were found in pretests on GPAs or persistence, the literature has indicated that the ESL level in which ELs begin college is a predictor of ESL program completion and graduation (Belcher, 1988; Patthey-Chavez et al., 2005). Of the race/ethnicity categories, there were only enough Hispanic students to include in the equations. The literature has suggested that Hispanics have fared more poorly than average in American higher education (Hagedorn et al., 2007; Hagedorn & Lester, 2006; Santos, 2005). In addition, Hispanic ELs at EPCC were the only ethnicity category to have a significant difference with a significantly lower first fall GPA than the rest of the group: $t (123.38) = 2.38$, $p = .02$. With access to the country of origin information in the database, I applied Hispanic codes to nonresidents as well in order to make the comparisons more robust.

Other variables were eliminated from the equations. I eliminated Pell receipt due to low numbers in the data, nonsignificant results on preliminary *t* tests on GPAs and enrollment between ELs receiving and not receiving Pell grants, and mixed results in the literature using Pell receipt as a variable in quantitative analyses (Ewers, 2007; Pascarella & Terenzini, 2005; Tinto, 1993). Even though enrollment status has been shown to have an impact on goal completion in college (Schmid & Abell, 2003), this variable was eliminated due to low numbers and no significant results in the *t* tests. In addition, even though there were enough numbers, sex was excluded since the literature has yielded mixed results in quantitative analyses (Ewers, 2007; Tovar & Simon, 2006), and there were no significant differences in *t* tests. Finally, although nonresidents had significantly higher first fall GPAs, $t(114.94) = -2.62$, $p = .01$, the number of nonresidents was not enough to be included in the logistic regressions. Finally, frequencies, means, and regressions were calculated on the matched samples of ELs and non-ELs in terms of their graduation, persistence, and final fall GPAs.

Results

ELs' Overall Patterns of Success

Table 11.2 presents descriptive statistics on the performance of the whole group of ELs. Although completion and persistence rates were quite low, GPA means were rather high albeit with standard deviations equivalent to at least one whole letter grade indicating a high degree of variance. The final fall GPA means were significantly lower than the first fall GPA means, $t(160) = 2.61$, $p = .01$. In further investigation of general trends across the college (not just FF), it was found that higher grades were issued in ESL courses (3.16 average, equal to about a B+) than the college as a whole (2.73 average, equal to about a B–). Nevertheless, for their final fall GPA, a majority of ELs (86%) earned at least a 2.00 (equivalent to a "C" letter grade), which is the minimum required for graduation, and almost half (49%) earned at least a 3.00 (equivalent to a "B" letter grade) which is often enough to meet transfer requirements. The mean of the final fall GPA, 2.75, was higher than the rest of the cohort as well ($n = 6,968$), 2.15 ($SD = 1.27$). In other words, whether they were graduating, transferring, meeting their goals, or dropping out, ELs did so while they were performing well academically.

TABLE 11.2 Descriptive Statistics for ELs

ELs	Completed ESL	Graduated	First fall GPA M	SD	Final fall GPA M	SD	M falls enrolled	SD
161	60 (37%)	21 (13%)	2.86	1.14	2.75	1.03	1.13	1.25

Also in Table 11.2, the mean for the number of falls enrolled was 1.13 (*SD* = 1.25), implying that ELs enrolled an average of just over one subsequent fall semester. However, the standard deviation was higher than the mean, indicating a high degree of variance. In addition, the mean of the falls enrolled did not appear much different than the rest of the cohort of non–ELs, (*n* = 6,968), 1.10 (*SD* = 1.17). However, in another view, the data showed that only 30% of ELs attended the following fall semester, bearing in mind that some returned in later fall semesters. The EL graduation rate was 13%, significantly lower than EPCC's overall rate of 23%, χ^2 (1, *N* = 9000) = 9.1, *p* = .01. The ESL program completion rate was 37%. There were an additional 10 students who started in ESL, did not finish the ESL program, but still graduated, indicating that they had tested out of ESL. With this number taken into consideration, there were then 70 (43%) students who started in ESL and successfully either passed the program or simply went on with their studies and graduated. Additionally, there were 18 students currently enrolled at the time of analysis with the potential to graduate. This still left 73 (45%) ELs unaccounted for. Students may have left with the intention of transferring or beginning employment, but as records did not provide this information, causes for departure remain unknown.

In addition, students who graduated were generally more successful in receiving high grades, and they persisted longer than those who did not graduate (Table 11.3). Independent *t* tests showed that graduates had significantly higher first fall GPAs *t* (47.61) = 4.04, *p* < .001, with a large effect size, *d* = 1.2, higher final fall GPAs, *t* (43.28) = 3.04, *p* = .004, with a large effect size, *d* = 0.9, and higher number of subsequent fall semesters enrolled, *t* (30.92) = 6.41, *p* < .001, with a large effect size, *d* = 2.3. Standard deviations indicated a high degree of variance for each variable, especially for non-graduates.

Differences among ELs

Descriptive statistical results for ESL program completion, graduation, GPAs, and number of falls enrolled were calculated for certain groups among ELs (Table 11.4). In terms of students' entering proficiency level, it appeared that the lower the level of ESL in which students began, the poorer they performed in every area. As with the whole group, GPAs went down from first to final fall

TABLE 11.3 Comparison of GPA and Enrollment Between EL Graduates and Non-Graduates

	First fall GPA M	SD	Final fall GPA M	SD	M falls enrolled	SD
Graduated (n = 21)	3.43★	.59	3.12★	.59	2.38★	.92
Did not graduate (n = 140)	2.77	1.18	2.69	1.07	0.94	1.19

Note. ★p < .05.

TABLE 11.4 Descriptive Statistics of ELs by Characteristics

Variable	n (%)	Completed ESL	Graduated	First fall GPA M	SD	Final fall GPA M	SD	M falls enrolled	SD
Level 1	38 (24%)	7 (18%)	3 (8%)	2.68	1.08	2.52	0.97	1.16	1.31
Level 2	69 (43%)	18 (26%)	6 (9%)	2.81	1.22	2.73	1.11	1.04	1.27
Level 3	43 (27%)	25 (58%)	9 (21%)	3.03	1.03	2.96	0.91	1.16	1.17
Level 4	11 (7%)	10 (91%)	3 (27%)	3.05	1.24	2.86	1.11	1.45	1.37
Age 18–24	72 (45%)	36 (50%)	16 (22%)	3.12	0.87	2.93	0.81	1.40	1.27
Age 25+	89 (55%)	24 (27%)	5 (6%)	2.64	1.28	2.60	1.16	0.91	1.19
Part–time	130 (81%)	43 (33%)	12 (9%)	2.82	1.15	2.71	1.05	1.05	1.26
Full–time	31 (19%)	17 (55%)	9 (29%)	3.01	1.08	2.91	0.94	1.48	1.18
Nonresident	43 (27%)	16 (37%)	12 (28%)	3.17	0.80	2.99	0.82	1.19	1.16
Resident	118 (73%)	44 (37%)	9 (8%)	2.74	1.22	2.66	1.08	1.11	1.29
Hispanic	50 (31%	21 (42%	4 (8%)	2.50	1.23	2.55	1.02	1.18	1.34
White	42 (26%)	14 (33%)	4 (10%)	2.91	1.18	2.64	1.12	1.05	1.10
Asian Am.	16 (10%)	6 (38%)	1 (6%)	3.11	1.10	2.98	1.05	1.56	1.71
African Am.	1 (1%)	1 (100%)	0 (0%)	3.70		3.70		0.00	
Unknown	9 (6%)	2 (2%)	0 (0%)	2.56	1.50	2.67	1.35	0.33	0.50
Men	57 (35%)	17 (29%)	9 (16%)	2.60	1.21	2.61	1.10	1.11	1.24
Women	104 (64%)	43 (41%)	12 (12%)	2.97	1.09	2.82	0.98	1.14	1.27
Pell	34 (21%)	16 (47%)	7 (20%)	2.95	1.12	2.78	0.95	1.50	1.30
No Pell	127 (79%)	44 (35%)	14 (11%)	2.83	1.15	2.74	1.05	1.03	1.23

Notes. Percents in the first column are of all ELs.
Percentages in second and third columns are of the respective category.
Empty cells indicate that information is not applicable.

semester for every level, again probably having to do with higher ESL grades. The standard deviations also indicated a high degree of variance. The category of sex had mixed results where women exceeded men in completing the ESL program and in their first and final fall GPAs, but then graduated at a slightly lower rate even though they enrolled for a slightly higher average of fall semesters. Traditionally-aged students outperformed nontraditionally-aged students in every area, as did full-time students over part-time students, nonresidents over residents (except with ESL program completion where they equaled each other), and students receiving Pell over those who did not.

Some of these results could be anticipated considering previous literature indicating that part-time students (Tinto, 1993), nontraditionally-aged students (Sorey & Duggan, 2008), and students who begin in lower levels of ESL (Belcher, 1988) are at a disadvantage. However, one might expect that students receiving Pell, an indicator of low SES, would not perform as well. As noted above, Pell receipt is not always a precise predictor of college success; on the one hand, Pell eligible students may be at an economic disadvantage while, on the other, grants may aid in retention by promoting access to college (Pascarella & Terenzini, 2005). At EPCC Pell grants seem ultimately to aid access by giving financial stability.

Table 11.4 also presents results by race and ethnicity for residents. Students self-identifying as Hispanic, White, and Asian American students represent the largest groups. Asian American students had the highest GPAs, enrolled the most falls but graduated the least. However, these differences did not prove significant in preliminary t tests. Hispanic students' GPAs were lower than White and Asian American students but they had the highest ESL program completion rates whereas White students enrolled in the fewest falls, completed the ESL program the least, but graduated the most. For the regressions that follow, the categories of traditional and nontraditional ages, Hispanic (including nonresidents) and all other ethnicities, and high and low levels were used. Table 11.5 gives the descriptive statistics for these characteristics.

Linear Regression.   Linear regressions were used to compare the first and final fall GPAs and number of falls enrolled among ELs by age, ethnicity, and level. Based on descriptive findings (Table 11.5), preliminary analyses, and previous literature, I had hypothesized that nontraditionally-aged students, Hispanic students, and students who started in the two lower levels of ESL would have significantly lower GPAs and number of falls enrolled than their counterparts. In the first linear regression, the variables of age, ethnicity, and level accounted for only 8% of the variance in the first fall GPA, implying that there were unknown variables that account for the variance (Table 11.6). Only age and ethnicity were significant ($p = .02$ and $p = .03$ respectively), but age ($B = -0.43$) had more of an effect than ethnicity ($B = -0.40$) as nontraditionally-aged students had lower GPAs. There were no significant findings in the second

TABLE 11.5 Descriptive Statistics by Age, Ethnicity (Including Nonresidents), and ESL Level

Group	n (%)	Completed ESL	Graduated	First fall GPA M	SD	Final fall GPA M	SD	M falls enrolled	SD
Age 18-24	72 (45%)	36 (50%)	16(22%)	3.12	0.87	2.93	0.81	1.40	1.27
Age 25+	89 (55%)	24 (27%)	5 (6%)	2.64	1.28	2.60	1.16	0.91	1.19
Hispanic	64 (40%)	25 (39%)	6 (9%)	2.59	1.20	2.62	0.97	1.09	1.26
Others	97(60%)	35 (36%)	15(16%)	3.03	1.06	2.82	0.96	1.15	1.25
Levels 1-2	107 (66%)	25 (23%)	9 (8%)	2.77	1.17	2.65	1.06	1.08	1.28
Levels 3-4	54 (34%)	35 (65%)	12 (22%)	3.04	1.06	2.94	0.94	1.22	1.21

TABLE 11.6 Linear Regression Results on GPAs and Enrollment by Three Characteristics

Dependent variable	R^2	Independent variable	B	SE B	β	t	p
First Fall GPA	0.08	Age (nontrad. = 1, trad. = 0)	-0.43*	0.18	-0.19	-2.35	.02
		Ethnicity (Hispanic = 1, others = 0)	-0.40*	0.18	-0.17	-2.25	.03
		Level (low = 1, high = 0)	-0.10	0.19	-0.04	-0.54	.59
Final Fall GPA	0.06	Age	-0.24	0.16	-0.12	-1.51	.13
		Ethnicity	-0.15	0.15	-0.08	-1.00	.32
		Level	-0.33	0.17	-0.16	-1.97	.05
Falls enrolled	0.04	Age	-0.50*	0.21	-0.20	-2.41	.02
		Ethnicity	-0.03	0.20	-0.01	-0.14	.89
		Level	0.01	0.22	0.01	0.07	.95

Note. * $p < .05$.

linear regression on final fall GPAs. The third linear regression was performed on number of falls enrolled (Table 11.6). Nontraditionally-aged students enrolled significantly fewer fall semesters by about 0.50 of a subsequent fall than their counterparts. In other words, even when ethnicity and level were controlled for, it appeared that on average nontraditionally-aged ELs enrolled half of an additional fall semester less than traditionally-aged ELs. However, these findings accounted for only 4% of the variance in final fall GPAs.

Logistic Regression. For the logistic regressions, I hypothesized that nontraditionally-aged students, Hispanic students, and students who started college in lower levels of ESL would be less likely to complete the ESL program or graduate. Table 11.7 indicates that students who began in the two lower levels were five times less likely ($e^b = 5.214$) to complete the ESL program than students who began in the two higher levels. It might be expected that a student who began in level four had a greater chance than one who started in level one. However, that lower levels were five times less likely to finish seems to be an outstanding difference. For the logistic regression on graduation, nontraditionally-aged students were 3.9 times less likely to graduate than traditionally-aged students, even when controlling for ESL course level (Table 11.7).

ELs' Graduation, GPA, and Enrollment Compared to Non-ELs

Frequencies of graduation, means of final fall GPAs, and means of number of fall semesters enrolled were calculated for EL and non-EL samples matched by race/ethnicity, age, and enrollment status (Table 11.8). First fall GPAs were not used since ESL courses, which ELs would take in at least the first semester,

TABLE 11.7 Logistic Regression Results for Those Less Likely to Complete ESL Program and Graduate

Variable	Less likely to complete ESL program					Less likely to graduate				
	B	SE	Wald	p	e^b	B	SE	Wald	p	e^b
Age (Nontrad. = 1, trad. = 0)	0.66	0.37	3.16	.08	1.93	1.35	0.56	5.87	.02★	3.87
Ethnicity (Hispanic = 1, others = 0)	-0.38	0.37	1.05	.31	0.68	0.46	0.53	0.75	.39	1.59
Level (Low = 1, High = 0)	1.69	0.38	19.62	.00★	5.21	0.77	0.50	2.34	.05	2.16

Notes. ★p < .05
Students who completed (n = 60) were coded "0" and students who did not complete (n = 101) were coded "1." Goodness of fit (-2LL) was 182.346. Nagelkerke R square was 0.234.

TABLE 11.8 Results for Matched ELs and Non-ELs

Matched groups	Graduated	Final fall GPA M	SD	M Falls enrolled	SD
EL (n =139)	16 (12%)	2.72★	1.04	1.13	1.25
Non-EL (n = 139)	20 (14%)	2.32	1.37	0.86	1.24

Note. ★p = .01

issued higher grades than other courses. ELs had significantly higher GPAs than non-ELs in the last fall semester, t (256.87) = 2.76, p = .01, with a medium effect size (d = 0.3). There were no significant differences found in the number of falls enrolled between ELs and non-ELs.

To investigate differences in graduation between the groups, I conducted a logistic regression hypothesizing that ELs would be less likely to graduate than non-ELs, since ELs' percentage was lower (Table 11.8). However, the differences were not significant (Table 11.9). In addition, both samples had lower graduation rates than the whole group of non-ELs, whose graduation rate was 23%, as well as the college as a whole, also 23%.

Discussion and Conclusion

Before discussing the impact and relevance of these results, it is important to note some limitations of this study, mostly regarding the data. Since transcript data did not contain student goals, it was unknown whether students wanted to complete the ESL program only, graduate, or transfer and seek a bachelor's degree. There was also no information on why students left EPCC: whether they became employed, transferred, or simply quit out of discouragement. The data were limited in terms of information on student race/ethnicity, identifying students only in categories such as Asian American or Hispanic and not specific ethnolinguistic groups within them. Data were also not available on whether students were generation 1.5 or first generation college students. As noted earlier, data also lacked spring enrollment information and showed only the total number of fall semesters enrolled. Although there were enough participants for many statistical tests, the low number in some categories restrained the use of

TABLE 11.9 Logistic Regression Results for Those Less Likely to Graduate, ELs Compared to Non-ELs

Variable	B	SE	Wald	p	e^b
Language learning status (EL = 1, Non-EL = 0)	0.256	0.359	0.509	.48	1.292

Notes. Graduating was coded as "0" and not graduating as "1."
Goodness of fit (-2LL) was 213.787
Nagelkerke R square was 0.003.

logistic regression, especially with the low number of nonresidents who had a significantly higher first fall GPA mean than residents in preliminary tests.

These limitations lead to research implications regarding community college data and record keeping. Specifically, it may be worthwhile to invest in more accurate database systems, to ask more questions on application forms, and to build relationships with four-year institutions to track student transfer. Perhaps student transcript requests could be used to initiate contact with students who potentially transferred. It may also serve community colleges well to perform exit interviews asking students why they are leaving and if they know the steps to take to re-enroll, and link this information in the database immediately to prevent having to retroactively solicit information from former students.

Despite data limitations, certain results demand attention and certainly justify further study in this line of inquiry. First, it is alarming that ELs performed well in terms of their GPAs but did not complete ESL or academic programs at a high rate. Findings were not as dire as those found in Belcher (1988), but the graduation rate of 13% was significantly lower than that of the college at 23% and lower than that of community colleges across the nation at 25% (Sorey & Duggan, 2008). Although goals for these participants were unknown, the majority of ELs at this college have expressed that they wanted to at least graduate from EPCC with an associate degree (Almon, 2010). In addition, attending just one subsequent fall semester would not have given much time for ELs to graduate or even complete the ESL program. Whereas there is little previous research on the persistence of FF ELs, general trends of persistence have shown that 16% of community college students depart from college in their first year (Sorey & Duggan, 2008). In this study, although some returned in a later semester, 70% of ELs did not persist to the subsequent fall.

One explanation for the incongruity of high performance yet high dropout rates could be derived from the high degree of variance among EL groups. First, graduates of the college had higher GPAs than non-graduates, suggesting that academic underpreparation is a factor in not completing. Two other groups among ELs who seemed to present risk were students who began college in lower levels of ESL and nontraditionally-aged students. ELs who began in lower levels were five times less likely to complete the ESL program, a finding consistent with Belcher (1988) and Patthey-Chavez et al. (2005). Nontraditionally-aged ELs were of most concern as they had significantly lower first semester GPAs, had significantly fewer fall semesters enrolled, and were almost four times less likely to graduate even when level was taken into account. Sorey and Duggan (2008) viewed lower persistence and graduation rates as likely consequences of these learners having to face more financial obstacles than traditionally-aged students. Hispanic ELs had significantly lower GPAs but showed no significant differences for final fall GPA, persistence, or graduation indicating that this group was more successful than Hispanic community college students studied in previous literature (Hagedorn et al., 2007; Hagedorn & Lester, 2006; Santos, 2005).

Unfortunately, not enough of the variance was explained by the regressions, indicating that other factors are at play. Aside from the fact that some groups which could be at risk were not represented in the data, there could be other explanations for student departure. In interviews and surveys from Almon (2010), most students reported that the outside factors including lack of financial resources, full-time employment, and family obligations led to their leaving college. In addition, ELs also spoke of linguistic difficulties, the alienating status of being an EL at the college, and lack of procedural knowledge about college processes as having an impact on their engagement and enrollment.

It should also be noted that when matched in age, enrollment status, and race/ethnicity, ELs performed as well as and sometimes better than a sample of non-ELs. Specifically, ELs had significantly higher final fall GPAs but no significant differences in persistence or graduation. Nevertheless, both matched samples had lower graduation rates than those for the college and nation, possibly due to their sharing high risk groups of nontraditionally-aged, part-time, and Hispanic students. ELs' greater performance could have stemmed from ELs feeling more support from the college than non-ELs (Almon, 2010). However, that support was insufficient as some ELs were still unaware of college procedural knowledge that could have assisted them in remaining enrolled such as waivers for graduation requirements and appeals to reinstate Pell grants (Almon, 2010). In sum, research on community colleges with a larger enrollment of ELs could make even more of an impact by incorporating inferential statistics as those presented here and following up with interviews on those ELs to explore reasons for their success or attrition and seek ways to prevent dropout of this important subgroup of their population.

Notes

1. Minors and cases with missing ages were omitted from the data as per IRB agreement.
2. Crosstabs in SPSS were used to categorize the desired number of the three characteristics and draw random samples for each category among non-ELs to match each category in the ELs. Note $n = 139$ due to lack of non-ELs in some categories.
3. Since this was an exploratory inquiry, I used the entire sample of ELs, unequal variances in all. When Levene's test indicated unequal variances, I used the significant results associated therein as well as the appropriate t and df when calculating effect sizes. This will make the df appear not as the expected $n - 1$.
4. Due to unequal variances, the df in parentheses does not appear as the typical $n - 1$.

References

Almon, C. (2010). *English language learner engagement and retention in a community college setting* (Doctoral dissertation). Available from ProQuest Dissertation and Thesis database. (Publication No. AAT 3408684)

Belcher, M. (1988). *Success of students who begin college by enrolling in English as a second language* (Research report No. 88-90). Miami, FL: Miami-Dade Community College. Office of Institutional Research. Retrieved from ERIC database. (ED296763)

Brown, J. D. (2001). *Using surveys in language programs.* New York, NY: Cambridge University Press.

Curry, M. J. (2001, April). *Adult ESL students in the contact zone: Exploring the effects of multiple educational attainment levels on the community college writing classroom.* Paper presented at the annual meeting of the American Educational Research Association. Seattle, WA. Retrieved from ERIC database. (ED454706)

Dowd, A., & Melguizo, T. (2008). Socioeconomic stratification of community college transfer access in the 1980's and 1990's: Evidence from HS&B and NELS. *The Review of Higher Education, 31*(4), 377–400.

Ewers, E. B. (2007). *The power of faculty, staff, and peer interactions: Impact on community college student retention* (Doctoral Dissertation). Available from ProQuest Dissertation and Thesis database. (Publication No. AAT 3269340)

Hagedorn, L. S., & Lester, J. (2006). Hispanic community college students and the transfer game: Strikes, misses, and grand slam experiences. *Community College Journal of Research and Practice, 30*(10), 827–853.

Hagedorn, L. S., Chi, W., Cepeda, R., & McLain, M. (2007). An investigation of critical mass: The role of Latino representation in the success of urban community college students. *Research in Higher Education, 48*(1), 73–91.

Kolajo, E. (2004). From developmental education to graduation: A community college experience. *Community College Journal of Research and Practice, 28*(4), 365–371.

Kuo, E. (1999). English as a second language in the community college curriculum. *New Directions for Community Colleges, 108,* 69–80.

Lew, J., Chang, J., & Wang, W. (2006). UCLA community college review: The overlooked minority: Asian Pacific American students at community colleges. *Community College Review, 33*(2), 64–84.

Lewis, C., & Middleton, V. (2003). African Americans in community colleges: A review of research reported in the Community College Journal of Research and Practice: 1990–2000. *Community College Journal of Research and Practice, 27*(9), 787–798.

Licht, M. (1995). Multiple regression and correlation. In G. Grimm & P. Yarnold (Eds.), *Reading and understanding multivariate statistics* (pp. 19–64). Washington, DC: American Psychological Association.

Lujan, L., Gallegos, L., & Harbour, C. P. (2003). La tercera frontera: Building upon the scholarship of the Latino experience as reported in the community college journal of research and practice. *Community College Journal of Research and Practice, 27*(9), 799–813.

Maxwell, W., Hagedorn, L. S., Cypers, S., Moon, H. S., Brocato, P., Wahl, K., & Prather, G. (2003). Community and diversity in urban community colleges: Coursetaking among entering students. *Community College Review, 30*(4), 21–46.

Miller, M. T., Pope, M., & Steinmann, T. (2005). Dealing with the challenges and stressors faced by community college students: The old college try. *Community College Journal of Research and Practice, 29*(1), 63–74.

Pascarella, E., & Terenzini, P. (2005). *How college affects students, volume 2: A third decade of research.* San Francisco: Jossey-Bass.

Patthey-Chavez, G., Dillon, P., & Thomas-Spiegel, J. (2005). How far do they get? Tracking students with different academic literacies through community college remediation. *Teaching English in the Two Year College, 32*(3), 261–277.

Santos, M. (2005). The motivations of first-semester Hispanic two-year college students. *Community College Review, 32*(3), 18–34.

Schmid, C., & Abell, P. (2003). Demographic risk factors, study patterns, and campus involvement as related to student success among Guilford Technical Community College students. *Community College Review, 31*(1), 1–16.

Song, B. (2006a). Content-based ESL instruction: Long-term effects and outcomes. *English for Specific Purposes, 25*, 420–437.

Song, B. (2006b). Failure in a college ESL course: Perspectives of instructors and students. *Community college Journal of Research and Practice, 30*(5), 417–431.

Sorey, K. C., & Duggan, M. H. (2008). Differential predictors of persistence between community college adult students and traditionally-aged students. *Community College Journal of Research and Practice, 32*(2), 75–100.

Spurling, S., Seymour, S., & Chisman, F. (2008). Pathways & outcomes: Tracking ESL student performance. A longitudinal study of adult ESL Service at City College of San Francisco. Retrieved from Council for Advancement of Adult Literacy website: http://www.caalusa.org/pathways-outcomes/pathways-outcomesfull.pdf

Sylvia, C., Song, C., & Waters, T. (2010). Challenges in calculating two-year college student transfer rates to four-year colleges. *Community College Journal of Research and Practice, 34*(7), 561–575.

Tinto, V. (1993). *Leaving college: Rethinking the causes and cures of student attrition.* (2nd ed.). Chicago: The University of Chicago Press.

Tovar, E., & Simon, M. S. (2006). Academic probation as a dangerous opportunity: Factors influencing diverse college students' success. *Community College Journal of Research and Practice, 30*(7), 547–564.

Townsend, B., Donaldson, J., & Wilson, T. (2005). Marginal or monumental? Visibility of community colleges in selected higher-education journals. *Community College Journal of Research and Practice, 29*(2), 123–135.

Wright, R. (1995). Logistic regression. In G. Grimm & P. Yarnold (Eds.), *Reading and understanding multivariate statistics* (pp. 217–244). Washington, DC: American Psychological Association.

12

CONTEXTUALIZING THE PATH TO ACADEMIC SUCCESS

Culturally and Linguistically Diverse Students Gaining Voice and Agency in Higher Education

Melissa Holmes, Cristina Fanning, Amanda Morales, Pedro Espinoza, and Socorro Herrera

> Language is power, life and the instrument of culture, the instrument of domination and liberation.
>
> *(Angela Carter, 1997, p. 43)*

For decades, we as a nation have struggled to answer age-old questions regarding the purpose and practice of educating linguistic minorities in the United States. As evidenced in seminal reports such as The Unfinished Education (1971) and The Excluded Student (1972) published by the U.S. Commission on Civil Rights (USCOCR), the educational plight of immigrant populations and their lack of access to full, meaningful participation in schools is long-standing.

The extensive and torrid history of education as a means for colonization of culturally and linguistically diverse peoples in the United States can be traced back to the 1700s (Crawford, 2004; Spring, 2005). Linguistic and cultural domination, initiated by the British, had an impact on every indigenous and immigrant population in the New World. Africans, Chinese, American Indians, Latinas/os, and even Germans have undergone purposeful "deculturalization" at various points in our history (Spring, 2005, p. 183). According to Spring (2005), the imposition of the English language was used as a tool for "cultural transformation" (p. 124) in efforts to prevent cultural pluralism.

A push to *Americanize* the non-White and non-English speaker through schooling flourished in the 1800s and continued to affect immigrant populations throughout the 1900s (Crawford, 2004). For example, German immigrants were said to be "aliens" who neither spoke nor thought "American" (Crawford, 2004, p. 90); therefore, legislative mandates for English-only instruction were passed, doing away with all foreign language instruction. Though in this case the Supreme Court ruling *Meyer vs. Nebraska* (1923) overturned these laws, the passing and later retracting of oppressive policies continues to be a recurrent theme in U.S. educational history.

In theory, today educational discrimination founded on race, class, and linguistic difference does not exist, as a result of judicial rulings such as *Mendez vs. Westminster* (1946), *Brown vs. Board of Education* (1954), *Lau vs. Nichols* (1974), and *Plyler vs. Doe* (1982). However, it is argued that educational policies and practices continue to marginalize immigrant and linguistic minority students at every level (Ladson-Billings, 1998; Macedo, 2006; USCOCR, 1971, 1972). This is despite the fact that between 1995–1996 and 2005–2006, the K–12 English learner population increased by 57.2% while over the same period the total student enrollment increased by only 3.7% (National Clearinghouse for English Language Acquisition, 2007). Currently, foreign-born students constitute 45% of English learners in K–12 classrooms (Lachat, 2004). According to the Pew Research Center, the U.S. educational system can expect a significant increase in immigrant students in the years to come. Pew researchers Passel and Cohn (2008) claim that "nearly one in five Americans (19%) will be an immigrant in 2050, compared with one in eight (12%) in 2005" (p. i).

It is clear from the literature that this rapid increase in number of English learners, the majority (77%) of whom are Spanish speakers (Kindler, 2002), presents many challenges to traditional policy and practice in education (Alliance for Excellent Education, 2009; Holmes Group, 1995; Howard, 2010). Baugh (2009) establishes the term "linguistic stereotype threat" to describe the educational risks and challenges experienced by students who lack fluency in Standard English as the dominant language. In addition to the blatant denial of access, as in the *Lau vs. Nichols* case, more subtle forms of linguistic stereotype threats exist at the interpersonal level. As Baugh (2009) states, "When teachers, parents, and others who are involved in children's education harbor false linguistic stereotypes, they may—often inadvertently—overlook or devalue the intellectual potential of students" (p. 280). This misperception of linguistic minorities often leads to poor curriculum, ineffective ESOL programming, biased testing, and ability tracking at the K–12 level.

The damaging effects of such factors are seen at the college level as well. As stated by Castellanos and Gloria (2007), "Out of 100 Latina/o elementary students, only 21 will go to college, 8 will earn a graduate degree, and less than .2% will earn a doctoral degree" (p. 380). Despite the dramatic increases in Latino/a populations over the past several decades, from 1976–77 through 2007–08, the percentage of bachelor's degrees conferred to Latinas/os only increased from 2.0% to 7.9% (with percentage of total students enrolled increasing from 3.5% to 11.4%) (National Center for Educational Statistics, 2009). This discrepancy between enrollment and graduation highlights the challenges related to retaining the Latina/o students that are recruited into higher education.

In light of these grim statistics, many argue that schools are failing English learner students, not English learners failing schools (Alliance for Excellent

Education, 2009; Hurtado, Carter, & Spuler, 1996; Romo, 2005; Valenzuela, 1999). As a result of anti-immigrant, hegemonic social discourse and the resulting lack of acceptance of English learners on predominantly White college campuses, scholars (see, e.g., Da Silva Iddings, 2005; Macedo, 2006) contend that linguistic minority students often carry with them substantial feelings of self-doubt and isolation throughout their educational careers. This lack of integration due to a negative campus climate serves as a significant threat to their resiliency at the college level (Gay, Dingus, & Jackson, 2003; Herrera, 1995; Locks, Hurtado, Bowman, & Osegueara, 2008; Solorzáno, Allen, & Carroll, 2002). Although many studies consider the impact of schooling on culturally and linguistically diverse (CLD) students and students from poverty, few focus specifically on perceptions of language as an indicator for risk in immigrant student education (Baugh, 2009). The researchers of this study seek to address this gap in the literature using language as the interpretive lens for understanding Spanish-speaking immigrants' educational experience in college.

Purpose of the Study

This ethnographic case study documents the experiences of culturally and linguistically diverse (CLD) first-generation immigrant students as they developed their sense of voice and personal agency at a predominantly White, midwestern university. The study is framed within the larger context of an ongoing, longitudinal study on the BESITOS (Bilingual/Bicultural Education Students Interacting To Obtain Success) model of recruitment and retention (Herrera & Morales, 2005; Herrera, Morales, Holmes, & Terry, 2011–2012), which was developed in 1999 to address the multifaceted assets and needs of Latina/o learners in higher education. The model takes into account literature on CLD student recruitment and retention (e.g., Ceja, 2001, 2004; Gay, Dingus, & Jackson, 2003; Hobson-Horton & Owens, 2004), second language acquisition (e.g., Cummins, 1991; Krashen, 1991; Thomas & Collier, 1997), and ecologies of care and respect (e.g., Delpit, 1995; Gay, 2000; Ladson-Billings, 1999; Nieto, 2004).

The BESITOS scholarship program is funded by the Office of English Language Acquisition and implements the BESITOS model within the College of Education. The overarching goal of the BESITOS scholarship program is to increase the number of teachers, especially those from underrepresented backgrounds, who are prepared to effectively address the needs of CLD students and families. Efforts to meet the program's overarching goal have been guided by a strong commitment to first understand and respect the identities of the students who participate in the program. Faculty and staff look beyond the parameters often set by universities of what it means to care and provide a safe environment for students who are learning to navigate a place that is foreign and often unwelcoming to students who are perceived to have "gaps" in academic background, rather than assets that must be used to accelerate learning. Students' identities, perceived self, culture, language, and cross-cultural experiences are viewed as central to their participation in the program.

One of the structural components of the program identified most frequently by participants as instrumental to their retention is an identity/advocacy seminar. Opportunities to learn from professionals in the field through readings and guest speakers raise questions of oppression, discrimination, and marginalization. The seminar readings and assignments are catalysts for difficult conversations that provide space for participants to reveal their "hidden" self: experiences of the past and present that often reflect inequalities in schools, in their own communities, and in the larger society.

Since 1999, 191 individuals have gained access to higher education through funding made possible through one of five Title VII/III grants. The first semester after acceptance into the BESITOS scholarship program is essentially a trial semester in which the participant and program staff members determine if the program is the right fit for the student. Students, for example, might decide that teaching is not the career they would like to pursue. The majority, however, continues with their studies to become future teachers, and 74% are retained within the program (excluding those who must drop for extenuating medical/family circumstances). Although each student's path to and through the university is different, this study sought to identify commonalities among the experiences of one subgroup of English learner participants. Specifically, the researchers sought to document the lived experiences of native Spanish-speaking, immigrant Latina/o college students as they made sense of, and continued to forge, their linguistic identities.

Theoretical Framework

Building on the work of Thomas and Collier (1997) and their conceptualization of the prism model, Herrera and Murry (e.g., Herrera, 2010; Herrera & Murry, 2005; Herrera, Murry, & Cabral, 2007) use *CLD student biography* to refer to the totality of a student's identity. This biography includes four interrelated dimensions—sociocultural, linguistic, cognitive, and academic—and is situated within the sociopolitical context of U.S. schools, K–16. Herrera and Murry extend upon the notion of multiple factors simultaneously contributing to the development of CLD students and emphasize the challenges and processes related to each biographical dimension.

The four dimensions of the CLD student biography can be summarized briefly as follows:

- *Sociocultural Dimension:* Relates to students' ways of life in and out of school and those things that bring them laughter and love. This dimension encompasses affective influences (e.g., motivation, anxiety, self-esteem) as well as social interactive phenomena (e.g., bias, prejudice, discrimination).

- *Linguistic Dimension:* Involves the processes that students use for comprehension, communication, and expression in both their native language (L1) and second/target language (L2).
- *Cognitive Dimension:* Relates to the culturally influenced ways students know, think, and apply their learning.
- *Academic Dimension:* Encompasses students' past and current access to a high-quality education, their engagement in classroom learning, and their hope for both academic achievement and life success.

Method

Data Collection

The researchers collected data in the form of surveys, semi-structured interviews, and student artifacts. Individuals who at any point in their educational careers had been involved in a scholarship program that utilized the BESITOS model were surveyed about their K–16 educational experiences in the United States. Contact with 106 students was made utilizing email and an online social networking system. A total of 58 students responded to the electronic survey, yielding a response rate of 54.7%. Twenty-nine respondents (50%) met the study criteria of being native Spanish speakers who immigrated to the United States. Of these 29 participants, 90% were first-generation college students. Countries of origin represented by these participants included El Salvador, Honduras, Mexico, Nicaragua, and Puerto Rico. The average age upon arrival to the United States was 15.

From those survey respondents who met the study criteria, the researchers selected a purposive sample (Teddlie & Yu, 2008) of six participants for semi-structured interviews. Care was taken to select individuals who represented within-group diversity related to funding period, recency of immigration, age at time of study, and region of home community within the state. An additional interviewee who met the study criteria was selected based on the alignment between her response to a seminar assignment and the focus of the study. Together, six females and one male participated in the interviews. Six of the participants emigrated from Mexico; one emigrated from Puerto Rico. One interviewee is a current undergraduate student; six of the interviewees obtained bachelor's degrees in education between the years 2003 and 2008. Three of these individuals have since earned advanced degrees, and one is taking coursework toward an advanced degree. Each of the interviewees was interviewed once for an average of 20 minutes. The interviews were audio recorded and then transcribed. Pseudonyms are used throughout this chapter to refer to all students, including the seven interviewees: Esmeralda, Francisco, Mariana, Paola, Patricia, Teresa, and Victoria.

The researchers also collected student artifacts, such as reflective essays and written responses to open-ended questions on assignments generated within the structured curriculum of the identity/advocacy seminar offered each spring and fall semester. The researchers included the artifacts to give voice to the larger population of Spanish-speaking immigrant learners with whom they have interacted over the course of the program (1999–present).

Data Analysis

The researchers conducted two rounds of analyses. They initiated analysis by first coding each piece of data according to the four dimensions (socio-cultural, linguistic, cognitive, and academic) of the CLD student biography framework (e.g., Herrera & Murry, 2005). Second, the researchers employed a form of qualitative construction of categories driven by existing research in Latino/a education (e.g., recruitment and retention, second language acquisition, etc.) and the meanings derived from the student voices in the study (Merriam, 1998). This allowed for direct interpretation of the data, which Creswell describes as a "process of pulling the data apart and putting them back together in more meaningful ways" (1998, p. 154). This process led to the establishment of patterns (Creswell, 1998) and enabled the researchers to identify emergent themes and subthemes. Triangulation of the data as well as peer debriefing (which included discussions and consensus in establishing the final themes and subthemes) among all five researchers bolstered the trustworthiness of the study (Lincoln & Guba, 1985).

Findings

Four overarching themes emerged from the analysis of the data: (a) rejection and alienation, (b) compartmentalization of language, (c) bilingualism as a blessing, and (d) the establishment of student's sense of agency. These themes worked together to capture students' linguistic journey into and through college.

Rejection and Alienation

Feelings of rejection and alienation based on one's language have historical roots in this country. It is not surprising, therefore, that one of the most salient and present themes that emerged from the participants' voices was that of rejection and alienation in the educational environment. Students experienced these feelings at different points in their educational careers. For some, the feelings originated during their K–12 education and continued through their university experience. Others did not experience these feelings in a linguistic sense until college. Some participants continued to report issues of rejection and alienation as bilingual Latinas/os even into their professional careers.

Participants indicated that the hegemonic practices of educational institutions attempted to separate them as linguistic minority students and deny their equitable access to appropriate educational materials, information, and teaching. The following remark exemplifies this separation at the university level:

> No nos dejaron tomar clases de la universidad [cuando entramos en el colegio] solamente clases de ESL para que nos ayudaran a aprender el segundo idioma un poco mas. Eso lo vi yo un poco negativo de que sólo porque hablábamos español nos apartaron un poquito. Claro que las maestras nos trataban bien, pero uno sentía ese rechazo, esa forma de aislamiento—clases en otro edificio, actividades en otro lugar.
>
> *(Victoria, interview)*

> [They did not let us take university classes (upon entering college). Our classes were more like ESL classes to help us learn the second language a little bit more. I saw that a little bit negative because just because we spoke Spanish they separated us a little bit. Of course the teacher treated us well, but we felt that rejection, that form of isolation—classes in a different building, activities in a different place.]

This participant's voice highlights the negative consequences of approaches that attempt to address the needs of students whose first language is not English by removing the learners from the general educational setting through pullout programs or special programs designed to teach English or remediate reading and writing skills. Students' descriptions of these types of programs provided a collage of the often subtle, yet powerful messages sent regarding the native language and its place within institutional settings (see Kanno & Grosik, this volume; Shapiro, this volume).

Participants began to internalize the messages, both hidden and overt, about their native language. For example, Patricia shared:

> High school was just like I rejected my language cuz it's how they [teachers] made me feel when I was in high school ... all of my teachers were like, "That's [Spanish is] negative. That's making you not to learn the language [English]. Plus you're not learning the subject." ... Until today I still feel like my language has been rejected.
>
> *(Interview)*

Participants relayed similar experiences at the university. For example, they shared instances when professors chided them in the hallway for speaking Spanish. Participants even revealed rejection of the native language when use of the language was the intent of the communicative environment, as in a modern language methods course. Susana, herself a bilingual learner, explained the injustice that she witnessed and described her response:

> Last Tuesday, in one of my classes, we had to do a microteach in Spanish. All the students have to give a positive feedback and a suggestion to

improve our teaching skills.... One of the Latino students [a fellow BESI-TOS student] received a note stating that she spoke too much Spanish during her microteach. I could not understand that suggestion because during the teaching, we are supposed to speak the target language. At that moment I felt attacked just because we speak Spanish and we are different. The rest of the students did not receive the same type of feedback. It was time to take action about this matter.

I decided to talk to the instructor of the class and made her aware of some of the comments. I asked her if she could talk to the class and ask the students to be tactful in their comments. Immediately she realized that she needed to address this issue with the class next week because we will present another microteach. A year ago, I could have thought of not even getting involved because I am very close to graduation and I will not see these people anymore. I needed to do this for my friend and all the Latino students at [Midwestern University]. I needed to do it for my children who will be attending college in the near future. They need to learn to advocate for others and themselves. I needed to do it for those students that I will teach one day. They will need an advocate and a person who they can trust in this world. It was not an easy decision but I am happy that I addressed this issue. I know this is just the beginning of my journey but it feels good to do the right thing.

(Student artifact)

Through her comments, Susana illuminates the reality that linguistic discrimination, though often subtle, is deeply entrenched at the university. Although fluent use of Spanish in this context should have been celebrated, the peer comments and instructor's apparent unawareness of the issue reflect the notion of tolerance for only "acceptable levels" of native language use. Although not directly affected by the incident, Susana recognized the need to take action on behalf of others, knowing that without such efforts future generations of bilingual learners will continue to experience the same kinds of rejection and alienation.

For many of the participants, the non-acceptance of their native language in school was a certainty and, as preservice and inservice educators, they anticipated their students' inevitable experiences with similar rejection. In her interview, Paola provided the following interpretation when reflecting on her students' understanding of potential negative repercussions associated with native language use: "They don't know any better. Until they go through that experience of that shock—that first shock of where you are told, 'You are not welcome, your language is not welcomed here.'" Many interviewees described the feelings of rejection and alienation that resulted from such initial moments of shock; they relayed the unpredictable responses of school personnel to their inability to fully participate in the English language. These circumstances led participants to begin to see their native language as a *carga*, or burden, that must be carried as they navigated the educational system in search of academic achievement.

Even participants who today are highly accomplished professionals continue to carry the weight of this burden. Paola described her feelings of rejection and alienation in the following way:

> You know there are certain occasions when you are in your professional setting, you know, politics and certain meetings or people that you encounter—and you know that this is not the place [to use Spanish] because of the politics surrounding the context.... [You know because of] a lot of the nonverbal clues. You can sense it. When you walk in, um, you sense the air. It gets very thick.... Sometimes within conversation there are some clues given, um, that, um, the culture is not welcome. The tense—that sometimes it's not very friendly.

Paola's experiences spoke of the importance of developing the ability to detect clues given through nonverbal communication regarding when one's use of native language, as an embodiment of culture, is unacceptable.

The participants described their native language and culture as central to their identity; therefore, when their language was rejected, they *themselves* felt rejected. Paola's words provide a window into this phenomenon:

> I always knew that language was part of my culture, and that that was very, very important because that made up my identity as a person. So when I came from Puerto Rico at the age of 12, even though I was made fun of for speaking Spanish and I was made very uncomfortable, it was still a requirement from my family not to lose a sense of where I came from.... So not speaking my language meant that I was almost denying where I came from or who I was. Wherever I step, whatever I do, my language—my culture—is part of me.

Because language is tied to every other dimension of one's biography, the view or message of educators and society that the native language is inconsequential often results in only a fragmented, partial understanding of students, both cognitively and academically. Mariana reflected on the education system's rush to "mainstream," noting the resulting lack of information that educators had about the strengths she possessed in the native language, a language that she recognized had won her awards in the past. She stated:

> At school, I was in everything in Mexico. I mean, I was sent to un concurso de recitaciones [recitation contest] and it was in first grade and I would sit with third graders. And, I mean, I was so bright and here nobody knew, and I don't think the elementary school ever found out how bright I was because they were trying to mainstream.

Evidence of teachers' lack of preparation and knowledge related to language and the hidden academic potential it carried left many English learners in the periphery, with their academic potential untapped.

Participants related similar instances in which their cognitive and academic abilities seemed to be overlooked or doubted at the university. They shared examples of how college peers seemed to doubt their abilities to fully participate in the curriculum. One student, for example, described an instance in which her comments about ways a group project might be improved were not acted on by the rest of the group until the instructor reiterated the same points. Esmeralda relayed how even her university-appointed advisor seemed to have lower expectations for her:

> I was having a hard semester so I was complaining about how hard and time consuming my math class and I told that to my [university-appointed] advisor and he said the same thing my [high school] counselor has said to me before. "Why don't you do Spanish it would be easier for you." I felt stupid once again but I didn't quit because I was going to demonstrate him and myself that I was capable of doing math and so I stick with math until now. I just don't understand why both of them thought that math was too hard for [me] maybe just because my English is not the best so they thought they were giving me a favor by recommending what they thought it was easier for me, but little do they know me.
>
> *(Student artifact)*

Many other participants related to this idea of being shocked by the way they were initially perceived by peers or faculty and the subsequent feeling that they then must prove wrong the low expectations others held for them.

Compartmentalization of Language

The second theme that emerged from participants' voices was what resulted in educational settings where use of the native language was unacceptable. Participants who were successful in navigating the alienation, isolation, and other consequences recognized that one way to survive the situation was through the compartmentalization of their language. Realizing that at times the use of the native language was allowed and at other times was punished, participants quickly reacted by trying to separate the linguistic halves of themselves.

Navigating the contradictory dynamics of language use in schools, participants recognized that their native language was not perceived as an "asset" in the educational setting; rather, it became a commodity that was "useful" in some circumstances, yet should be hidden in others. Paola described the situation in the following way:

> I don't think it was ever—You know, when you think of the word "asset," you think of something that is celebrated—something that somebody

looks at as, uh, something that is big and awesome. I don't think it was ever looked at as an asset. I think it was *used*, the word is *used*, K–12. When there was another Hispanic kid that came in with no English I was *used* as a student to be that translator, to be the person that helped out the teacher.… I don't ever think my teacher ever celebrated my language or my culture or where I came from. It was more of here is how we celebrate what you bring because we *need* you.

(Original emphasis)

Such commonly experienced scenarios often led to participants becoming social actors, assigned to perform roles (e.g., language broker) based on the sociopolitical dynamics of acceptable time, place, and purpose for native language use.

Participants' compartmentalization of language was often the response or reaction to understanding that benefits could be gained from "playing the game." For many participants, use of the native language was suppressed for survival purposes, on the one hand, or used to ground and maintain a sense of self, on the other. To illustrate, the compartmentalization of the native language manifested responses of survival among participants that related to "fitting in" and "coping" after they had internalized that their native language did not have a place in the U.S. classroom. Mariana stated in her interview:

You know, because I wanted to fit in, I learned to speak English without an accent, and I think that by listening to that, it was like a coping mechanism—like "I can speak English like you can so therefore I might be as smart as you are."

The need to not have an "accent" and "be as smart as" made it necessary for Mariana to present a public persona in the classroom that would lead others to see her as monolingual, and therefore worthy of success.

At times participants felt that their relationships with others were threatened if they insisted on speaking the native language in the presence of monolingual English speakers. This notion of "offending" those around them significantly limited participants' use of the native language. They continually monitored for how "appropriate" it would be to use the native language in specific situations. Teresa, who works with CLD families in her position, described the pressure to speak English in the workplace by saying:

Not that I thought that it [speaking Spanish] was not appropriate. It was just more like not causing any problems for people who didn't understand it. I was using Spanish for, to do my work … But, yes, there were times where I felt … it was best not to use Spanish so the people around me wouldn't feel offended. Not that I was offending them, but they felt that way.

(Interview)

The struggle to determine where and when to use the native language, and for what purposes, caused for some participants an acute sense of shame associated with native language use. They felt the need to assimilate: to talk, act, and think like those around them. One participant stated:

> Growing up and while working on my Bachelor's, I did not feel like I could be myself around other people because if I was, then I would not fit in with the rest of the group. I had to learn to assimilate and act like the majority of the group. There was a point in my life when I was even ashamed [of] speaking Spanish.
>
> *(Saul, survey)*

Participant voices vividly documented the rollercoaster ride that many of these individuals experienced in coming to terms with how their culture, language, and thus identity fit within the educational setting. At the same time, however, they remained cognizant of the importance of using the native language to ground their sense of self and maintain connections to their family and cultural heritage. They recognized that despite the challenges they faced across the educational landscape, they needed to remain connected to the language for their own sense of belonging. Speaking passionately about what her native language meant to her, Mariana shared: "My native language was my family, and it was who I was. It was my, it was my whole being. My person, the way we communicated, how we communicated, love in our family, tradition" (interview). Another participant recognized that speaking her native language reflected to others the pride that she continues to feel in her culture: "The purpose of using my native language is because I am proud of knowing both languages and that I'm able to communicate in these languages.... I am proud of my roots and speaking two languages" (Maria, student artifact).

Bilingualism as a Blessing

The third theme that emerged from participants' collective voice was the notion of seeing bilingualism, with all the challenges that come with being a second language learner, as a blessing. The words of Maria, a preservice teacher, exemplify this theme:

> Being bilingual has influenced me in many ways, because I have the blessing of speaking two languages. I have been granted the opportunity to learn a new language and know Spanish[;] this has influence[d] me in being able to help others that need my assistance. Being bilingual is going to open many doors for me in the future when I become a professional. It makes me proud to be bilingual because I know I can use it to help others.
>
> *(Student artifact)*

Ana, an older student who is both a wife and a mother, similarly recognized and wrote about the benefits of knowing two languages, using "privilege" to express the gratitude she felt in being able to communicate with others around the globe as she continues to develop personally and professionally.

> It is a privilege to speak and understand more than one language. I call this a privilege because I can communicate with people from other countries (not just Americans) and I can learn about their cultures, values, education, way of life, styles, etc.

> Being bilingual has helped [me] to live in this country, I have been able to work and do what I like in another context, giving me the opportunity to grow and be a professional.

> *(Student artifact)*

Subthemes reflected in participants' voices related to the benefits of the native language for self and for others. One participant described the benefits of being bilingual to his overall learning process. Explaining his use of Spanish and English, Francisco said:

> I use both languages, actually, to learn new stuff. I always try to, if I learn a new word in either language, I always look up that word in the equivalent language. It is a great resource because you can make connections—historical connections, linguistic connections.

> *(Interview)*

Many participants similarly commented on their use of cognates as a tool for learning. This strategy has shown potential for bilingual learners, especially in the areas of second language reading comprehension and vocabulary development (Freeman & Freeman, 2004; Goldenberg, 2008).

At other times participants shared how their bilingualism is a gift that they can use to help others. For example, Teresa talked about how her own language learning experiences have given her the ability to empathize with others' struggles and encourage them along the way:

> I'm glad that I went through that because now I can understand how people feel and why they hesitate to do things sometimes. Cuz I felt like that many times. And every time I had to speak to people or to students, I tell them, "You have no idea how many times I entered into a class, the first day of class, and I felt like just going back to home (laughs) and not coming back." Because when I saw the syllabus, honestly it was scary to me—I'm not going to be able to accomplish everything, especially when I saw those big words. I understood the words; it was just intimidating for me. And I just felt like going back and not coming back. But, uh, I tried, I stayed, and I was able to finish. And now that experience, uh, gives me

the confidence to encourage people to do it. Cuz I know they're gonna be able to accomplish it. But they can see that I believe in them, and therefore they go ahead and they try.

(Interview)

Patricia spoke about how she knew that her ability to speak two languages would enable her to better help future students, their parents, and other school faculty. This desire to help children kept her moving forward to achieve her educational goals:

When I first started, I applied for elementary teacher, and then they took us one semester … to elementary schools. And I would just have so many kids frustrating [sic] because they don't know what the teacher was saying. And I always wanted to be a teacher, and then there were days I said, "I hate it. I don't want to be a teacher." But that whole semester when we went to the schools, and I see those kids just crying and saying, "I don't understand the teacher, I just want to go home," when they just got here from different countries—Guatemala, El Salvador, Mexico. It was just, that just broke my heart. And I just, I don't want the kids to suffer like they are. So, um, [it's] just wonderful that I know an extra language. I wouldn't say that I know all of them, but that just gives me a step more than other teachers to be able to communicate with them.

(Interview)

Pointing to the need to help end the cycle of linguistic silencing and suffering, participants such as this young woman continue to find strength to battle the waves of linguistic intolerance to pave the way for the academic success of Latina/o immigrant bilingual learners.

Establishing Sense of Agency

The fourth and final theme that emerged from participants' voices was the development of students' sense of personal and collective agency as Latino/a English learners. For example, participants often times turned painful linguistic challenges into a source of personal motivation as they pushed forward to prove wrong those who doubted their academic abilities. Patricia explained her situation at the university in this way:

Many times they [educators] were like I'm not in the right place.… So those are days [that] make me feel like, yes, I'm not smart enough. This is not where I'm supposed to be. College is not for me. I'm not capable of following the career.… But then those same people make me push myself harder, like prove to them that I was capable of doing, and better then what they were doing.

(Interview)

For Patricia, the struggle to learn the English language and succeed in college classes pushed her to continue when she desperately wanted to quit. She refused to let others silence her or destroy her dreams of becoming a teacher. She went on to say:

> I finally accept who I am and I'm proud of who I am. And even though I have my accent real sharp, I wouldn't change it. And I don't care what other people say. That's who I am, and I wouldn't change it for anything.

> *(Interview)*

For many participants, their ability to see their native language as a *regalo* (gift) was strengthened by, if not indelibly tied to their participation in the BESITOS program and the opportunities it provided for emotional connectedness and for reflection upon issues of language use, status, hybridity, and discrimination as well as other aspects of their identity. Acceptance into the program during her second year of college represented a turning point for Paola, who felt as though she was "a reject and a failure coming to college" in her first year at the university:

> It wasn't until it [Spanish] was appreciated by the BESITOS program that I felt it was an asset. Because writing papers, giving presentations, it never was. It just got in the way.... So, not until I got to BESITOS is when my self-esteem started being built—a building block, one block at a time. From my teachers ... from everybody.... It was like being with family, ... They were building our self-esteem as we went along—"Don't be afraid." You know, "You are who you are, and you have to be proud." And it was the building our self-esteem while they were building our academic level. The two went hand in hand. It wasn't that now you have to take a class ... [Interviewer: It wasn't remediation.] Right. It was both at the same. It wasn't leaving one separate from the other.... Somebody got to, tapped into my talent in college ... and you exploded that talent into something that I could attain.... And so [now] I am supposed to be doing something bigger, because I've always been told that. You have to be an advocate, and you have to fight, and you have to do this, and, you know, you have to help. And that was instilled in me.

Paola experienced healing in the acceptance that she found within the program among people who accepted her and her native language. Today, she is a Director of English Language Arts for a nationally recognized foundation where she utilizes her agency to direct CLD youth on their college-bound educational journeys.

Discussion and Conclusions

Findings suggest that in order to support Latina/o, immigrant English learners' academic achievement in education at the elementary, secondary, and postsecondary levels, support cannot be one-dimensional (Elenes, González, Delgado Bernal, & Villenas, 2001; Holmes Group, 1995). Efforts must target all four dimensions of the student's biography—sociocultural, linguistic, cognitive, and academic. This study allowed the researchers to explore intersections of the linguistic dimension with each of the other three dimensions.

As exemplified in the first theme, *rejection and alienation*, students' sociocultural dimension is intimately tied to their native language. Perceptions of (non) acceptance within the educational community by peers and educators both influence the degree to which students view themselves as capable learners (as evidenced in the cognitive dimension) and color the way they interpret and respond to future interactions related to their use of the native language and the dominant English language. English learners who experience rejection and alienation due to their primary language in their formative years are at significant risk of academic struggles (Baugh, 2009).

Students quickly become savvy about which contexts allow and value use of their native language and which do not. The second theme of *compartmentalization* reveals the outward splintering of students' identities. Though their biographies remain constant, they selectively choose which aspects of their identity they will share with others and in which situations and circumstances. One of the most detrimental consequences of such compartmentalization of self is the failure of educators and the students to draw on the full range of sociocultural, linguistic, cognitive, and academic assets available for use in the learning process. What students in higher education often need, then, are opportunities to see their native language being respected, valued, and encouraged in the educational arena by those with whom they interact on a daily basis (e.g., instructors, peers) in addition to those who provide students with support services (e.g., recruitment personnel; financial aid, enrollment, and advising staff).

Students who have decided for themselves how their language fits into their personal identity spoke to the third theme of *bilingualism as a blessing*. These students emerged from their struggles with linguistic discrimination and disenfranchisement with a stronger sense of who they are, finally unashamed to share their voice. Students' statements further illustrate how some used their dual language abilities as a tool to leverage their success in various contexts.

The notion of student voice is alluded to in many of the selected excerpts throughout this chapter. More specifically, as Latino/a English learners within the BESITOS program, students related an increased *sense of agency* as they progressed through college. This fourth theme was indicated by students' increased understanding of not only their personal experiences as immigrant, English learners in school but also of their ability as learners and future educators to challenge language discrimination and marginalization they see in educational settings.

Given the country's historic struggles to effectively educate linguistic minorities, educators at all levels must actively seek new approaches for responding to the unique needs of immigrant students learning English as an additional language. Students entering higher education need to see the value they place on their native language and culture reflected in the atmosphere and expectations of the campus learning environment. Until English learners are accepted as full members of the academic community, colleges and universities will continue to overlook the wealth of linguistic, sociocultural, cognitive, and academic assets that CLD students bring.

The BESITOS model is designed to increase the recruitment, retention, and graduation of culturally and linguistically diverse students. The success of BESITOS program participants over the last decade is due, in large part, to the ability of faculty and staff to recognize the relevance of situating the students' academic success within their individual biographies. Program staff members strive to create conditions for participants' exploration and affirmation of identity. As linguistic minority students establish their voice and develop their sense of agency, they demonstrate ever-greater persistence in navigating the university's systems to achieve their academic aspirations.

References

Alliance for Excellent Education. (2009). *Factsheet: Latino students and U.S. high schools*. Retrieved from: http://www.all4ed.org/files/Latino_FactSheet.pdf

Baugh, J. (2009). Linguistic diversity, access, and risk. *Review of Research in Education, 33*, 272–282.

Brown v. Board of Education, 347 U.S. 483 (1954).

Carter, A. (1997). Notes from the front line. In J. S. Uglow (Ed.), *Shaking a leg: Collected journalism and writings* (pp. 36–43). London: Chatto & Windus.

Castellanos, J., & Gloria, A. M. (2007). Research considerations and theoretical application for best practices in higher education: Latina/os achieving success. *Journal of Hispanic Higher Education, 6*(4), 378–396.

Ceja, M. (2001). *Applying, choosing, and enrolling in higher education: Understanding the college choice process of first-generation Chicana students*. Unpublished doctoral dissertation, University of California, Los Angeles.

Ceja, M. (2004). Chicana aspirations and the role of parents: Developing resiliency. *Journal of Hispanic Higher Education, 3*(4), 338–362.

Crawford, J. (2004). *Educating English learners* (5th ed.). Los Angeles: Bilingual Educational Services.

Creswell, J. W. (1998). *Qualitative inquiry and research design: Choosing among the five traditions*. Thousand Oaks, CA: Sage.

Cummins, J. (1991). Interdependence of first- and second-language proficiency in bilingual children. In E. Bialystok (Ed.). *Language processing in bilingual children* (pp. 70–89). Cambridge, UK: Cambridge University Press.

Da Silva Iddings, A. C. (2005). Linguistic access and participation: English language learners in an English-dominant community of practice. *Bilingual Research Journal, 29*(1) 165–183.

Delpit, L. (1995). *Other people's children: Cultural conflict in the classroom*. New York: New Press.

Elenes, C. A., González, F. E., Delgado Bernal, D., & Villenas, S. (2001). Chicana/Mexicana feminist pedagogies: Consejos, respeto, y educación in everyday life. *International Journal of Qualitative Studies in Education, 14*(5), 595–602.

Freeman, D. E., & Freeman, Y. S. (2004). *Essential linguistics: What you need to know to teach reading, ESL, spelling, phonics, and grammar.* Portsmouth, NH: Heinemann.

Gay, G. (2000). *Culturally responsive teaching: Theory, research, and practice.* New York: Teachers College Press.

Gay, G., Dingus, J. E., & Jackson, C. W. (2003). *Recruiting teachers of color.* Denver: Education Commission of the States.

Goldenberg, C. (2008, Summer). Teaching English language learners: What the research does—and does not—say. *American Educator, 32*(2) 8–44.

Herrera, S. G. (1995). *Junior high school teachers and the meaning perspectives they hold regarding their Mexican American students: An ethnographic case study.* Unpublished doctoral dissertation, Texas Tech University, Lubbock.

Herrera, S. (2010). *Biography-driven culturally responsive teaching.* New York: Teachers College Press.

Herrera, S. G., & Morales, A. R. (2005, April). *From remediation to acceleration: Recruiting, retaining and graduating future CLD educators.* Paper presented at the annual conference of the American Educational Research Association, Montréal, Canada.

Herrera, S. G., Morales, A. R., Holmes, M. A., & Terry, D. H. (2011-2012). From remediation to acceleration: Recruiting, retaining, and graduating future culturally and linguistically diverse (CLD) educators. *Journal of College Student Retention: Research, Theory & Practice, 13*(2), 229–250.

Herrera, S. G., & Murry, K. G. (2005). *Mastering ESL and bilingual methods: Differentiated instruction for culturally and linguistically diverse (CLD) students.* Boston: Allyn and Bacon.

Herrera, S. G., Murry, K. G., & Cabral, R. M. (2007). *Assessment accommodations for classroom teachers of culturally and linguistically diverse students.* Boston: Allyn and Bacon.

Hobson-Horton, L. D., & Owens, L. (2004). From freshman to graduate: Recruiting and retaining minority students. *Journal of Hispanic Higher Education, 3*(1), 86–107.

Holmes Group. (1995). *Tomorrow's schools of education.* East Lansing, MI: Author.

Howard, T. C. (2010). *Why race and culture matter in schools.* New York: Teachers College Press.

Hurtado, S., Carter, D. F., & Spuler, A. (1996). Latino transition to college: Assessing the difficulties and factors in successful college adjustment. *Research in Higher Education, 37*(2), 135–157.

Kindler, A. (2002). *Survey of the states' limited English proficient students & available educational programs and services 1999–2000 summary report.* Retrieved from National Clearinghouse for English Language Acquisition and Language Instruction Educational Programs website: http://www.ncela.gwu.edu/files/rcd/BE021854/SEALEPSurvey9900.pdf

Krashen, S. (1991). Bilingual education and second language acquisition theory. In C. F. Leyba (Ed.), *Schooling and language minority students: A theoretical framework* (pp. 51–79). Los Angeles: Evaluation, Dissemination and Assessment Center, CSULA.

Lachat, M. A. (2004). *Standards-based instruction and assessment for English language learners.* Thousand Oaks, CA: Corwin Press.

Ladson-Billings, G. (1998). Just what is critical race theory and what's it doing in a nice field like education? *International Journal of Qualitative Studies in Education, 11*(1), 7–24.

Ladson-Billings, G. (1999). Preparing teachers for diverse student populations: A critical race theory perspective. *Review of Research in Education, 24*, 211–247.

Lau v. Nichols, 414 U.S. 563 (1974).

Lincoln, Y., & Guba, E. (1985). *Naturalistic inquiry.* Newbury Park, CA: Sage.

Locks, A. M., Hurtado, S., Bowman, N. A., & Oseguera, L. (2008). Extending notions of campus climate and diversity to students' transition to college. *The Review of Higher Education, 31*(3), 257–285.

Macedo, D. (2006). *Literacies of power: What Americans are not allowed to know.* Boulder, CO: Westview Press.

Mendez v. Westminster School District, 64 F. Supp. U.S. 544 (1946).

Merriam, S. (1998). *Case study research in education: A qualitative approach.* San Francisco: Jossey-Bass.

Meyer v. Nebraska, 262 U.S. 390 (1923).

National Center for Education Statistics. (2009). Table 285, data from Higher Education General Information Survey (HEGIS), "Degrees and Other Formal Awards Conferred" surveys, 1976–77 and 1980–81; and 1989–90 through 2007–08 Integrated Postsecondary Education Data System, "Completions Survey" (IPEDS-C:90-99), and Fall 2000 through Fall 2008; Table 227, data from Higher Education General Information Survey (HEGIS), "Fall Enrollment in Colleges and Universities" surveys, 1976 and 1980; and 1990 through 2008 Integrated Postsecondary Education Data System (IPEDS), "Fall Enrollment Survey" (IPEDS-EF:90), and Spring 2001 through Spring 2009. Washington, DC: U.S. Department of Education.

National Clearinghouse for English Language Acquisition. (2007). *The growing number of limited English proficient students, 1995/96-2005/06.* Retrieved from www.ncela.gwu.edu/files/uploads/4/GrowingLEP_0506.pdf

Nieto, S. (2004). *Affirming diversity: The sociopolitical context of multicultural education* (4th ed.). Boston: Allyn and Bacon.

Passel, J. S., & Cohn, D. (2008). *U.S. population projections 2005–2050.* Retrieved from Pew Research Center website: http://pewhispanic.org/files/reports/85.pdf

Plyler v. Doe, 457 U.S. 202 (1982).

Romo, J. (2005). Border pedagogy from the inside out: An autoethnographic study. *Journal of Latinos and Education, 4,* 193–210.

Solorzáno, D., Allen, W. R., & Carroll, G. (2002). Keeping race in place: Racial microaggressions and campus racial climate at the University of California, Berkeley. *Chicano-Latino Review, 23,* 15–46.

Spring, J. (2005). *The American school: 1642–2004.* Boston: McGraw Hill.

Teddlie, C., & Yu, F. (2008). Mixed methods sampling: A typology with examples. In V. L. P. Clark & J. W. Creswell (Eds.), *The mixed methods reader* (pp. 199–228). Los Angeles: Sage.

Thomas, W. P., & Collier, V. P. (1997). *School effectiveness for language minority students* (NCBE Resource Collection Series No. 9). Washington, DC: National Clearinghouse for Bilingual Education.

U.S. Commission on Civil Rights (USCOCR). (1971). *The unfinished education.* Washington, DC: Author.

U.S. Commission on Civil Rights (USCOCR). (1972, Spring/Summer). The excluded student: Educational practices affecting Mexican Americans in the Southwest. *Journal of Mexican American Studies, 1*(3-4), 192–200.

Valenzuela, A. (1999). *Subtractive schooling: U.S.-Mexican youth and the politics of caring.* Albany, NY: SUNY Press.

13

BENEFITS AND COSTS OF EXERCISING AGENCY

A Case Study of an English Learner Navigating a Four-Year University

Ronald Fuentes

English learners (ELs) have progressively become a prominent and fast growing population on many university campuses. ELs are defined here as students whose first language is not English and who may be in need of English language support. These students have been identified by educational institutions as having limited English proficiency. ELs represent 10.8% of the total U.S. K–12 public school enrollment (National Clearinghouse for English Language Acquisition, 2011). In the United States, approximately 13% of undergraduate students speak a language other than English at home (NCES, 2002). These demographic trends raise critical questions regarding ELs' progression, barriers, and equality in higher education institutions. Information regarding these students' experiences is vital in the pursuit of social equality for linguistic minorities.

Research into linguistic and ethnic minority students' experiences has mostly centered on socioeconomic class, limited English language proficiency, gender, and race/ethnicity as factors affecting their academic and social progression within educational institutions (Centrie, 2004; Lee, 2005; Leki, 2007). Similarly, institutional culture is a significant factor that can powerfully shape students' performance and engagement by ultimately facilitating or hindering their academic and social performance, engagement, and goals (Pascarella & Terenzini, 1991). Institutional culture refers to a set of taken-for-granted beliefs, values, and assumptions. It is an ideological system composed of continually competing visions and values that marks people's thinking within an educational institution.

The purpose of this chapter is to examine how institutional culture influences and shapes ELs' behaviors and ideological beliefs, what tensions arise, and how they respond to institutional culture in a higher education setting. I chronicle one female undergraduate EL's (Nasim)[1] perceptions and experiences of her university culture and how certain features affected her academic and social life at a public university. Success at the university largely depended on the assimilation and resistance strategies she developed in response to university culture. I argue that although the coping strategies used by ELs like Nasim to navigate the university system can further EL marginalization and alienation, these same strategies can also lead to EL success.

Literature on School Culture

Research on school effectiveness has found school culture to be a significant factor affecting students' performance (Reynolds & Teddlie, 2000; Smylie & Hart, 1999). A study by Brady (2006) found that school culture influenced academic achievement and student engagement among secondary school students. Hu and Kuh (2002) and Pascarella and Terenzini (1991) concluded that school culture had a considerable impact on student academic development as well as student engagement with the institution. Focusing on students' academic and social integration, researchers have examined students' experiences and involvement in courses, programs, disciplines, interactions with peers and instructors from a student's perspective (Hermanowicz, 2005; Marcoulides, Heck, & Papanastasiou, 2005). These studies reveal that student experiences with school culture can be an important determinant of student academic and social achievement.

At the university level, research examining the relationship between institutional culture and students tends to focus on the experiences and perceptions of racial or ethnic groups. Since most American universities tend to reflect and reproduce the values and attitudes of the White monolingual middle class, racial minority students often experience values and situations inconsistent with their conduct and beliefs (Jones, Castellanos, & Cole, 2002). Ancis, Sedlacek, and Mohr (2000) found that African Americans described more negative accounts of the university than Asian American, Latino/a, and White student groups. Concretely, African Americans reported racial/ethnic hostility, pressure to conform to academic performance and behavior stereotypes, pressure to adopt language and dress standards, unequal treatment by university faculty and staff, and faculty racism. Studies by Cabrera and Nora (1994) and Hurtado (1992, 1994) found that Hispanics' experiences with elements of university culture produced a state of disorientation, confusion, social isolation, and racial tension.

Although university culture has been examined in relation to other student populations, there is little investigation of the interaction between university culture and ELs. Research regarding ELs' experiences in university frequently documents and describes their learning processes and strategies in ESL skills-based and discipline-specific courses (Buttaro, 2003; Zamel & Spack, 2004);

yet, little scholarship is specific to ELs and university culture. The present study intends to fill the gap in knowledge regarding ELs and higher education by examining an EL's experiences of institutional culture, the role it may play in her academic and social engagement and endeavors, and how individual agency converges with institutional culture.

Theoretical Framework

The definition of university culture that I present draws on definitions of school culture by the following scholars: Maslowski (2006), Fullan and Hargreaves (1996), and Kuh and Hall (1993). I define university culture as a set of taken-for-granted beliefs, values, and assumptions. It is an instrument, frequently invisible, through which ideological and cultural transmission occurs, and it is often undergirded by an educational institution's policies and practices. It is an ideological system made up of a set of constantly negotiated ideas and beliefs that characterizes individuals' thinking within an educational institution. Through this system institutional members share and develop a common interpretive lens used to make decisions about appropriate and inappropriate actions and behavior. The nature of this frame of reference is to guide and give meaning to the actions and behaviors of an educational institution and the individuals within it. University culture is developed, disseminated, and maintained over time by multiple stakeholders' beliefs and social interactions and a university's declared and undeclared policies and practices. With its amalgam of competing and negotiated beliefs and wide ranging contradictions and tensions, university culture can be a powerful and distinctive instrument affecting student achievement, integration, and persistence.

In the present study, the term *university culture* reflects a multidimensionality, fragmentation, and plurality by embracing the *moving mosaic* metaphor, coined by Toffler (1990) and adopted by Hargreaves (1994) and Hargreaves and Macmillan (1995). Toffler (1990) asks his readers to imagine "a moving mosaic composed not on a flat solid wall, but on many shifting see-through panels, one behind the other, overlapping, interconnected, the colors and shapes continually blending, contrasting, and changing" (p. 221). Like a mosaic, a university is comprised of individual pieces that take the form of various faculties, departments, and organizations. Individuals within each division and subdivision may have a distinctive culture and thus be in conflict with one another. Students, faculty, and administrators may have conflicting understandings and visions of university culture. A university may not have a single and unified vision of institutional culture; rather a university can have multiple cultures which are continually competing for legitimacy and negotiated by stakeholders with conflicting interests and views. These stakeholders' beliefs and values give shape to fragmented perceptions and visions of university culture instead of a single and unitary one. While recognizing that multiple perceptions of culture may exist among various stakeholders in a university, many commonalities in the ways these stakeholders perceive culture may also exist. The differences in perception do not necessarily hinder the formation of commonalities among various stakeholders or the day-to-day functioning of an institution.

I adopt Bourdieu's (1986, 1997) theory of cultural reproduction, which provides a means of analyzing the day-to-day struggles, failures, successes, and interactions of individuals in response to elements of university culture. Bourdieu's theory of cultural reproduction employs the concepts of *capital, habitus,* and *field* in analyzing language in education and its subsequent role in the process of social reproduction. Cultural capital refers to the knowledge, skills, and qualifications that individuals possess, use, and acquire; habitus references individuals' set of dispositions or mood—i.e., how they should think or act in certain situations; field refers to the spheres of interaction (e.g., education) where individuals engage in a specific set of practices. Since educational institutions retain a significant influence over the way individuals learn to speak, listen, and interact, Bourdieu's cultural reproduction concepts become pivotal in linking the social conditions of the production and reproduction of a variety of subtle, common, taken-for-granted practices to universities' culture.

Following the work of several scholars adopting reproductive frameworks, this study also examines the role of agency (Canagarajah, 2004; Davidson, 1996; Gibson, 1988; Luykx, 1999; Portes & Rumbaut, 2001; Willis, 1981). Levinson and Holland (1996) state that cultural production "provides a direction for understanding how human agency operates under powerful structural constraints. Through the production of cultural forms, created within the structural constraints of sites such as schools, subjectivities form and agency develops" (p. 14). Individuals do not simply accept schools' ideology and practices, but rather there exists a constant tension in which schools' norms, values, and identity options are assimilated or resisted. For example, Gibson (1988) demonstrates how Sikh immigrants consciously accommodate and acculturate to dominant group ways in an American high school without losing their Sikh identity and culture. Gibson uses the term *accommodation* to refer to the instances in which Sikhs consciously choose to adopt the ways of the dominant group over their own when they believe this to be in their best interests. Her study reveals that Sikh students exercise agency by adopting many aspects of the dominant American culture while actively resisting others. Similar to Gibson's notion of accommodation, Portes and Rumbaut (2001) adopt the term *selective acculturation* to demonstrate the instances whereby immigrant youth selectively acquire dominant cultural practices while deliberately preserving their own ethnic culture and values. Merging cultural reproduction and agentive perspectives allows for the examination of schooling within a specific context and its relationship to students' attitudes and practices.

Method

Nasim, the subject of this chapter, is part of a larger project that examines ELs' experiences of university culture and how this institutional feature affects their academic and social life at a public university (Fuentes, 2009). Among my participants, I chose Nasim as the focus of this study because of her distinct ethnic, linguistic, and religious background and varied educational experiences. Since this study examines how an EL perceives and experiences university culture and how one responds to it, Nasim described such perceptions and experiences more extensively than the other participants. Located in an urban setting, Northern Green University (NGU) is a public university with approximately 45,000 students and 7,000 faculty members. Out of a 33-participant pool, 5 undergraduate nonnative English-speaking participants enrolled in a number of ESL courses, including Nasim, were recruited from Kanno and Varghese's (2008, 2010) study on immigrant ELs in higher education. I adopted the method of maximum variation sampling (Patton, 2002) for participant selection because it details the unique characteristics of each subject while simultaneously identifying similar themes and patterns across the subjects. The selection and recruitment of participants was based on their background, including first language, ethnicity, gender, age of arrival in the United States, parental education level, and English proficiency level (as indicated by their previous and/or current enrollment in ESL classes). I wanted to maximize the sample within each group in terms of these characteristics, and I wanted approximately half of my participants to be first-generation college students and the other half of participants not to have this attribute.

By NGU's standards, ELs were those students who do not have American citizenship and do not speak English as a first language (see also Shapiro, this volume). NGU did not require all entering students to demonstrate English language proficiency; rather only non-U.S. citizens were required to do so. Once students were categorized as ELs, they were required to demonstrate proficiency by submitting a minimum score on one of several qualifying standardized tests (e.g., 237 on TOEFL or 490 on SAT) or completing mandatory courses in the Academic ESL Program (AEP). Students needing to satisfy the English language proficiency requirement had to continue to register for AEP courses each succeeding academic quarter until the sequence of courses is completed. Since the participants in this study did not meet the university's English proficiency criteria, all of them were required to take AEP classes in addition to their other coursework.

AEP classes did not count toward graduation credits; yet, they were graded and tabulated into students' grade point average (GPA). Also, these courses entailed an additional cost of approximately $1,000 per course above regular university tuition. Approximately half of the AEP students were freshmen and sophomores; the other half upper level students and graduate students. AEP classes consisted of a sequence of five courses: 100A, 100B, 100C, 101A and 101B. Non-U.S. citizen students might be required to take all or some of these courses depending on the English proficiency level they demonstrated at the time of their admissions to NGU.

Nasim

Nasim was a 21-year-old senior student completing a B.A. in Painting and Drawing. In 2002, she arrived in the United States as a refugee from Iran. Nasim was Azeri, the largest ethnic minority in Iran, and she belonged to a persecuted and discriminated religious minority, the Baha'i. Since Baha'is were prohibited from attending higher education institutions in Iran, her parents decided to immigrate to the United States. Nasim enrolled in Grade 11 and successively took ESL courses during her junior and senior years of high school. She attended a community college for two years, where she took one ESL course. At NGU, Nasim was required to take AEP classes to satisfy the university's English language proficiency requirement. In addition to AEP courses, Nasim took several painting and drawing classes. She also took pre-optometry courses at a community college. Nasim lived at home and she primarily financed her studies through student loans and grants. She was applying to optometry schools in the United States and awaiting her American citizenship.

Data Collection

Data collection approximately spanned an academic year (mid-September 2007 to mid-June 2008). It consisted of two sets of EL interviews (pre-shadow and post-shadow observation interviews), five shadow observations, EL journal logs, email exchanges, and data-clarification sessions. Selection, recruitment, and qualitative in-depth structured pre-shadow observation interviews of the participant occurred at the beginning of the academic year. Shadow observations were performed for the participant's on-campus, school-day activities throughout a 20-week period for five entire non-consecutive school days. Post-shadow observation interviews took place after the completion of the five shadow observations.

Data Analysis

Grounded theory guided the process of data analysis (Strauss & Corbin, 1994). Theory development emerged from the process of collecting, transcribing, coding, contrasting, and comparing the data. The development of theory was grounded in localized and detailed narratives and experiences. The interviews and observations in this study generated and illuminated, in Denzin's (1994) terms, individuals' *epiphanies* (i.e., defining life experiences). This lens allowed me to examine how Nasim construed her on-campus experiences with NGU's institutional culture.

Prior to conducting my data analysis, all interview recordings, shadow observations, and hand-written fieldnotes were transcribed fully as they materialized. In adopting the perspective that "analysis is a cyclical process and a reflexive activity" (Coffey & Atkinson, 1996, p.10), I produced reflective journal entries throughout the data collection and transcription period that not only conceptualized but also raised questions about the data. Data segments were collected and grouped around salient patterns; I entered interview transcripts, shadow observation fieldnotes, researcher and participant journals, and email exchanges into the ATLAS.ti (Version 5.0) computer program.

The concept of narrative inquiry was used to capture and transmit Nasim's experiences at NGU. Wolcott states, "qualitative researchers need to be storytellers" (1996, p. 17). Adopting a narrative inquiry approach placed Nasim and her experiences at the forefront, and it provided a platform from which she recast her perspectives and day-to-day life experiences. Hence, like stories, a participant's experiences are structured modes of conveying information (Coffey & Atkinson, 1996). It is through this narrative framework that Nasim's experiences are chronicled.

University Culture Experiences

Nasim reported that her experiences and perceptions of NGU's institutional culture impacted her academic and social achievements, integration, sense of belonging, and overall engagement at the university. Two dimensions of university culture were perceived as affecting her integration and sense of belonging: high academic standards and the primacy of English.

High Academic Standards

Nasim cited high academic standards and the resulting competitive spirit among students as important and unique elements of NGU's institutional culture. The exigency of outstanding academic achievement was a source of constant pressure and anxiety for Nasim. "They make you work hard because the standards are high but sometimes you get overwhelmed and you feel like you don't belong here," she lamented. The high academic demands and high stakes environment, especially in NGU's science courses, cultivated in Nasim feelings of anxiety and resentment towards the university, causing her to take pre-optometry courses at a local community college. Nasim was an academically capable student who, even though having maintained a 3.4–3.5 GPA, decided to opt for community college courses because she could not accept and cope with the academic demands of NGU's science courses.

In Nasim's view, some students such as native-English speakers (NESs) could more easily meet the university's high academic standards because they were more likely to possess the cultural and linguistic capital to do so; ELs on the other hand faced more difficulties in achieving those standards because they tended to lack the cultural and linguistic capital. This difference in capital made it more difficult for ELs to succeed at the university, which in turn produced feelings of discouragement in ELs and led some of them to discontinue their university studies. Nasim explained:

> If you're a good student, if you do like good all the time, then like it doesn't matter but then in general it discourages a lot of people.... Like lot of people just give up and they can do well ... I think should like no human being should be compared to someone else. It's like you are your own person, you are who you are and you shouldn't be compared to someone else.

Nasim believed that NGU's high academic standards led students to compare each other's abilities resulting in a division of two student groups: those who met (e.g., NESs) and those who did not meet (e.g., ELs) the university's strict academic standards. For ELs, "it just depends what position you are in," said Nasim. According to her, *position* referenced ELs' sociocultural environment and predispositions such as student's ability and motivation to perform well, socioeconomic status, cultural upbringing, and English language proficiency. This lack of NES cultural capital and habitus, which Nasim seemed to reference, made achieving success at NGU more difficult for her and other ELs. In Nasim's view, since the university conferred value upon the cultural capital of NESs, ELs' success at the university largely depended on their acquisition of NES cultural capital and habitus. The likelihood of attaining a high academic standing, and ultimate academic success, at the university largely depended on ELs being in a similar position as NESs: i.e., sharing their dispositions and attributes. For Nasim, inability to attain such academic performance standards led to discouragement, disappointment, and disengagement from the university. She minimized her academic and social engagement with the university not because she believed she was academically incapable but because she objected to the entire value system of the university. Nasim tended to show disdain for American behaviors and attitudes, and oftentimes expressed her sense of superiority to American students. She commented, "There are [American] things that as Persian I cannot accept it and I guess that what makes me different than an American."

Nasim often considered discontinuing her education: "Sometimes, I feel like I can't do it. I should think of something else, something different." She believed that the university's high academic standards, which included native-like English proficiency in reading, writing, and class discussions affected ELs like herself more negatively than any other student group; they heightened her insecurities, sense of not belonging, and sense of marginalization when unable to meet such high demands. These high academic standards primarily reflected the characteristics and experiences of dominant group members at the university—e.g., NESs—which in turn facilitated their acquisition of knowledge and academic progress. ELs like Nasim, who were not members of the dominant group, therefore became disadvantaged because the institutional culture did not reflect their historical, cultural, and social experiences. University culture not only invalidated ELs' capital but also highlighted ELs' lack of NES capital. It heightened ELs' sense of not belonging for their lack of valued capital, and thereby ensured the reproduction of NESs' dominant group position at the university.

The Primacy of English

For Nasim, NGU was a monolingual institution that did not value other languages besides English. The primacy of English is not particular to NGU's university culture but rather marks American university culture in general. More importantly, it suggests how normalized and taken for granted the status of English is in American universities. "There are people who speak different languages but like everybody speaks English here," she said. Walking through campus grounds, Nasim reported that most signs, if not all, were in English. The absence of displays in other languages besides English reinforced the dominant position of English at NGU. Nasim critiqued English monolingualism as the dominant norm even though many NGU students were multilingual. In her view, multilingual students' knowledge was viewed as deficient while the knowledge of the dominant NES group was considered the only knowledge of value. Nasim wrote in her journal:

> One thing they say is that they value diversity, but I think this is not true (to some extent) because I as an ESL student think that the fact that I have to take ESL classes, or in writing classes, my writing is being compared to an American student is not fair.

For Nasim, mastery of the English language was as an important element of NGU's institutional culture. She frequently referred to the university's exceptionally stringent English requirements as an obstacle in her educational goals because they incurred additional stress, finances, and study time. "The biggest obstacle I have is just English language," she stated. Nasim felt that the university's English language requirements were unfair to ELs. These requirements not only intensified her indifference towards improving her English skills in AEP classes but also intensified her aversion towards the university and the United States in general. The difficulty of meeting such high English standards caused her to feel alienated and marginalized. She avoided classes that required her to speak, give presentations, and write extensively. Nasim sought ways to sidestep oral communication in her classes. For example, during a group presentation for an art history class, Nasim was the only member of her group to not present. She had agreed with her peers that she would prepare the presentation materials in lieu of presenting. Nasim explained:

> I'm not comfortable speaking English. Sometimes it's hard. Like you don't know how people are gonna think about you … since they're talking to someone, you feel like "Oh, if I say something wrong, what's gonna happen?" "What are they going to think of us?" And since it's like biggest school and everybody thinks that everybody here is perfect and they know everything. And since I don't know the English language perfectly, I feel like oh, if I say something, if I don't say right, then it will look bad.

Nasim was an academically competent student but she strongly objected to the university's English language requirements and competitive academic environment. Her belief that she was required to speak English proficiently led her to minimize her academic and social engagement with the university, causing her to be a quiet and distant individual and producing feelings of not belonging.

Nasim struggled to understand why NGU made a distinction among students based on citizenship and why it did not require all students to demonstrate English language proficiency. When asked to explain her response at having to take AEP courses, Nasim stated, "At first, I was a little mad. But then I was like OK that's how it is. I should be happy that I'm here and if they make me do something, I gotta do it. This is not my country." She seemed to conclude that since she was not an American citizen, she did not have the right to protest against the university's English language proficiency requirements. This statement seemed to contradict earlier statements in which Nasim expressed her extreme opposition, bitterness, resentment, and anger towards AEP coursework. For instance, when asked to characterize her experiences in AEP classes, Nasim adamantly responded: "I hated it; it's wrong; I didn't learn anything." Commenting on the usefulness of AEP courses, she said, "They're repeating the things that you know and I already know the stuff. I just need to practice more and I'm not going to learn it in three months, so just leave me alone."

University Interactions and Involvement

Nasim commented that NGU's institutional culture severely hampered her interactions at and involvement with the university. "I think they have made things very hard that you don't have time to socialize. Even though, they want you to socialize in class, to find friends, and study, and make a study group and all that," she stated. While Nasim believed that NGU provided students with various opportunities and outlets for socialization such as student organizations, clubs, and study groups, she found it difficult to balance her academic obligations and university social life. Due to the importance NGU placed on high academic achievement and English language proficiency, Nasim felt that she could only dedicate her time to either academic or social pursuits. She decided to devote most of her time and energies to academic endeavors which constantly made her feel tired and overwhelmed. Establishing relationships with peers and instructors is important not only for socialization but also for academic performance (Leki, 2007). The lack of social interaction at the university heightened Nasim's disengagement from the university.

Nasim's on-campus interactions were few. She spent very little time on campus; most of it was spent frequently alone and in silence in a university café studying and preparing for the upcoming class. Nasim often expressed a sense of alienation and a sense of not belonging to NGU, which she principally attributed to the university culture and her EL status:

> As a second language or as a nonnative I never think that I belong. I'm very happy to be in this country. I have a lot of opportunities but I never think that I belong to this place. It's just like a plant that is used to a pot and if you take it out of the pot, then the plant, it's hard for that plant to grow again.

Nasim perceived that NESs were unsympathetic or did not understand the difficulties she experienced as an EL at NGU. For instance, NESs did not comprehend how Nasim was a NGU student if she did not have superior English skills. She described interactions with NESs:

> It depends who you're dealing with. Some of them are very open, some of them aren't.... As for some of them, it's just like you tell them that you're not from here and your English isn't as good as it should be and they're like "Oh no, if you're at NGU you gotta know it. How come you don't know it?"

This lack of understanding contributed to Nasim's disassociation with NESs. She found it hard and uncomfortable to associate with NESs primarily because of English language difficulties. Nasim believed she could not make any linguistic mistakes when interacting with NESs; she felt stressed and ill at ease. Conversation and interaction with NESs threatened her academic and social endeavors because she perceived that peers and instructors tended to equate EL status with weak academic ability.

Nasim also experienced cultural stereotyping at the university. NESs were often apprehensive when meeting Nasim because of her Iranian ethnicity. "Some of them [keep their] distance, some of them are scared. Some of them think 'Oh my God, you're from that region.' when you say like I'm from Middle East," she explained. Students' preconceptions and fears of people from the Middle East as well as their English proficiency expectations contributed to Nasim's state of unease and anxiety when interacting with NESs. She projected this sentiment onto incoming ELs by telling them:

They are going to face a lot of kind of like not discrimination, it's just like they might not be treated the same way as Americans are treated and they should not take that personal. I guess it's just the way it is. It's how the world works.

A sense of resignation, pessimism, and unhappiness sprang from Nasim when discussing not only her university interactions but also her university experience in general. The university's institutional culture limited her on-campus interactions, making her feel alienated and marginalized. This in turn heightened her unwillingness to participate in university life.

Student Resistance: Paving a Path to Success

Despite such intense feelings of alienation, Nasim nonetheless persisted and eventually graduated from NGU. Central to her success was her selective acculturation (Gibson, 1988; Portes & Rumbaut, 2001) strategies in regards to the university's institutional culture. She selectively accepted and rejected elements of university culture. This strategy allowed her to preserve her home culture while simultaneously assimilating new cultural and ideological knowledge. For example, Nasim had similar beliefs to those of NGU, particularly in regards to the university's hard-work ethos and self-reliance ideology before her NGU attendance. This theme was prominent among the university's faculty and administrators. Dr. Heathers, Provost of the university advised ELs:

> Take advantage of as much as they possibly can. This university has programs that are so diverse, so rich, so broad, so deep that I would hope a nonnative speaker would ask all the time, use their advisors to introduce to them the different kinds of opportunities that are open to them.

While previously being exposed to such ideas, Nasim became more aware of the importance of assimilating more deeply these beliefs and values at NGU if she were to achieve her goals of graduating from NGU and attending an optometry school. At the university she had learned to believe that through hard work and perseverance one could achieve anything:

> I learned that if I work hard no matter what it is I can overcome the obstacles. It's just a matter of working hard and having faith in what you're doing.... And I learned that you need, like you should have a goal. If you don't have a goal ... you [are] lost.

Attending NGU was a means to an end for Nasim. Her goal was to obtain an NGU undergraduate degree and attend an optometry school. She had this agenda prior to attending the university, and she navigated the institution in ways that would help her accomplish that agenda. NGU deemed that students', and particularly ELs' success, depended on their ability to take charge of their education. This was voiced by several NGU administrators such as Mr. Davids, Director of Recruitment and Outreach. He advised ELs:

> Take ownership of their education. And so, it's a place where you reach out for the resources that you need. If it's from the professor, you demand the resource. 'Cause it's your education and you're paying and so you should be getting what you need out of it. And so, that's just the general advice. Depending on the student, I would refer them to maybe some different offices writing centers and things like that. But just generally take ownership.

The university favored a system that called on students to actively participate in and assume ownership of their actions and overall education. This not only reduced the university's direct involvement in students' education but also lay most of the responsibility of students' educational successes and failures on students themselves. In these terms, NGU functioned on a system that measured student progress primarily on individual ability. In this meritocratic system, students were ultimately sorted into varying degrees of academic proficiency that legitimated and reinforced inequality. ELs, like Nasim, who may have lacked English language proficiency, familiarity with the American schooling system, and the necessary cultural capital were more likely to have difficulty in attaining success at NGU than NESs.

While agreeing with the meritocratic principles espoused by the university, Nasim disagreed with and refuted certain elements of university culture. She resisted the university's insistence on high academic achievement. The high academic demands not only created stress and anxiety but also made it more difficult for her to earn the high GPA necessary to attend an optometry school. This academic ethos presented Nasim with obstacles that interfered with the realization of her goals. Nasim declared: "I would not take science class at NGU anymore. I've taken it once and I would not take it anymore because it affects my grade and my GPA and I don't want to get a low grade." Rather than take science courses at NGU, Nasim opted to complete these courses at a local community college. This act of resistance and her overall selective accultura-tion strategies allowed her to obtain her goal—high GPA and admittance to an optometry school—and to achieve ultimate success. On the whole, Nasim was unhappy with her NGU experience. Her main concern was "getting out of this school and going to optometry school. Become an optometrist and start working ... I don't like this school."

Discussion

Two dimensions of institutional culture were identified by Nasim as potentially affecting her full participation and sense of belonging at the university: high academic standards and the primacy of English. Scholarship suggests that concerns regarding one's sense of belonging can directly affect one's achievement (Gibson, Bejínez, Hidalgo, & Rolón; 2004; Koyama, 2007). A sense of not belonging can make students avoid school resources such as professors' office hours, tutorial centers, and counseling and can potentially lead to attrition. Research demonstrates that school culture can powerfully affect both positively and negatively students' academic and social performance (Dewit et al., 2000; Voelkl, 1994; Wang, Haertel, &Walberg, 1997). In this respect, institutional culture can be viewed as a significant factor affecting ELs' sense of belonging and, ultimately, degree completion.

Student agency played a pivotal role in Nasim's experiences of university culture. In response to NGU's institutional culture, Nasim developed a selective acculturation strategy to achieve her goals within the university. This strategy allowed Nasim to adopt institutional culture elements that best suited her needs and interests and to resist those elements that conflicted with her cultural and individual beliefs. She developed a critical awareness of the limits and possibilities she faced at the university. Nasim not only identified the obstacles impeding her success but also developed strategies to cope with and overcome them. She weighed the benefits of her strategies against the cost of those strategies in terms of attaining her goals at the university. At times, her actions incurred great losses on a social and personal level; yet, she principally viewed that the gains made by these actions outweighed the losses because it allowed her to achieve her overall objectives. Nasim's exercise of agency successfully allowed her to achieve them.

Nasim articulated success in a way that reflected one of the fundamental messages of the institutional culture: The opportunity to achieve success was the result of one's individual effort. She firmly believed that she was responsible for taking ownership of her education and the subsequent actions leading to her successes as well as failures. Nasim believed in high academic performance but rejected the value system the university attached to it. The high academic standard orientation and the resultant competitive academic environment were not conducive to the pursuit of her goals. Nasim's decision to take pre-optometry courses at a community college was a means of attaining a high GPA but also rejecting the behavioral practices and value-laden ideology ascribed to high grades by the university. This action ultimately brought her success in that she attained the high GPA to be admitted to optometry school.

One area of agency involved Nasim's approach to oral and literacy development. She recognized the importance of having strong oral and literacy skills. However, she purposely avoided taking any courses with a demanding writing component because the extra time and work needed to be successful in these courses could hurt her academic standing. Nasim exercised silence and nonparticipation in her courses. Active participation revealed and accentuated the linguistic differences between herself and her NES classmates. These differences often led instructors to deduct grade points from students' work because of their inability to reproduce the proficiency level of their NES peers. In adopting self-censorship (Kanno & Varghese, 2010) and nonparticipation strategies, Nasim avoided being identified as EL and the possibility of being penalized with lower grades. She pursued anonymity and nonparticipation because it allowed her to better achieve her academic goals and it was more in-tune with her behavior and cultural background. These actions did not hinder the achievement of Nasim's goals but rather helped her achieve them—albeit at the cost of being alienated from university life.

The coping strategies used by Nasim to navigate a university system furthered her marginalization and alienation. While her strategies produced negative results such as social isolation, she considered that the gains made by these strategies far outweighed the losses because it allowed her to achieve her objectives. Research demonstrates that students who exercise agency can increase their marginalization and contribute to the reproduction of social inequality (Fordham, 1993; Holland & Eisenhart, 1988; Weis, 1985, 1990; Willis, 1981). Although Nasim's actions led to her marginalization in the university, they did not lead to the reproduction of social inequality. Despite her rejection of the university culture and its value system, Nasim was able to acquire the necessary cultural capital (i.e., a bachelor's degree) to attend an optometry school. Coping strategies, such as those adopted by Nasim, may be viewed as challenging institutional practices of the dominant class; yet, they simultaneously hamper ELs' engagement with university activities. In Nasim's case, the exercise of agency in the form of resistance led to her success.

Conclusion

The questions set forth in this chapter are fundamentally questions about the interactions of students and schooling. Based on Nasim's experiences, institutional culture was reported as a significant factor affecting her participation, engagement, and a sense of belonging in a university setting. Even though Nasim experienced, in some cases, great problems with university culture that made her contemplate discontinuing her education, she persevered. To examine ELs' experiences of institutional culture is to examine how attitudes toward school and mainstream sociocultural values, on the part of ELs, are assimilated and resisted. Nasim consistently exercised agency in negotiating her subject positions in specific environments. The actions she took largely depended on how she perceived herself in relation to a specific context. Nasim's actions, which may be in accordance and/or conflict with the university's institutional culture, were made in terms of achieving her goals and ultimate success. While the institutional culture had largely hindered Nasim's engagement within the university, her agentive strategies contributed further to her alienation from university peers and overall university disengagement. Nonetheless, rather than hinder her trajectory, Nasim's exercising of agency through resistance allowed

her to obtain the necessary cultural capital to achieve her goals, ultimately leading to her overall success. ELs' decisions to assimilate and resist the cultural and
ideological trappings in schools is an area that can further our understanding
of the pressures, aims, and constraints of linguistic minority students within
tertiary institutions.

Note

1. Pseudonyms are used for participants and university.

References

Ancis, J. R., Sedlacek, W. E., & Mohr, J. J. (2000). Student perceptions of campus cultural climate
by race. *Journal of Counseling and Development, 78*(2), 180–185.

Bourdieu, P. (1986). The forms of capital. In J. G. Richardson (Ed.), *Handbook of theory and research
for the sociology of education* (pp. 241–258). Westport, CT: Greenwood Press.

Bourdieu, P. (1997). The forms of capital. In A. H. Halsey, H. Lauder, P. Brown, & A. S. Wells
(Eds.), *Education: Culture, economy, and society* (pp. 46–58). Oxford, UK: Oxford University
Press.

Brady, P. (2006). Inclusionary and exclusionary secondary schools: The effect of school culture on
student outcomes. *Interchange, 36*(3), 295–311.

Buttaro, L. (2003). Adult ESL in higher education: Balancing academic learning, speech science
and English language arts. *Perspectives: The New York Journal of Adult Learning, 2*(1), 4–17.

Cabrera, A. F., & Nora, A. (1994). College student perceptions of prejudice and discrimination
and their feelings of alienation: A construct validation approach. *Review of Education/Peda-
gogy/Cultural Studies, 16*(3-4), 387–409.

Canagarajah, S. (2004). Subversive identities, pedagogical safe houses, and critical learning. In
B. Norton & K. Toohey (Eds.), *Critical pedagogies and language learning* (pp. 116–137). Cambridge, UK: Cambridge University Press.

Centrie, C. (2004). *Identity formation of Vietnamese immigrant youth in an American high school.* New
York: LFB Scholarly Publishing.

Coffey, A., & Atkinson, P. (1996). *Making sense of qualitative data: Complementary research strategies.*
Thousand Oaks, CA: Sage.

Davidson, A. L. (1996). *Making and molding identity in schools: Student narratives on race, gender, and
academic engagement.* Albany: State University of New York Press.

Denzin, N. K (1994). The art and politics of interpretation. In N. K. Denzin & Y. S. Lincoln
(Eds.), *Handbook of qualitative research* (pp. 500–515). Thousand Oaks, CA: Sage.

Dewit, D. J., Offord, D. R., Sanford, M., Rye, B. J., Shain, M., & Wright, R. (2000). The effect
of school culture on adolescent behavioural problems: Self-esteem, attachment to learning,
and peer approval of deviance as mediating mechanisms. *Canadian Journal of School Psychology
16*(1), 15–38.

Fordham, S. (1993). "Those loud black girls": (Black) women, silence, and gender "passing" in the
academy. *Anthropology and Education Quarterly, 24*(1), 3–32.

Fuentes, R. (2009). *ELLs' experiences of university culture.* Unpublished dissertation, University of
Washington, Seattle, WA.

Fullan, M. G., & Hargreaves, A. (1996). *What's worth fighting for in our school?* New York: Teachers
College Press.

Gibson, M. (1988). *Accommodation without assimilation: Punjabi Sikh immigrants in an American high
school.* Ithaca, NY: Cornell University Press.

Gibson, M. A., Bejínez, L. F., Hidalgo, N., & Rolón, C. (2004). Belonging and school participation: Lessons from a migrant student club. In M. A. Gibson, P. Gándara, & J. P. Koyama

(Eds.), *School connections: U.S. Mexican youth, peers, and school achievement* (pp. 129–149). New York: Teachers College Press.

Hargreaves, A. (1994). *Changing teachers, changing times: Teachers' work and culture in the postmodern age.* New York: Teachers College Press.

Hargreaves, A., & Macmillan, R. (1995). The balkanization of secondary school teaching. In L. S. Siskin & J. W. Little (Eds.), *The subjects in question: Departmental organization and the high school* (pp. 141–171). New York: Teachers College Press.

Hermanowicz, J. C. (2005). Classifying universities and their departments: A social world perspective. *The Journal of Higher Education, 76*(1), 27–55.

Holland, D., & Eisenhart, M. (1988). Women's ways of going to school: Cultural reproduction of women's identities as workers. In L. Weis (Ed.), *Class, race, and gender in American education* (pp. 266–301). Albany: State University of New York Press.

Hu, S., & Kuh, G. D. (2002). Being (dis)engaged in educationally purposeful activities: The influences of student and institutional characteristics. *Research in Higher Education, 43*(5), 555–575.

Hurtado, S. (1992). The campus racial climate: Contexts of conflict. *Journal of Higher Education, 63*(5), 539–569.

Hurtado, S. (1994). The institutional climate for talented Latino students. *Research in Higher Education, 35*(1), 21–41.

Jones, L., Castellanos, C., & Cole, D. (2002). Examining the ethnic minority student experience at predominantly White institutions: A case study. *Journal of Hispanic Higher Education, 1,* 19–39.

Kanno, Y., & Varghese, M. (2008, March). *The EL factor in higher education.* Paper presented at the American Educational Research Association (AERA) Annual Meeting, New York.

Kanno, Y., & Varghese, M. (2010). Immigrant and refugee ESL students' challenges to accessing four-year college education: From language policy to educational policy. *Journal of Language, Identity, and Education, 9*(5), 310–328.

Koyama, J. P. (2007). Approaching and attending college: Anthropological and ethnographic accounts. *Teachers College Record, 109*(10), 2301–2323.

Kuh, G. D., & Hall, J. E. (1993). Using cultural perspectives in student affairs. In G. D. Kuh (Ed.), *Cultural perspective in student affairs work* (pp. 1–20). Lanham, MD: University Press of America.

Lee, S. J. (2005). *Up against Whiteness: Race, school, and immigrant youth.* New York: Teachers College Press.

Leki, I. (2007). *Undergraduates in a second language: Challenges and complexities of academic literacy development.* Mahwah, NJ: Erlbaum.

Levinson, B. A., & Holland, D. (1996). The cultural production of the educated person: An Introduction. In B. A. Levinson, D. E. Foley, & D. C. Holland (Eds.), *The cultural production of the educated person: Critical ethnographies of schooling and local practice* (pp. 1–54). Albany: State University of New York Press.

Luykx, A. (1999). *The citizen factory: Schooling and cultural production in Bolivia.* Albany: State University of New York Press.

Marcoulides, G. A., Heck, R. H., & Papanastasiou, C. (2005). Student perceptions of school culture and achievement: Testing the invariance of a model. *The International Journal of Educational Management, 19*(2/3), 140–152.

Maslowski, R. (2006). A review of inventories for diagnosing school culture. *Journal of Educational Administration, 44*(1), 6–35.

National Center for Education Statistics (NCES). (2002). *Profile of undergraduates in U.S. postsecondary institutions: 1999–2000 Statistical analysis report.* Retrieved from http://nces.ed.gov/pubs2002/2002168.pdf

National Clearinghouse for English Language Acquisition. (2011). *NCELA FAQ: How many school-aged Limited English Proficient (LEP) students are there in the U.S.?* Retrieved from http://www.ncela.gwu.edu/faqs/view/4

Pascarella, E. T., & Terenzini, P. T. (1991). *How college affects students.* San Francisco: Jossey-Bass.

Patton, M. Q. (2002). *Qualitative research and evaluation methods* (3rd ed.). Newbury Park, CA: Sage.

Portes, A., & Rumbaut, R. G. (2001). *Legacies: The story of the immigrant second generation.* Berkeley: University of California Press.

Reynolds, D., & Teddlie, C., with Creemers, B., Scheerens, J., & Townsend, T.. (2000). An introduction to school effectiveness research. In C. Teddlie & D. Reynolds (Eds.), *The international handbook of school effectiveness research* (pp. 3–25). London: Falmer Press.

Smylie, M., & Hart, A. (1999). School leadership for learning and change: A human and social capital perspective. In J. Murphy & L. K. Seashore (Eds.), *Handbook of research on educational administration* (pp. 421–441). San Francisco: Jossey-Bass.

Strauss, A., & Corbin, J. (1994). Grounded theory methodology: An overview. In N. K. Denzin & Y. S. Lincoln (Eds.), *Handbook of qualitative research* (pp. 1–18). London: Sage.

Toffler, A. (1990). *Powershift: Knowledge, wealth, and violence at the edge of the 21st century.* New York: Bantam Books.

Voelkl, K. E. (1994). School warmth, student participation, and achievement. *Journal of Experimental Education, 63*(2), 127–138.

Wang, M. C., Haertel, G. D., & Walberg, H. J. (1997). Learning influences. In H. J. Walberg & G. D. Haertel (Eds.), *Psychology and educational practice* (pp. 199–211). Berkeley, CA: McCuthan.

Weis, L. (1985). *Between two worlds: Black students in an urban community college.* Boston, MA: Routledge & Kegan Paul.

Weis, L. (1990). *Working class without work: High school students in a de-industrialized economy.* New York: Routledge.

Willis, P. (1981). *Learning to Labor: How working class kids get working class jobs.* New York: Columbia University Press.

Wolcott, H. F. (1996). *Transforming qualitative data: Description, analysis, and interpretation.* Thousand Oaks, CA: Sage.

Zamel, V., & Spack, R. (Eds.). (2004). *Crossing the curriculum: Multilingual learners in college classrooms.* Mahwah, NJ: Erlbaum.

14

CITIZENS VS. ALIENS

How Institutional Policies Construct Linguistic Minority Students

Shawna Shapiro

Each year, millions of aspiring freshmen fill out college applications that ask, "Are you a U.S. citizen?" Many students are accustomed to answering this question for school, work, or travel; they may see it as mere administrative procedure. Yet there are situations in which the boundary between "citizen" and "resident" has significant implications, and may result in the denial of particular benefits and privileges. This is the case at Northern Green University (pseudonym), where U.S. permanent residents (i.e., non–U.S. citizens) were subject to a distinct set of expectations for language proficiency. These linguistic minority students have been, in the most literal sense, *alienated* from their peers.

This chapter explores the conditions and effects of this institutional alienation, as well as its ideological underpinnings. In cases like Northern Green, the institutional response to linguistic minority students reflects an ideology of deficit: Linguistic difference is seen as a liability, rather than an asset, to institutional excellence (Rose, 1985; Canagarajah, 2002; Ferris, 2009). This deficit-focused ideology results in policies and programs that emphasize student remediation, rather than institutional support. The case of Northern Green University illustrates these dynamics in powerful ways. It shows how a set of policies worked to demarcate linguistic minority students as "deficient" and in need of "remediation." As a result, these students felt increasingly alienated from the academic community.

Theoretical Framework: Institutional Citizenship vs. Alienation

The theoretical framework that I employ in this chapter builds on the work of scholars such as Vincent Tinto, whose research examines the nature of institutional integration and the causes of student departure (1975, 2006; Engstrom & Tinto, 2008). While space prohibits a lengthy discussion of this work here, some key findings are particularly applicable to my analysis. The first of these is that academic success is closely tied to institutional belonging. Students who experience a high degree of institutional isolation or incongruence are much more vulnerable to academic failure and/or departure. Another key finding is that both social and academic factors have an impact on students' sense of institutional belonging. Academic experiences are particularly important for students who reside off-campus (as is the case with most linguistic minority students at Northern Green University), since those students may not be as involved in campus social life. Tinto (2006) has outlined a variety of institutional practices that facilitate integration for "at-risk" students. He finds that the most successful initiatives increase student involvement in academic life, by creating smaller "learning communities." As students find a place in these micro-communities, they also feel more validated as members of the larger institution (Tinto, 2006). Tinto's more recent work has called for more attention to institutional climate, policies, structures, and curricula as comprising the context for academic integration and student learning (2006; Tinto & Englstrom, 2008).

This chapter builds on Tinto's work in several ways. First, it applies Tinto's insights toward a specific population of students: U.S. linguistic minorities. Although Tinto has occasionally referenced "ESL students" as one group for whom retention is a concern, his work does not discuss the particular experiences and needs of this population. This project also responds to Tinto's call for more attention to contextual factors that impact the integration process. In this case, institutional policies are an important part of the context for student experiences. Finally, this study moves beyond the question of retention vs. attrition to consider the ethical implications of institutional practice. My work, like Tinto's, is undergirded by the assumption that all students who have been admitted to the institution deserve to be treated equitably—that, as Engstrom and Tinto (2008) put it, "Access without support is not opportunity" (p. 50). I argue here that when policies discriminate against a particular group because of linguistic background (and, in this case, because of national citizenship), they not only hinder the institutional integration of those students, but also call into question that institution's commitment to equity and diversity. If linguistic minority students are recruited and admitted under the assumption that they have something valuable to offer, then the institution must treat them as "promises" instead of "problems" (Van Meter, 1990, pp. 4–5). Language policies that are deficit-focused do precisely the opposite: They construct students as unwelcome aliens, rather than as institutional citizens.

Institutional citizenship is a particularly applicable framework for examining the case of Northern Green University, since NGU's policies actually conflate nation of origin with language proficiency, as will be discussed later in this chapter. This framework allows for a critical perspective on the

relationship between linguistic minority students and their institutions of practice: It assumes that all students—including linguistic minorities—should have
rights that are *inalienable*. This also raises questions about what role is served by
academic support programs (such as ESL) in the integration process. Are they
student advocates or institutional "border control"?

Language Programs as Border Control

To understand the dynamics of this case, it is important to consider how institutions use remedial education as a political mechanism. Remedial programs tend
to function as institutional gate-keepers, creating and preserving a distinction
between students who are "deficient" and those who are not (Soliday, 2002).
This allows universities to admit more students from diverse educational, linguistic, and cultural backgrounds, without having to enact institutional change
to accommodate them. By creating a program that will "remedy" students'
linguistic "deficiencies," the institution can claim that it has increased access
while still maintaining traditional standards (Soliday, 2002, pp. 13, 57). In the
remedial equation, in other words, it is the students who must change to meet
the needs of the institution, not the other way around.

Surveys of programs at many institutions reveal that ESL instruction often
operates from this remedial model. Policies are a particularly salient indicator: In a remedial ESL program, courses tend to be mandatory, rather than
voluntary. The program usually decides which courses students must take, and
may actually block students from taking other (mainstream) courses until the
remedial requirement has been fulfilled (Williams, 1995). As a result, students
may be confined to an "ESL ghetto" until they have been deemed proficient
enough for mainstream courses (Valdés, 1998). In addition, coursework is usually non-credit—an important sign, according to Jean Van Meter (1990), that
those courses are not seen as equal in academic rigor to those in the mainstream. Many of the decisions for placement, evaluation, and completion of
remedial ESL courses are made via standardized testing, rather than using multiple forms of assessment. This is in part because student "deficits" (and the
"remedy" administered by the program) must be measurable, and such measures must be seen as objective.

All of these policies imply a high degree of institutional marginalization,
not only for students, but for ESL programs themselves. From her survey
of 78 institutions, Jessica Williams (1995) concluded that ESL programs are
rarely treated as integral to the campus community. Most of those in her study
were only loosely (if at all) affiliated with academic departments; as a result,
they lacked both institutional support and disciplinary allies. Instructors and
administrators in such programs often express a high degree of alienation and
inefficacy. A study by Jan Ignash (1995), for example, found that institutional
constraints, rather than student needs, were driving much of the decision-

making in remedial ESL programs. Similarly, Amy Blumenthal (2002) found that many administrators knew full well that their policies prioritized expediency over ethics. This, says Mary Soliday (2002), is one of the primary characteristics of remedial programs: They serve the needs of the institution more than those of students. Indeed, remedial education has been found to have a number of potentially negative effects on students. It diverts resources (time, energy, money) away from other endeavors and undermines students' confidence at a time when they most need it to be reinforced (Shor, 2001; Soliday, 2002). Hence, remedial education can easily become an obstacle to institutional integration. This was the case with the Academic ESL Program at Northern Green University, where deficit-focused policies exacerbated the institutional alienation already experienced by linguistic minority students.

The Institution

Northern Green University is similar to many other public research institutions: It has been listed as a "public ivy" (Greene & Greene, 2001) and has more than 40,000 students, most of whom are undergraduate state residents. According to publically available statistics from 2006–2007, NGU's undergraduate student body is comprised of approximately 35% students of color. Asians are the largest minority group, comprising approximately 26% of undergraduates. Hispanic and Black students comprise approximately 5% and 3%, respectively. NGU has been recognized for placing particular emphasis on socioeconomic diversity in its recruitment initiatives, and ranks highly for numbers of low income students compared with its peer institutions.[1]

NGU's institutional culture can be characterized as prioritizing disciplinary autonomy and political decentralization. Departments—and the faculty in them—drive most institutional decision-making. Few if any campus-wide standards exist for admission, assessment, and graduation. As might be imagined, crafting language policies within this decentralized framework is a challenging task. In fact, NGU has no general language requirement that applies to all students. Rather, it has (until very recently) had specific policies that only apply to non-U.S. citizens. At the time of my study (2006–09), approximately 14% of NGU's student body fit this description: More than half of these (8%) were international students—often in graduate programs. The other portion (6%) was comprised of permanent residents, most of whom were undergraduates who transferred to NGU from local community colleges. This chapter focuses in particular on the latter group of U.S. linguistic minority students.

Research Methods and Participants

This chapter is part of a larger case study project looking at the academic experiences of students in NGU's Academic ESL Program in 2006–2009. It draws from a number of data sets: The first is comprised of survey and interview responses from faculty, staff, and teaching assistants in a variety of departments with high numbers of linguistic minority students. An online survey was distributed via email and completed by 89 participants in 2007. Interviews were also conducted with seven faculty and staff members who work closely with linguistic minority students were also interviewed. The second data set includes surveys, interviews, and participant observation within the Academic ESL Program from 2006–2009. A third and final data set consists of surveys, focus groups, and semi-structured interviews with students who were required to take courses in the Academic ESL Program. Surveys were completed in-class without the instructor present, in spring of 2006. The response rate was 56% (129 out of the 231 students enrolled).[2] From survey respondents, 10 students were recruited to participate in a 1 hour semi-structured interview. (See Appendix for interview questions.)

I will draw from all of these data sets in this chapter, but focus in particular on the experiences of five of the student interview participants. All five are female, permanent residents who have been in the state for at least 4 years and have family connections there. Four of the five transferred from local community colleges, while one entered as a freshman. All five were placed into NGU's Academic ESL program (AEP) at either the lowest or second-lowest level. I chose to focus on these five women because they embody several of the values NGU claims are central to its institutional vision: diversity, community, and global citizenship (NGU website, 2009). These students are in-state residents, a population NGU is expected to prioritize. They contribute to the institution's ethnic, cultural, and socioeconomic diversity. In addition, they plan to invest in the local community by pursuing professions in medicine, social work, and business. They would seem, then, to be the ideal institutional "citizens." Yet they are treated instead as institutional "aliens." (See Table 14.1 for additional information about these interview participants.)

Before discussing the nature and impact of the NGU's ESL-related policies, I will describe some of these women's initial experiences at the institution. I wish to show that institutional alienation is already a prevalent phenomenon. This lays the groundwork for showing how this alienation is exacerbated by language policies and instruction.

Findings

Crossing the Institutional Border

Scholarship on the experiences of linguistic minority students transitioning into postsecondary education has revealed that institutional alienation is quite common (e.g., Leki, 2007). For entering students, the institution often feels large and unfamiliar. Many students report feeling lost in their first semes-

TABLE 14.1 Key Participants

Name (Pseudonym)	Linguistic/Educational Background	LOR in U.S.[a]	Educational History at NGU
Phuong	Vietnamese and some Mandarin. Came to U.S. in high school with family.	7 years	Entered as freshman. Finished Biology degree. Planning to pursue future studies in public health or pharmacy
Lois	From mainland China (speaks Mandarin and Cantonese). Married to U.S. engineer.	6 years	Transferred from community college. Finished Biochemistry degree. Pursuing medical assistant licensure.
Sun-hi	South Korean. Came to U.S. in high school with older siblings. Parents joined later.	8 years	Transferred from community college. Finished Biochemistry degree. Planning to pursue dentistry.
Eunyoung	South Korean. Came to U.S. in high school with parents.	9 years	Transferred recently from community college. Planning to major in Business.
Sakimi	Japanese. Recently married U.S. citizen whom she had met in Japan.	4 years	Transferred from community college. Pursuing Psychology degree.

a Length of residence in the U.S. (at the time of the interview).

ter. These students were often at the top of their classes in high school and/ or community college, and assume that their acceptance to the university is validation that they have what it takes to be successful. Yet when they experience struggles early on, they start to wonder if they truly belong. While many incoming undergraduates experience these kinds of challenges (Engstrom & Tinto, 2008), linguistic minority students are particularly vulnerable, since their educational, linguistic, and cultural backgrounds may be quite different from those of their peers, yet they are often not recognized as a special population by their institutions (Gray, Rolph, & Melamid, 1996; Ortmeier-Hooper, 2008; Roberge, 2009). In addition, a majority of linguistic minority students at universities like NGU have transferred from local community colleges. This creates additional challenges to institutional integration, as the opportunities for social interaction and orientation to the campus community are usually more limited for transfer students (Tinto, 2006). These students may also be at a significant disadvantage compared to their classmates, who (if they entered as freshmen) have had two additional years to build a social network, as well as to become familiar with the institution's norms, expectations, and resources.

The experience of linguistic minority students at NGU illustrates many of these trends. With its more than 30,000 undergraduates, NGU can feel quite intimidating to newcomers. Classes of more than 200 students are not uncommon, particularly in the natural sciences. Many of the participants in my study commented on class size as a significant factor in their academic experience. Phuong, who entered as a freshman, was "so proud," about her acceptance to NGU, since she had only been in the United States for 3 years. But when she arrived on campus, she said, "I was like 'Oh my god! I'm so scared!' because the class is so big and everything is big, big, big." After struggling significantly throughout her first quarter, Phuong began to feel "really nervous." She says it was not until she chose a major several quarters later that she began to feel a sense of belonging at the institution.

The transfer students also faced significant challenges in their first year. Like those in a recent study by Kanno and Varghese (2010), they felt that they had not been adequately prepared for much of their NGU coursework. Sun-hi, for example, lost much of her "self-confidence" when she encountered unanticipated difficulties with course readings and class discussion. Similarly, Lois had thought that the sciences would be her strong point, but she struggled a great deal in her first year of biochemistry at NGU. She found the experience "humiliating." Both she and Sun-hi were dismayed to find that even laboratory work was a struggle, since the instructions were difficult to follow.

Eunyoung, who came to NGU to study in the Business School, came to the conclusion that her reading skills were "horrible … but not as horrible as writing." She felt "depressed" after receiving poor grades on some of her earliest assignments. Eunyoung also struggled to comprehend course lectures, despite having high listening comprehension overall. She eventually realized that the professors were assuming a great deal of background knowledge about the U.S. government, as well as foundational concepts in economics that other students (most of whom entered NGU as freshmen) likely learned in their first two years. Other studies have confirmed that it is not only language proficiency, but also background knowledge, that prevents L2 students from grasping course material (e.g., Erten & Razi, 2009; Leki, 2007; Spack, 1997).

As is often the case with linguistic minority students, the social dynamics of the classroom were also a challenge (Leki, 2007). Sakimi found it difficult to communicate with classmates on group projects. "I hate it," she said, "Because there's always someone who is not responsible." Even those who do their share, she says, "tend to wait til the last minute." Similarly, Phuong described a project for which she was placed into a group with eight other members. It was nearly impossible to get the group together for work sessions, and they barely finished on time. Eunyoung said she felt particularly uncomfortable when her professors asked students to choose their own group members: She was rarely chosen, because most of her classmates (who had entered as freshmen) already knew each other and formed groups accordingly.

Perhaps the most alienating aspect of these women's classroom experience, however, was testing, particularly in courses where exams comprised a significant portion of the final grade. As discussed by Hamp-Lyons and Kroll (1996) and Kanno and Varghese (2010), linguistic minority students are often highly disadvantaged in timed testing situations, as they need more time to read and respond to questions. They may also lack the cultural frames of reference that are employed in "real-world" scenarios (Hamp-Lyons & Kroll, 1996; Leki, 2007). Eunyoung said that her most difficult course was one in which the grade rested almost entirely on two exams. She ran out of time on both tests, particularly on the essay questions. Lois had similar experiences: "I feel frustrated in the exam … My understanding is a big problem—the ways they put the questions—I think I understand maybe 80 percent." "Most of [my friends] are native speakers," she said, "so they don't have such problems." Sun-hi also felt that most of her peers did not have the same challenges: "The Americans understand the questions," she explained. Sakimi felt alienated by a different testing situation: She failed the Business School's writing exam, because "you have to look at [famous] sayings and write about it … so maybe if you grew up here, most of the quotes are familiar, but if you didn't grow up here, you have to guess. It's really hit-and-miss."

Some of the assumptions made by these students, such as that "Americans" or "native speakers" do not have the same struggles during exams, may have been inaccurate. Yet they reflect the high degree of alienation felt by these students: These women *perceive* themselves to be at a significant disadvantage because of their linguistic, cultural, and academic backgrounds. Compounding this sense of alienation is the fact that many professors claim they cannot provide individualized assistance to linguistic minority students. On an anonymous online survey in which NGU faculty and teaching assistants discussed their teaching practices in response to ESL students, I received a number of comments such as: "With large classes of 300+ in the intro level and 100+ at the 400 level, we don't have the resources needed to provide ESL students individual support" (Faculty in Biology); "I try to evaluate them relative to their background, but I don't think it is appropriate for me to actually change the class to accommodate the ESL students" (Faculty in Business); and "With writing classes in particular, paying special attention to ESL students means losing the non-ESL students" (Faculty in Business).

Some respondents explained that they are willing to offer addition help, but only if approached directly by students: One faculty member in Anthropology said, "I put the university notice in my syllabus and announce the first day of class a willingness to offer support of any kind. *I almost never have had a student request support*" (original emphasis). Other responses were quite similar: "Without a request there is little effort to adapt to ESL students' needs when it comes to the preparation and delivery of in-class materials" (TA in Communication); "I ask our TAs to identify ESL students early in the course to encourage them to make use of office hours. The problem is that most students don't take advantage of this" (Faculty in Biology).

Hence, another point of potential alienation is at work: Professors expect students who are struggling to seek help in a particular way and are confused, perhaps even offended, when this expectation is not met. Sun-hi wanted to ask professors for help but was too intimidated. She also explained that "Asians tend not to ask." Lois said that when she did approach her professors after class, they usually told her to ask the teaching assistant or to come by during office hours. She felt that these responses were dismissive and made her "pull back a little bit." Similarly, Phuong commented that her professors "always seem busy." Some had a policy by which they would only communicate with students via email, and even then, she says, they often took several days to respond. Most of these women tended to blame their struggles almost entirely on what Phuong called "personal issues." They occasionally mentioned curricular or pedagogical factors that might have had an impact, but they seemed resigned to the conclusion that, as Eunyoung put it, "American professors don't care about ESL." She and Sun-hi actually expressed sympathy for their professors, saying that ESL students were probably "difficult" to teach.

None of these findings are particularly unusual. The experience of these students parallels much of what existing literature has revealed about the experiences of linguistic minority students at large universities (e.g., Leki & Carson, 1997; Roberge, Siegal, & Harklau, 2009). What is particularly worrisome in the case of NGU, however, is that the ESL program into which these students were placed executed a set of policies that actually exacerbated students' sense of institutional alienation.

ESL Policies as Institutional Alienation

As at other institutions, the ESL program at NGU operated from a remedial, deficit-oriented model, and tended to be institutionally marginalized at the same time that it marginalized students. The program's 2007 Operations Manual (since revised) explained that one of its goals was to help students improve their English so that they "do not pose an excessive burden to instructors." This would also "ensur[e] that students who graduate … possess adequate English language skills that maintain the university's academic standards and reputation." While the program did not have a say in who is admitted to NGU in the first place, it did have a significant impact in determining who graduated and at what cost. For some linguistic minority students, this cost was quite high. In the sections that follow, I will first describe the policies implemented by the AEP for selection, placement, tuition, credit, and assessment. Then, I will discuss the impact of these policies on linguistic minority students, highlighting indicators of increased institutional alienation.

Perhaps the most unusual aspect of NGU's policies is that they conflated citizenship and language proficiency: All non–U.S. citizens, with the exception of those from countries where English is the primary language, were marked as having a "language proficiency requirement" to fulfill prior to graduation. Before the 1980s, of course, "non–U.S. citizen" referred almost exclusively to international students. By 2006, the undergraduate student body came to include more U.S. permanent residents than international students, but the policy remained the same, and did not distinguish between the two groups. Both were categorized as "aliens" by the Office of the Registrar and therefore had to prove that they were proficient in English.

As is the case with many remedial programs, testing was at the center of the AEP's placement and assessment procedures. Only standardized test scores (usually the SAT or TOEFL) were accepted as evidence of language proficiency. If a student with the proficiency requirement could not submit an acceptable score, he or she was required to enroll in the AEP before registering for other (mainstream) classes. Placement in the program was determined via the AEP's own "diagnostic test." Completion of each course also depended on testing: Students needed an 80% on the final exam in order to be passed to the next level.[3] According to the Operations Manual, this testing-heavy design was in place so that "all sections of each course observe the same exit criteria." Elsewhere in the manual, it was explained that "The AEP is an alternative to more standardized measures of English ability such as the TOEFL." This fit with the aforementioned responsibility of the program to "ensur[e]" that graduates "possess adequate English skills."

Several other aspects of the program indicated that it operated from a remedial model. For example, each course costs more than $1,000 in additional tuition on top of regular matriculation and fees, a cost that the AEP attributed to higher administrative costs for the program. All of the courses were non–credit. Finally, although the focus of this chapter is policy rather than pedagogy, it is noteworthy that the curriculum for the AEP focused heavily on grammatical accuracy: The standardized course objectives aimed for student "mastery" of grammatical concepts, as evidenced by lack of error at the sentence and paragraph level. The course sequence includes little if any extensive reading or writing, and no direct instruction in speaking.

Student Reactions

News of the language proficiency requirement came as quite a shock to most students, particularly incoming transfer students who had only needed transcripts and no test scores to be admitted to the university. These students found it confusing that their community college GPA was sufficient for admission, but not for language proficiency. Similarly, freshmen were baffled to find that while NGU used a holistic admissions process with no minimum standardized test scores to admit them, the university nevertheless used their test scores to judge their language proficiency. Students' prior academic accomplishments seemed somehow invalidated. Eunyoung, for example, felt that the policies treated her "wrong[ly]" as if she had "no English skills." She had placed out of ESL at her community college, yet was no longer considered proficient in English, once she arrived at NGU.

Exacerbating students' anxiety is the fact that they were blocked from registering for other (mainstream) classes until they had enrolled in the AEP. Many students did not realize this until they tried to register for the first time. Advisors were often the ones who were tasked with explaining the policy. Tara, an advisor who specializes in helping in-state students with residency documentation, often served as a de-facto advisor for the AEP: "It's frustrating," she explained. "I try to let the students know that most often I'm on their side … but we didn't make the rules."

While some students scrambled to take an SAT or TOEFL exam before classes begin, most resigned themselves to joining the program. They then chose either to begin with the lowest AEP course or to take the program's diagnostic test, a 20-year-old instrument whose origins were unknown to all of the members of the curriculum committee, including the Assessment Coordinator. Students often complained about the difficulty of the test, and question whether it placed them appropriately. Sun-hi claimed that the diagnostic test was actually "harder than TOEFL," and far more difficult than what was required in the courses themselves. Both Sun-hi and Sakimi said they had been placed into courses that were "too easy." Tara, the advisor, confirmed that this was a frequent student complaint. The exam-based model for course completion also angered many students. As explained by one anonymous survey participant, "I think the final grade should base on the homeworks and midterms. I always feel very nervous on the final." Some students reasoned that that if the exam was all that matters, then the class sessions should be targeted toward test preparation. As one survey respondent commented, "You should focus on teaching us how to pass the final. It is no use letting students consider what the best way to study English by themselves. I feel waste of time and money for taking this class." Once they realized that the AEP was funded and administered independently, some students began to question the ethics of these testing policies. The program relied on the presence of student "deficiencies" in order to ensure its own survival; yet, it was allowed to construct the exams that identified such deficiencies. As one veteran AEP teacher admitted ruefully in a staff meeting, "We're like the fox guarding the henhouse."

This indeed is how many students perceived the program. A number of my research participants expressed serious concerns about the AEP's testing measures. As one survey respondent put it, "The passing score for final exam is too high. I felt that the object of AEP course is not help to improve English skills for student, [but] making a money instead." Sadly, these suspicions are not unfounded. Although programmatic documents from the AEP did not discuss financial issues, they did offer some evidence that an expectation of failure is built in to the program: One discussion of "Operating Constraints" in the Operations Manual claimed that the program aimed to see "80% mastery in each course by 80% of the students who show sufficient effort." Since mastery is determined via the final exam, it was assumed that approximately 1 in 5 students (i.e., 20%) would fail—this in addition to expected failure by those who do *not* put in "sufficient effort." It was not uncommon, in fact, for a student to repeat a single course several times before passing the final exam.

Alienation Effects

The overall impact of these policies on linguistic minority students varied widely. For some students, the AEP requirements felt more like an annoyance than a burden. Joanna, who directed a learning center for first-generation students (some of whom are linguistic minorities) explained that many students saw the AEP coursework as a tedious game: "A lot of students start to feel like this is a hoop I have to jump through. I fill out these little exercises, get the right answers, and then get out of here as quickly as I can ... They see it as kind of wheel-spinning." This "wheel-spinning" effect may not seem like a significant problem: Students simply played the game and moved on. It is important to remember, however, that only non-U.S. citizens were required to "play" in the first place. The policy discriminated not only between native and non-native speakers, but between U.S. and non-U.S. citizens. This struck many students as illogical. One survey respondent noted, "This school only assign non-citizen to take this course but they forget that [citizens vs. non-citizens] won't have any differences in their English knowledge." Another commented, "Please assign an English course for all non-native speakers." A focus group participant observed, "My roommate is American, and she asks me, 'Why do they make you learn this? It's not relevant.'" In fact, as the study concluded one student was threatening to sue the university, claiming discrimination on the basis of "nation of origin."

This most literal "alienation effect" of the program is only one piece of the puzzle, however. Being placed into the AEP alienated students from their peers in a number of other ways. This was often felt most acutely in the first week of classes. Although the AEP sent a letter to new students during the summer notifying them of the language proficiency requirement, many students—particularly the most vulnerable ones—did not notice it amidst the stack of other paperwork. Hence, they arrived on campus already somewhat apprehensive, and then discovered to their dismay that they had been blocked from registration. Tara (the aforementioned residency advisor) told me that many students came to her in a panic, because "Somehow or another, the information is not getting out to them." By the time they reached her office, they had been "passed around a lot," trying to figure out how to remove the registration hold.

For newcomers, the confusion and sense of being singled out was compounded by the location of the AEP's offices a mile off-campus. One student told me that those first few weeks were "the nightmare of my life," but declined to discuss the experience further.

The diagnostic test was another particularly alienating aspect of the program. As was mentioned earlier, many students questioned the accuracy of their placements, suspecting that the test was intentionally difficult. As Lois explained, "We thought that the program made the test really hard, [so] only the most excellent can pass." One survey participant wrote that "The AEP test is bias. It seeks our failure, not our success." Another suggested during a focus group conversation that "You should make ... all English professors ... take the diagnostic test." He was convinced that even they would not perform well. It is also important to remember that this entire placement process happened at the beginning of each quarter, when students were already working hard to complete all of the administrative procedures necessary for a successful start to the school year. AEP students lost valuable time and energy, while their non-AEP peers were more able to focus on other aspects of college adjustment.

Of course, the additional financial burden was also a significant concern, particularly for students who are already socioeconomically disadvantaged. Somehow, these students had to figure out how to pay an additional (and unanticipated) $1,000 per quarter. Although they did not discuss their financial situations directly with me, Sun-hi and Eunyoung both said they were planning to re-take the TOEFL as soon as possible in order to try to meet the score for exemption from the AEP. They would have liked to continue their English language studies, but as Sun-hi explained, "[the tuition] is too much for us." The additional cost for courses was particularly problematic when considered in light of NGU's stated commitment to attracting more low-income, first-generation students. Midway through my study, a local newspaper ran a short editorial by a community college professor whose former students had transferred to NGU and were required to pay for AEP courses, despite being on scholarship as part of a socioeconomic diversity program. The author questioned the ethics of admitting low-income students and then requiring that they spend extra money for remedial ESL courses.

Another group of students likely to feel the financial burden of the AEP particularly heavily was undocumented immigrants. I did not speak with any of these students directly and could not locate any statistics on the size of this population at NGU. However, Tara mentioned that she had worked with members of this subgroup and was deeply concerned about the economic impact of AEP policies: "They don't have much money to begin with ... I'd think that some of these students would drop out. They can't come up with the cash."

To my knowledge, no research has been done on the part of AEP (or by NGU as a whole) to measure the impact of AEP tuition on students, or to examine attrition rates for AEP students in general. Do most students take out additional loans? Do they work extra hours? What do they give up in order to pay for the AEP? Although my data do not directly address these questions, they do reveal that many students experienced the program's tuition policy as discriminatory and punitive. Some of them came to suspect that NGU was actually taking advantage of their institutional vulnerability. Lois wondered, "Are you guys trying—I mean the program—to make more money out of the international students?" Another interviewee—an international student who had recently married an American—explained, "The impression I had was that [NGU thinks] international students have money. They can pay without questioning, and they don't have this option for us to question." The harshest criticism was seen in anonymous feedback. Comments such as, "This is about getting money from us," or "They cost way too much money and time, so the AEP courses should be abolished. You should consider this more seriously," or even "Stop stealing students money!" appeared frequently in my survey data, as well as in course evaluations.

AEP policies diverted other resources as well, such as the time and energy that students might have devoted to other academic or social endeavors. Phuong said that as a result of her placement in the AEP, "I would have to do [even] more work to keep up with classmates." Afraid of falling behind, Phuong decided one quarter to take 21 credits (including an AEP course) instead of the usual 15. That quarter, she failed her AEP course, which she had to take (and pay for) again the next quarter. This sort of experience—one that is not uncommon—is highly detrimental to students' self-confidence. As one survey respondent explained, "When I failed the final, I just wanted to quit school. I know that somebody who does not take AEP classes, doesn't understand AEP students feelings." Ironically, as students continued to take mainstream courses, they often felt increasingly alienated by the AEP requirement, since success in non-AEP courses was not counted as evidence of language proficiency. Tara said students often noted that "if they were able to get through and do fine, obviously their English was good enough." They began to suspect that they were being held to a higher standard than their native-speaking (and/or U.S. citizen) peers. As one survey participant admitted, "Often times, I feel I know more grammar than a native speaker." Indeed, because the AEP requirement was tied not only to registration but to graduation, there were occasional cases in which students had successfully completed all of their for-credit coursework, but not their AEP courses. I was told of at least one case in which a student's family members had already purchased airline tickets from overseas to attend graduation, but then had to cancel their trip last-minute when they discovered that he could not graduate. He had passed all of his regular courses but had failed the final exam for his AEP course.

Ultimately, for many linguistic minority students, the AEP was a hindrance, rather than a help, in the process of institutional integration. These students, who already had limited resources to begin with, now had even less to devote toward their involvement in the academic and social life of the institution. This is particularly problematic in light of the fact that many of these students were recruited as part of NGU's diversity initiatives. If they were claimed as assets to the institution, why were they treated as aliens? This is a question that has only very recently come to the forefront at NGU, as some of the policies described in this article are currently under review. In addition, soon after my study concluded, the AEP began revising its diagnostic test, as well as modifying the curricular content for some of its courses.

Implications

What implications does this case hold more broadly for the education of linguistic minority students? First, it is clear that institutional policies reflect institutional ideology. Policies that are punitive toward linguistic minority students are underwritten by the assumption that those students are deficient and perhaps even undesirable. As a result, such policies undermine students' sense of belonging. This is of particular concern in relation to transfer students, who already face a number of challenges to institutional integration in the first place. This case also illustrates how politics can overshadow pedagogy. An unintegrated, testing-heavy curriculum is unlikely to be seen by students as beneficial, particularly if its courses are noncredit and cost additional tuition. Remedial ESL courses may come to be seen as unwelcome "checkpoints" in a gate-keeping process, rather than as stepping stones toward academic success. Hence, what institutions call "support" might not be seen as such in the eyes of linguistic minority students.

This case also suggests that institutional reform must be long-term and multi-faceted. Reforming a single program such as the AEP is unlikely to result in a more equitable model of support, unless steps are taken to address more widespread institutional dynamics. Perhaps the most valuable function a program like the AEP can serve is not remediation, but mediation. Such programs can help facilitate dialogue among the many entities with a stake in the institutional integration of linguistic minority students. A nonremedial support model requires a major shift in institutional ideology: from deficiency to diversity. Universities like NGU must begin to ask the question: Why aren't linguistic minority students treated as contributors to institutional excellence? Many institutions, including NGU, have articulated a strong commitment to cultural diversity, socioeconomic equity, and global citizenship. Yet they treat linguistic minority students, who fit quite well with this vision, as institutional aliens. It is incumbent upon us, as teachers, scholars, and activists, to highlight this institutional hypocrisy, and to call for a more ethical and effective treatment of linguistic minority students.

Notes

1. This is based on Pell grant data, as well as 2007 meeting minutes from NGU's Diversity Council.
2. The majority of the survey was quantitative, asking students to identify which language skills and written genres were most relevant to their academic needs. The following three questions were qualitative, however, and are the focus for this chapter: (a) What parts of your AEP courses have been most helpful? (b) What parts of the AEP courses have not been as helpful? (c) [do you have] Other comments/questions?
3. Midway through my study, this was changed to 70%.

References

Blumenthal, A. J. (2002). English as a second language at the community college: An exploration of contexts and concerns. *New Directions for Community Colleges, 17*, 45–53.

Canagarajah, S. (2002). *Critical academic writing and multilingual students.* Ann Arbor, MI: University of Michigan Press.

Engstrom, C., & Tinto, V. (2008). Access without support is not opportunity. *Change, 40*, 46–50.

Erten, I. H., & Razi, S. (2009). The effects of cultural familiarity on reading comprehension. *Reading in a Foreign Language, 21*(1), 60–77.

Ferris, D. (2009). *Teaching college writing to diverse student populations.* Ann Arbor, MI: University of Michigan Press.

Gray, M. J., Rolph, E. S., & Melamid, E. (1996). *Immigration and higher education: Institutional responses to changing demographics.* Santa Monica, CA: Rand Corporation.

Greene, H., & Greene, M. (2001). *The public ivies: America's flagship public universities.* New York: HarperCollins.

Hamp-Lyons, L., & Kroll, B. (1996). Issues in ESL writing assessment: An overview. *College ESL, 6*(1), 52–72.

Ignash, J. M. (1995). Encouraging ESL student persistence: The influence of policy on curricular design. *Community College Review, 23*(3), 17–34.

Kanno, Y., & Varghese, M. (2010). Immigrant and refugee ESL students' challenges to accessing four-year college education: From language policy to educational policy. *Journal of Language, Identity, and Education, 9*(5), 310–328.

Leki, I. (2007). *Undergraduates in a second language: Challenges and complexities of academic literacy development.* Mahwah, NJ: Erlbaum.

Leki, I., & Carson, J. (1997). "Completely different worlds": EAP and the writing experiences of ESL students in university courses. *TESOL Quarterly, 31*(1), 39–69.

Ortmeier-Hooper, C. (2008) English may be my second language, but I'm not "ESL." *CCC, 59*(3), 389–419.

Roberge, M. (2009). A teacher's perspective on generation 1.5. In M. Roberge, M. Siegal, & L. Harklau (Eds.), *Generation 1.5 in college composition: Teaching ESL to U.S.-educated learners of ESL* (pp. 3–24). New York: Routledge.

Roberge, M., Siegal, M., & Harklau, L. (Eds.). (2009). *Generation 1.5 in college composition: Teaching ESL to U.S.-educated learners of ESL.* New York: Routledge.

Rose, M. (1985). The language of exclusion: Writing instruction at the university. *College English, 47*, 341–359.

Shor, I. (2001). Errors and Economics: Inequality breeds remediation. In G. McNenny & S. Fitzgerald (Eds.), *Mainstreaming basic writers: Politics and pedagogies of access* (pp. 29–54). Mahwah, NJ: Erlbaum.

Soliday, M. (2002). *The politics of remediation: Institutional and student needs in higher education.* Pittsburgh, PA: University of Pittsburgh Press.

Spack, R. (1997). The acquisition of academic literacy in a second language: A longitudinal case study. *Written Communication: A Quarterly Journal of Research, Theory, and Application, 14*(1), 3–62.

Tinto, V. (1975). Dropout from higher education: A theoretical synthesis of recent research. *Review of Educational Research, 45*(1), 89–125.

Tinto, V. (2006). Research and practice of student retention: What next? *College Student Retention: Research, Theory, and Practice, 8,* 1–20.

Valdés, G. (1998). The world outside and inside schools: Language and immigrant children. *Educational Researcher, 27*(6), 4–18.

Van Meter, J. (1990). Academic credit for ESL classes? *Review of Research in Developmental Education, 8*(1), 2–6.

Williams, J. (1995) ESL composition program administration in the United States. *Journal of Second Language Writing, 4*(2), 157–179.

Appendix: Student Interview Outline

1. Background Information
   a. What is your family and language background?
   b. Where are you in your studies?
   c. How are you feeling currently?
2. History at [NGU]
   a. Which courses were easiest/ most challenging for you?
   b. Which assignments were most challenging?
   c. Overall strengths, weaknesses, and areas of growth over time
   d. What did instructors/programs do that helped you? (How can an instructor support AEP students?)
   e. What other resources helped you?
3. AEP
   a. History—Which courses have you taken? When?
   b. What do you remember most? (about program and about individual courses)
   c. Specific skills you found useful/not useful for your other classes
   d. What did you think before/during/after course sequence? (about requirement, about courses, about self as learner)
4. Curriculum specifics—How important have the following been for you?
   a. Grammar (What helps you improve?)
   b. Writing (Has your writing improved over time? How/Why? How do you know?)
   c. Academic vocabulary
5. How do you think the AEP (and the university) might better support ESL students?

ABOUT THE CONTRIBUTORS

Cate Almon has over a decade of U.S. community college experience working with English learners in faculty and administrator roles. After receiving her doctorate from Temple University in 2010, she is now Test Centre Facilitator at Wits Language School, University of the Witwatersrand in Johannesburg, where she aims to continue research on ELs in higher education.

George C. Bunch is Associate Professor of Education at the University of California, Santa Cruz. He holds a Ph.D. in educational linguistics from Stanford University and an M.A. in TESOL and bilingual education from the University of Maryland Baltimore County. His research focuses on the ways that conceptions of academic language proficiency impact the education of linguistic minority students and those who are responsible for serving them, both in K–12 schools and higher education. He is currently the principal investigator of a 3-year project focusing on language testing and placement policies impacting linguistic minority students in California community colleges.

Rebecca M. Callahan is an Assistant Professor at The University of Texas at Austin. Her research focuses on the academic preparation of immigrant, linguistic minority adolescents as they transition from high school into young adulthood. She began her career as a K–12 bilingual teacher, an experience that continues to shape her present research agenda. Rebecca's recent publications explore a variety of factors shaping the achievement of immigrant adolescents including, but not limited to: ESL placement, primary language use, teacher practices, peer relations and school context. Her work appears in *American Educational Research Journal, Educational Policy, Social Science Quarterly, Theory and Research in Social Education,* and *Bilingual Research Journal.*

Ann K. Endris is Research Specialist and Project Manager for the Community College Project in the Education Department at the University of California, Santa Cruz, and adjunct faculty for the Digital Bridge Academy at Cabrillo College. She holds an M.A. in Latin American Studies from the University of California, San Diego, with a specialization in International Migration. Her research has focused on immigration and education policy, and she is currently managing a 3-year project investigating language placement and testing in California community colleges.

Pedro Espinoza is an Associate Director of Recruitment and Retention in the Center for Intercultural and Multilingual Advocacy (CIMA) at the College of Education, Kansas State University. His research focuses on strategies for recruitment and retention and educational access for diverse students and parent and family involvement. He is published in the *Journal of Enrollment Management*.

Cristina Fanning is Associate Director at the Center for Intercultural and Multilingual Advocacy (CIMA) in the College of Education at Kansas State University. Her professional experience includes instruction at the graduate and undergraduate level to develop the capacities of preservice and inservice teachers to critically reflect on their instructional practices with culturally and linguistically diverse students. Her research areas include sociohistorical foundations of education, culture and language in classroom practice, and the linguistics of second language acquisition. She is published in the *Journal of Hispanics in Higher Education*.

Ronald Fuentes is an Instructional Assistant Professor of Applied Linguistics at the University of Mississippi. His research interests include language policy in education, bilingual education, and language and identity. He is particularly interested in how multilingual learners experience language policies in different educational environments and how those experiences influence their engagement and integration into school life. His current projects include how English learners use agentive practices and strategies to achieve their academic and social goals in higher education settings and how these practices and strategies may reproduce the hierarchical and structural divisions present in such settings.

Sarah Arva Grosik is a doctoral student in TESOL at Temple University. Her research interests include the sociopolitical factors that impact English learners, educational policy issues within the K–12 realm, and English learners' educational opportunities. Sarah has worked as an EFL teacher abroad and has served as an ESL classroom teacher in Philadelphia.

Linda Harklau is a Professor in the Teaching Additional Languages program and Linguistics program at the University of Georgia. Her research focuses on second language academic development and qualitative research on adolescent and young adult immigrants. Her work has appeared in *TESOL Quarterly, Linguistics and Education, Educational Policy, Journal of Literacy Research,* and *Anthropology and Education Quarterly.* She was lead editor of *Generation 1.5 meets college composition* (Erlbaum, 1999) and coeditor of *Generation 1.5 in College Composition* (Routledge, 2009).

Socorro Herrera is Professor of Elementary Education and Director of the Center for Intercultural and Multilingual Advocacy (CIMA), College of Education at Kansas State University. Her research focuses on the preparation of future teachers to meet the needs of culturally and linguistically diverse students. Work with incarcerated high school males and recruitment and retention of immigrant populations have heavily influenced her work in language and literacy development. Current publications have appeared in the *Journal of Latinos and Education, Journal of Hispanic Higher Education, Bilingual Research Journal, Teaching Education,* and *Journal of Research in Education.* Her most recent book is *Biography-Driven Culturally Responsive Teaching* (Teachers College Press, 2010).

Melissa Holmes is an Instructor for the Center for Intercultural and Multilingual Advocacy (CIMA) in the College of Education at Kansas State University. For the past nine years, she has been a project coordinator for the Bilingual/ Bicultural Education Students Interacting to Obtain Success (BESITOS) recruitment and retention program. Her research focuses on the academic literacy development of culturally and linguistically diverse students in higher education and the development of advocacy skills among teacher candidates. Her work has been published in *Teaching Education, American Secondary Education,* and will soon appear in the *Journal of College Student Retention.* She recently co-authored the book, *Crossing the Vocabulary Bridge: Differentiated Strategies for Diverse Secondary Classrooms* (Teachers College Press, 2011).

Yasuko Kanno is an Associate Professor of TESOL in the College of Education, Temple University. She is interested in linguistic minority students' negotiation of identity and educational opportunities within institutional settings, and this interest has resulted in two books, *Negotiating Bilingual and Bicultural Identities* (Erlbaum, 2003) and *Language and Education in Japan* (Palgrave, 2008). Yasuko is currently working on several projects on linguistic minority students' access to college, including statistical analyses of the National Education Longitudinal Study of 1988 (NELS:88) and the Education Longitudinal Study of 2002 (ELS:2002), and an ethnographic study of linguistic minority high school seniors going to college.

Anysia P. Mayer is an Assistant Professor of Educational Leadership at the Neag School of Education at the University of Connecticut. She is also a member of the UConn Center for Education Policy Analysis. Her work examines education policy with a specific focus on understanding how we can advance low income, minority, and immigrant students to high achievement, with the goal of participation in a four-year college. Anysia has also worked as an ESL classroom teacher and a college counselor in California.

Shelly McClanahan is a doctoral student in Language and Literacy Education at the University of Georgia. Her research interests include community-based adult ESL programs and the educational needs of immigrant students in public schools. She has worked as an ESL teacher in Tennessee and Albania.

Amanda Morales is an Assistant Professor and the Graduate Program Advisor for Curriculum and Instruction in the College of Education at Kansas State University. Her research focuses on issues of recruitment and retention and educational access for diverse populations. She is published in *the Journal of Hispanics in Higher Education, Journal of Enrollment Management, Journal of College Student Retention, Texas Association of Bilingual Education Journal*, and her work will soon appear in *The Rural Educator* and the *Action in Teacher Education Journal*. She is the also the co-author of a book chapter, *Race, Culture, and Identity in Second Language Education*.

Eduardo Mosqueda is an Assistant Professor of Education at the University of California, Santa Cruz. His primary strand of research focuses on how school context factors such as course-taking patterns and the segregation of low-income students impact the mathematics achievement of English Learners. His current study investigates the experiences of immigrant students in continuation high schools to understand why Latino English learners drop out of high school at disproportionately high rates. He completed his doctoral studies at the Harvard Graduate School of Education where he was awarded the Spencer Dissertation Fellowship. He has taught both middle and high school mathematics.

Anne-Marie Nuñez is an Assistant Professor of Educational Leadership and Policy Studies at The University of Texas at San Antonio (UTSA). Her research addresses the influences on the college access and success of diverse students, including Latino, first-generation, and migrant students. Her recent publications include "Latino Students' College Transitions: A Social and Intercultural Perspective" in *Harvard Educational Review*, "Creating Pathways to College for Migrant Students: Assessing a Migrant Outreach Program" in the *Journal of Education for Students Placed at Risk*, and "Organizational Collaboration to Promote College Access: a P-20 Framework" in the *Journal of Hispanic Higher Education*.

Cristóbal Rodríguez is an Assistant Professor in the College of Education at New Mexico State University. Cristóbal has been formerly trained in education research, evaluation, and policy analysis with a K–12 focus, and has additionally experienced various secondary and postsecondary education roles around serving and preparing diverse students for academic success. As a doctoral student at The University of Texas at Austin, Cristóbal worked on numerous education policy research experiences that prepared him for a career in P-20 education pipeline policy research focused on access and performance of students from diverse backgrounds and settings, particularly in regions like the Texas Borderlands where concentrated diverse demographics are found.

Shawna Shapiro is a Visiting Assistant Professor at Middlebury College. She has taught a variety of courses and workshops in academic literacy, applied linguistics, and teacher education. Much of her research looks at the relationship between multilingual students and their academic institutions, considering ways in which institutional integration can be facilitated through collaborative program design, resource development, and classroom pedagogy. She has published articles in the *Journal of English for Academic Purposes* and *Teaching and Teacher Education*, and has book chapters in several volumes of TESOL's Classroom Practice Series.

Dara R. Shifrer is a doctoral student in Sociology at The University of Texas at Austin. Her research focuses on the academic, social, and social psychological experiences of minorities within the social institution of education, with a particular focus on students identified with disabilities and language minorities. Dara worked as a middle school math teacher for four years before entering academia.

P. Johnelle Sparks is an Assistant Professor of Demography and Organization Studies at The University of Texas at San Antonio (UTSA). Her research interests include racial/ethnic disparities in maternal health, child health, and breastfeeding patterns; spatial inequality; and rural–urban differences in education outcomes. Her recent publications include "Do Biological, Sociodemographic, and Behavioral Characteristics Explain Racial/Ethnic Disparities in Preterm Births?" *Social Science and Medicine* and "One Size Does Not Fit All: An Examination of Low Birth-Weight Disparities among a Diverse Set of Racial/Ethnic Groups" in *Maternal and Child Health Journal*.

Manka M. Varghese is an Associate Professor in Language, Literacy and Culture at the College of Education, University of Washington. Her research and her teaching have focused on language teacher education, language teacher identity, and most recently on the access to higher education of linguistic minorities. Her work has appeared in *TESOL Quarterly, Language and Education, Journal of Latinos and Education, Journal of Language, Identity and Education,* and *Equity and Excellence in Education*.

INDEX